WHEN THE TREE FLOWERED

Other books by John G. Neihardt
published by the University of Nebraska Press

ALL IS BUT A BEGINNING: YOUTH REMEMBERED, 1881–1901

BLACK ELK SPEAKS: BEING THE LIFE STORY OF A HOLY MAN OF
THE OGLALA SIOUX

THE DAWN-BUILDER

THE DIVINE ENCHANTMENT: A MYSTICAL POEM *AND* POETIC
VALUES: THEIR REALITY AND OUR NEED OF THEM

THE END OF THE DREAM AND OTHER STORIES

INDIAN TALES AND OTHERS

LYRIC AND DRAMATIC POEMS

THE MOUNTAIN MEN (Vol. I of A CYCLE OF THE WEST)

PATTERNS AND COINCIDENCES: A SEQUEL TO "ALL IS BUT A
BEGINNING"

THE RIVER AND I

THE SPLENDID WAYFARING. THE EXPLOITS AND ADVENTURES
OF JEDEDIAH SMITH AND THE ASHLEY-HENRY MEN, 1822–1831

THE TWILIGHT OF THE SIOUX (Vol. II of A CYCLE OF THE WEST)

WHEN THE TREE FLOWERED

The Story of Eagle Voice,
a Sioux Indian

by

JOHN G. NEIHARDT

New Edition

Introduction by Raymond J. DeMallie

UNIVERSITY OF NEBRASKA PRESS
Lincoln and London

First printing of this edition: 1991
Most recent printing shown by the last digit below:
10   9   8   7   6   5   4   3   2   1

Library of Congress Cataloging-in-Publication Data
Neihardt, John Gneisenau, 1881–1973
When the tree flowered: the story of Eagle Voice, a Sioux Indian / by
John G. Neihardt; introduction by Raymond J. DeMallie.—New ed.
p.   cm.
"A Bison book."
Includes bibliographical references.
ISBN 0-8032-8363-6 (pbk.)
1. Oglala Indians—Fiction.   I. Title.
PS3527.E35W4   1991
813'.52—dc20   90-19669 CIP

Reprinted by arrangement with the John G. Neihardt Trust. For this
new edition the subtitle has been changed from that used in the first Bison Book edition, *The Fictional Autobiography of Eagle Voice, a Sioux Indian*
to *The Story of Eagle Voice, a Sioux Indian*. The original subtitle was *An Authentic Tale of the Old Sioux World*.

♾

Contents

INTRODUCTION TO THE NEW EDITION
By Raymond J. DeMallie

John G. Neihardt (1881–1973), poet laureate of Nebraska, seems destined to be better remembered for his empathetic portrayal of the traditional Sioux way of life in *Black Elk Speaks* (1932) than for his epic poem *A Cycle of the West* (1915–41), which celebrates the triumph of the white race in the winning of the American West. Ironically, the former book required only four months to write, while the latter (originally published in five separate volumes and collected into one in 1949) occupied thirty years. On reflection, the irony has a further twist, for it was in celebrating the white American conquest of the West that Neihardt came to appreciate the full cost of that conquest for the native peoples who had for so long before inhabited the plains and mountains.[1]

In his youth, Neihardt, lyric poet and spinner of romantic tales, had published a number of short stories about Indian people, most set in the time before the white man spoiled the native harmony with nature, most highly romantic in theme, and most tinged with tragedy and loss. His inspiration came from long contact with Indian people near his hometown of Bancroft, Nebraska, where he worked for a time as clerk and collections agent for an Indian trader on the Omaha reservation.[2] The Omahas, in reference to his stature and in recognition of his spirit, named him Little Bull Buffalo, a name he carried with pride. But when he turned from romantic stories and lyric poetry to writing his epic poem, he began not with the Indian but with the frontiersman and adventurer.

The story of Neihardt's meeting with Black Elk has often been repeated.[3] At age fifty, living in Branson, Missouri, and working as a literary columnist for the *St. Louis Post-Dispatch,* he was preparing to write *The Song of the Messiah,* the final volume of *A Cycle of the West,* which chronicles the Ghost Dance as the last hope of the Plains Indians to resist the tide of white settlement threatening to engulf them. In the summer of 1930, accompanied by his son, Sigurd, Neihardt visited the Pine Ridge Reservation in South Dakota to find an Oglala Sioux Indian who had participated in the Ghost Dance and who could give him a believer's perspective on that religion of desperation. Circumstances led him to Black Elk, then sixty-six years of age, nearly blind, but prescient; he sensed the poet's coming, intuited his sincerity, and chose him to be his amanuensis. He bade Neihardt return in the spring, promising to tell him everything he knew about the other world of the spirit.

Neihardt did return in May 1931, accompanied on this trip by his daughters Enid and Hilda. Over the course of eighteen days, Black Elk told his life story, carefully translated into English by his son Benjamin and faithfully recorded in shorthand by Enid Neihardt. Black Elk took Neihardt as a son, giving him his second Indian name, Flaming Rainbow, in recognition of the great vision that had guided Black Elk's life from childhood. Hurrying home to Branson, Missouri, Neihardt used Enid's typed transcript of the interview notes as the basis for his telling of Black Elk's life story, writing at an inspired pace and completing the manuscript in October. He called it "The Tree That Never Bloomed," focusing even the title on the despair of Black Elk's failure to fulfill the promise of his great vision. The perplexed publisher objected to the title, and the simpler and more direct "Black Elk Speaks" was a compromise suggested to Neihardt by his wife, Mona.

Although *Black Elk Speaks* met with acclaim from the critics, it was not a popular success. Sales were not strong, and eventually the book was remaindered and allowed to go out of print. It was a stark contrast to Neihardt's volumes of the epic poem, all of which remained in print throughout his lifetime, moving from one edition to the next. In the meantime, he did not entirely lose touch with Black Elk. He tried for a while, without success, to stir interest in a motion picture based on *Black Elk Speaks,* and during the summer of 1934 he lived at Pine Ridge, camping with his daughters on Black Elk's land while he wrote the concluding portions of *The Song of the Messiah.*

During the 1940s, with the epic poem completed, Neihardt turned to a variety of projects to support his family. From 1944 to

1946 he worked for the Bureau of Indian Affairs, relocated to
Chicago during the years of World War II as director of the Divi-
sion of Information. During the winter of 1944 he was given the
opportunity to return to Pine Ridge, with the congenial assign-
ment of recording material to be used in writing a cultural history
of the Oglala Sioux. With his daughter Hilda acting as secretary,
transcribing interviews directly on the typewriter and thereby by-
passing the shorthand stage, they arrived late in November and
stayed three weeks. This was his last trip to Pine Ridge to record
material on Sioux history and culture, although he returned
again for very brief visits in the interests of the Bureau of Indian
Affairs in 1945 and 1946.

The 1944 trip was as rich as that of 1931 in terms of the material Neihardt was able to record. The typescripts found among
Neihardt's papers in the Western Historical Manuscripts Collection at the University of Missouri, Columbia, preserve the record
of Neihardt's interviews with three men during this visit. On November 27–29 and December 1, he interviewed Eagle Elk, who at
the age of ninety-three had a clear memory and told his life story,
a tale of the buffalo-hunting days, of adventures in war, and of
dedicating himself to his people in the Sun Dance. On December
5–8 and 11–13 Neihardt interviewed Black Elk, now eighty years
old—now truly the blind seer, bent with years, the very image that
Neihardt had somewhat prematurely drawn in *Black Elk Speaks*.
This time Black Elk spoke not about himself but about his people,
telling a history of the Sioux from the earliest tribal memories to
the coming of the whites, a sequence of sacred stories memorializ-
ing events sanctioned by visions: the origin of the knife, of the
bow and arrow, and of fire making; the naming of relatives, of the
directions, and of the animals; the dispersal of the people, the do-
mestication of dogs, the discovery of the horse, the creation of the
Sioux political system, and the prophecies of Wooden Cup, which
foretold the end of the old Sioux way of life. This was the sacred
charter, the cultural history that Neihardt had been charged to
record. Moreover, Black Elk told tales of mysterious adventures,
of warfare, humorous stories, and a long *ohunkakan* (winter-telling myth) that chronicles the adventures of Falling Star, an important mythic figure among the Plains peoples. In addition, on De-

cember 11, Andrew Knife told a long version of the popular story of Red Hail and her two suitors.

It was around these 1944 interviews that Neihardt fashioned his last book on the Sioux, *When the Tree Flowered* (1951).[4]

Neihardt began to write *When the Tree Flowered* in 1947, after returning from Chicago to his home in Branson. The following year, however, he and his family moved to Columbia, Missouri, purchasing a farm east of town that he named Skyrim. Then in 1949 he was invited to join the faculty of the English Department at the University of Missouri, and began to teach, further delaying progress on the book. By December 1950 the manuscript was completed—his second attempt to tell the story of the Sioux in prose, this time as a novel ("if it must be called so," he wrote to his daughter Hilda).[5] The key word in the subtitle is "authentic," for in this book Neihardt had reworked interview material, just as he had done in *Black Elk Speaks*. The difference was that in this case, Neihardt had merged Eagle Elk and Black Elk into a single character, the book's narrator, whom he called Eagle Voice, and had set what they had told him in the framework of a fictional plot.

The decision to use the pseudonym Eagle Voice seems to have been motivated not by a desire to signal him as a composite character, but rather as a way around the inevitable confusion of Eagle Elk with Black Elk: the names were simply too similar. At the same time, a fictional protaganist allowed for greater freedom to interpret the material, and it is in this that *When the Tree Flowered* differs most markedly from *Black Elk Speaks*. The earlier book had been a faithful telling of one man's life, and an attempt to interpret Black Elk's philosophy and personality as Neihardt understood them. He was aggravated when reviewers, instead of taking the book at face value as representative of the Sioux world-view, suggested that Neihardt had used Black Elk as a vehicle to express his own philosophy. In presenting Black Elk's life, he had minimized his own presence as author, relegating himself to a preface and a postscript, refraining throughout the text from introducing superfluous description and explanation.

Black Elk had to speak for himself, and it is this unembroidered directness, it might be argued, that led readers of the 1930s to reject the book as too far removed from their own experience to be credible, but led readers from the 1960s on to embrace it as representing the unmediated expression of a native voice. Both reactions missed the mark: Neihardt chose the direct first-person narrative to avoid the intrusion of himself as author (and the modern world at large) in order to bring a traditional Sioux perspective to the fore—hence the terseness—but he had not intended by this to obscure his creative role as author. He was equally cross with critics who considered *Black Elk Speaks* to be no more than a transcript of his interviews. The book did not write itself, and comparison with the actual interview transcripts published in *The Sixth Grandfather: Black Elk's Teachings Given to John G. Neihardt* (1984) allows for close determination of Neihardt's selectivity and invention in writing the book.

In the new tale to be woven from the 1944 interview notes, Neihardt had the opportunity to try once again to tell the story of the Sioux in such a way as to capture the popular imagination. Although there was thought in 1948 of bringing out another edition of *Black Elk Speaks*, nothing came of it. In 1954, when a German translation was being published, Neihardt wrote to request that the chapter "High Horse's Courting" be omitted. It was the only chapter of the book that seems to have had no basis in the Black Elk interviews, and it might be imagined he wished it deleted for that reason. Instead, however, the reason seems to have been far simpler: he had reworked the story in his new novel. Unfortunately, the German publisher replied, the type had already been set, and nothing could be done about it.[6]

This episode would be insignificant except that it reveals a fundamentally important perspective on the writing of *When the Tree Flowered*. The book would not compete with *Black Elk Speaks*, the latter being long out of print; rather, it would in a sense replace it, salvaging from it that which popular audiences seemed to like best, and minimizing the mysticism and personal visionary experience that seemed to prevent readers from empathizing with Black Elk as a real human being akin to themselves. The new book would provide more context, more description, and more connected plot. It would take up where the earlier work left off, trying to convey to non-Indian audiences the beauty and power of the old Sioux world and the tragedy of its destruction with the passing of the western frontier.

The plot of the book had long been simmering in Neihardt's imagination: the childhood affection between a little boy and girl, their long separation by the circumstances of their lives, and their eventual reunion in the aftermath of the Wounded Knee massacre. In a brief sketch of a scenario he proposed (apparently in the 1930s) for a motion picture based on *Black Elk Speaks*, Neihardt had outlined it succinctly: Black Elk, the little boy, hears voices and acts peculiarly. His only playmate is a little girl who loves him and becomes his confidante. After his great vision at the age of nine, it is with her alone that he shares his secret, and she has faith that he will grow up to become a great chief. At the Custer battle she encourages him to go out and fight the soldiers, secure in the protection provided by his vision powers. But after Black Elk, following the commands of the spirits, begins his career as a holy man, he becomes estranged from the girl and engrossed in the sacred powers. He travels with Buffalo Bill's Wild West show and in Paris becomes infatuated with a beautiful French girl, with whom he has a passionate affair. Visions of home call him back to Pine Ridge, where he is caught up in the fervor of the Ghost Dance. After the Wounded Knee massacre he charges on the soldiers, protected by the power of his sacred bow, in order to save a group of women and children captives. Among them is the girl he had loved so long before, and they are reunited at last. The plot, Neihardt wrote, was "romantic . . . with a decidedly modern cast" and could be worked out "without in any way falsifying the chief character or trend of the tale" of Black Elk's life.[7]

The life of Eagle Elk would fit well into this broad plot outline. One episode in particular made the connection obvious: Neihardt had been touched by the old Oglala man's romantic parting gesture toward his wife. As a youth, participating in the Sun Dance, Eagle Elk had been given a sacred quirt to protect him from harm all his life. Neihardt wrote to Mona: He *did* keep it all his long life until his wife died. Then when she was dead he slipped it down inside her dress against her bosom, & it was buried with her to have it for protection in her journey to the spirit world."[8] With only the smallest literary license, Eagle Elk's wife could be the little girl of the plot. The rest of the book would faithfully follow the adventures of Eagle Elk's life.

Perhaps Neihardt would have limited the book to Eagle Elk's own life story, but, unfortunately, the old man had related only his experiences up to the early 1880s. Happily, these included important battles that the Sioux fought against the army—Fetterman, Wagon Box, Rosebud, Little Big Horn—as well as stories of war parties against enemy tribes, and a long account of participating in the Sun Dance—which had been a major omission in the telling of Black Elk's life. But to bring the story down to Wounded Knee, Neihardt had to borrow from Black Elk's life, freely reworking material from *Black Elk Speaks*. Thus the trip with Buffalo Bill, the affair with the Parisian girl, the return to Pine Ridge, and the events of the Ghost Dance period strike readers of *When the Tree Flowered* who are familiar with *Black Elk Speaks* with a sense of déjà vu. Even the title of the new book was a reworking of Neihardt's original title for the book about Black Elk, "The Tree That Never Bloomed."

While retaining the first-person perspective of *Black Elk Speaks*, *When the Tree Flowered* is far richer in descriptive detail. In part this was made possible by the 1944 interviews with Black Elk, and his exegesis on the fundamentals of Sioux culture and history. Much of the material for the book originated in these interviews, but other details were taken from a great diversity of sources; attempting to trace all of Neihardt's sources would be a major undertaking.

In *Black Elk Speaks* the first-person narrator directly addresses the reader, but *When the Tree Flowered* utilizes a dialogical format by which the author, who serves in the book as unnamed recorder of Eagle Voice's story, stands between the narrator and the reader. This device allows for commentary on Eagle Voice's tale, both by means of the comments that the old man himself makes to the author outside the body of the narrative, and by the author's descriptions of Eagle Voice's actions and expressions. These comments serve most frequently to introduce chapters and maintain the flow of the narrative (for example, in the author's frequent impatient questions to Eagle Voice about the fate of the girl, Tashina Wanblee, his childhood sweetheart). The reader identifies with the author, who has come to record the old man's life story, and through the eyes of this outsider is given a glimpse into both the physical and the mental world of Eagle Voice. This dialogical format is especially effective in chapters XVII–XIX, where Eagle Voice gathers some of his cronies to tell stories. During the winter-telling tales the old men enter into the spirit of the storytelling session with childlike glee, playing the role of children themselves and participating through their responses in the action of the stories. These chapters evoke the dynamics of Plains Indian storytelling and are far more effective than the folkloristic studies of the day in suggesting the drama of the storyteller's art and the participatory role of the audience.

Importantly, the novelistic framework allowed Neihardt the freedom to use Eagle Voice to express his own interpretation of the Sioux experience. He took the vision of Wooden Cup as the organizing device. As Black Elk related the story to Neihardt, Wooden Cup had had his vision directly from the Great Spirit, who foretold the coming of the white race, the destruction of the buffalo, and the breaking up of the sacred hoop that symbolized the unity of the Sioux people. The fictional Eagle Voice comments, I think I did not believe what Wooden Cup said . . . for I was young and the world was new" (p. 8). In writing chapter VIII, which tells of Eagle Voice's vision, Neihardt incorporated one image from the vision experience related to him by Eagle Elk—the coup sticks with scalps hanging from them, swinging in the dust—but borrowed the remainder from Black Elk's visions. When Eagle Voice tells his vision to a holy man, the latter interprets it in a way that parallels the vision of Wooden Cup: You shall travel far and see strange peoples; but the sacred hoop of all the peoples under the flowering tree, you shall not see by the light of the sun" (p. 54). As in *Black Elk Speaks*, Neihardt here transforms the sacred hoop of the people into the sacred hoop of all peoples, extending Black Elk's vision symbol of the unity of the Sioux into a symbol of the unity of all humankind.

As the book progresses, Neihardt evokes a bittersweet mood by correlating the erosion of the Sioux way of life with Eagle Voice's own aging and the increasing confusion and disorganization of his world. When Eagle Voice tells the story of an old chief who forgave his young wife's infidelity, he ends by commenting, "All this was many snows ago, before the sacred hoop was broken, and when the people were still good" (p. 32). With Eagle Voice's advancing age comes wisdom and a kind of humility that seems to reflect as much of Neihardt as of Black Elk or Eagle Elk. Eagle Voice comments: "I am very old and I have learned so many things that I do not know much any more. Maybe I was wiser before my ears were troubled with so many forked words" (p. 42). Neihardt also picks up this theme to criticize the treatment of the Indian in the United States. After Eagle Voice tells of the killing of Fetterman's troops at Fort Philip Kearny in 1866, he says: "They all died, a hundred soldiers in the country that was ours. But the forked-tongued ones who sent them did not die. I think they are living yet" (p. 11). Neihardt uses Eagle Voice to comment critically on certain aspects of Sioux culture, as well. For example, in telling about the battle in which he first killed an enemy Crow, Eagle Voice reflects: "When I leaned down to take the man's scalp he looked at me once and then he died. I think I did not see that look until I was older" (p. 95).

Eagle Voice develops the theme of loss, both internal (for example, the breaking of the hoop), and external (the physical loss of land to the whites): We were living on a big island, and the Wasichus were like great waters washing all around it, nibbling off the edges, and it was getting smaller, smaller, smaller." Then Eagle Voice returns to the theme of prophecy: Our old men remembered Wooden Cup and what he saw and said before our grandfathers were born. But I was young" (p. 202).

Eagle Voice's perspective from old age takes on special meaning when one realizes that Neihardt did not begin writing the book until the age of sixty-six and did not complete it until he was near seventy. Yet age was not to be regretted, and as Eagle Voice finally sums it up in reference to his own life: "It was a good road that we walked together, Grandson. Sometimes we were hungry but it was a good road. Our children came to us, and when we were old, we saw our grandchildren too. It was a good road" (p. 248). In the end, Eagle Voice presents an image of dignity born of the cultural values of the past that give promise of strength for the future. In contrast to the defeated old man at the close of

Black Elk Speaks, the literary figure of Eagle Voice endures into the world of today, long after that happier time of *When the Tree Flowered*.

From its publication in 1951, *When the Tree Flowered* has been largely misunderstood. Reviewing the book in the *Westerners Brandbook*, Don Russell, respected newspaperman and western historian, wrote that Neihardt "warns us that this book is fiction," and quoted him, apparently from a letter, as saying: "The story is definitely a creation, but woven out of authentic materials. It would be naive to suppose that I merely wrote down what some old Indian told me." Russell added: "It would, of course, be quite a discovery if an Indian could have been found who witnessed the Fetterman fight, all the fights of 1876 including the Rosebud and the Little Big Horn, and on down to Wounded Knee." Noting that the book represents "authentic history . . . from an Indian point of view," he concluded, "Indian life has not been more sympathetically interpreted."[9]

The categorization as fiction made the book suspect to historians, and even more so since it presented an admittedly partisan perspective. Russell, like others at the time, did not understand the implications of Neihardt's designation of the book as "authentic," and failed to appreciate the extent to which it was based on primary material. Perhaps it was for this reason that when a British edition was published in 1953 under the title *Eagle Voice*, Neihardt added an introduction (reprinted in the present edition) discussing the sources for the book, as well as footnotes to identify concepts and places that would be unfamiliar to non-American readers. The real-life Eagle Elk had in fact participated in all the battles from the Fetterman fight through the Little Big Horn, and may have been at Wounded Knee as well; this we do not know, for his life story as told to Neihardt ended at the time he moved to the Pine Ridge Reservation in the early 1880s. Black Elk had been too young to take part in the fights of the 1860s, but had been at the Little Big Horn and Wounded Knee. The first-hand recollections of these men, their personal perspectives on events whose principal chroniclers had been on the side of the soldiers, not the Indians, enriched Neihardt's telling of the well-known tales of conflicts whose names have long been legendary in the history of the West. Theirs was an important perspective, as legitimate as that from the other side, and by combining what he learned from the Indian participants with the military's written records, Neihardt constructed well-rounded accounts that place these fights in very human context.

When the Tree Flowered is John Neihardt's mature and reflective interpretation of the old Sioux way of life. He served as a translator of the Sioux past whose audience has proved not to be limited by space or time. Through his writings, Black Elk, Eagle Elk, and other old men who were of that last generation of Sioux to have participated in the old buffalo-hunting life and the disorienting period of strife with the U.S. Army, found a literary voice. What they said chronicles a dramatic transition in the life of the Plains Indians; the record of their thoughts, interpreted by Neihardt, is a legacy preserved for the future. It transcends the specifics of this one tragic case of cultural misunderstanding and conflict and speaks to universal human concerns. It is a story worth contemplating both for itself and for the lessons it teaches all humanity. As the eagle encouraged Eagle Voice in his vision, "Hold fast; there is more."

NOTES

1. John G. Neihardt, *Black Elk Speaks: Being the Life Story of a Holy Man of the Ogalala Sioux* (New York: William Morrow, 1932; reprint, Lincoln: University of Nebraska Press, 1961, 1979); *A Cycle of the West* (New York: Macmillan, 1949). Biographical details are from Lucile F. Aly, *John G. Neihardt: A Critical Biography* (Amsterdam: Rodopi, 1977), and from discussions with Hilda Neihardt Petri, whose assistance and encouragement are gratefully acknowledged.

2. Neihardt told of his experiences with the Omahas in his *Patterns and Coincidences: A Sequel to "All Is But a Beginning"* (Columbia: University of Missouri Press, 1978).

3. Neihardt, Preface to *Black Elk Speaks* (1961 and 1979 eds.), pp. xv–xix; *The Sixth Grandfather: Black Elk's Teachings Given to John G. Neihardt,* ed. by Raymond J. DeMallie (Lincoln: University of Nebraska Press, 1984), pp. 26–29.

4. John G. Neihardt, *When the Tree Flowered: An Authentic Tale of the Old*

Sioux World (New York: Macmillan, 1951), published in Great Britain as *Eagle Voice: An Authentic Tale of the Sioux Indians* (London: Andrew Melrose, 1953).

5. Aly, *John G. Neihardt,* p. 270.

6. Joseph E. Brown to John G. Neihardt, October 29, 1953; Verlag Otto Walter to John G. Neihardt, May 17, 1954. Neihardt papers, Western Historical Manuscripts Collection, University of Missouri, Columbia.

7. Undated letter draft in the hand of John G. Neihardt addressed to Mr. Hobson, with "Suggestions For Screening *Black Elk Speaks*," Neihardt papers, Western Historical Manuscripts Collection, University of Missouri.

8. John G. Neihardt to Mona Neihardt, November 29, 1944. Photostatic copy in the Neihardt papers, Western Historical Manuscripts Collection, University of Missouri.

9. *Westerners Brandbook* (Chicago) vol. 8 (1951): p. 76.

INTRODUCTION TO THE BRITISH EDITION

I have been asked to furnish a brief Introduction to the following tale by way of suggesting the sources upon which I have drawn. This is a very large order, involving, as it does, a rather long lifetime spent in the American West.

Some of my most vivid boyhood memories are concerned with true pioneer life in north-western Kansas, where I lived with my covered-wagon grandparents in a sod house, with cow-chips" gathered from the fenceless prairie for fuel, and wicks in bowls of lard for lamps. . . .

In Nebraska, during my later boyhood and youth, I saw the frontier slowly vanish westward, being only vaguely aware of what was happening to my world.

The three most vital decades of my manhood were devoted to my *Cycle of the West,* designed to celebrate the great mood of courage characteristic of that epic time and country. I was never compelled to go in search of "local colour," which was all about me; and it was my privilege to know, as friends, many who had done their parts in the latter phases of that great Western epos—plainsmen, Missouri Rivermen, Red Indian fighters from privates to generals, scouts and Red Indians of the Plains.

More than half a century ago I was living among the Omaha Indians, a Siouan people, and (with the name of Little Bull Buffalo) I was truly one of them in heart. Later I became intimately acquainted with the Sioux Indians of the Dakotas, and through friendships with many of the unreconstructed "long-hairs" of the tribe, who knew no English, was enabled to enter into the consciousness of the once great nomadic people. I shared, in the closest terms of intimacy and understanding, their rich memories and their culture.

Perhaps the most illuminating experience of my life was my association with Black Elk—a Holy Man of the Sioux who, twenty-five years ago, made me his spiritual son (with the name Flaming

Rainbow) that he might teach me and that I, in turn, might pass his teaching on to an alien world; for "soon he would be under the grass" (he said), and what was given him for all men would otherwise be lost. Some of what he taught me is in the tale here told.

Our Eagle Voice—here speaking—is a composite character; but the tale he tells is based upon the life story of my old friend Eagle Elk, who died in 1945 at the age of ninety-four. The relationship that grew up between us is faithfully represented in this book. Eagle Voice *is* Eagle Elk in character, and in the idiom of his thoughts and speech. The adventures that I have added to his own, by way of giving a comprehensive view of the old Sioux world, are *all* authentic.

JOHN G. NEIHARDT
University of Missouri,
Columbia, Missouri, U.S.A.
1953.

WHEN THE TREE FLOWERED

"I Used to Be Her Horse"

A one-room log cabin, with an indolently smoking chimney, squatted in sullen destitution a hundred yards away. Before the door a ramshackle wagon stood waiting for nothing with its load of snow. Down yonder in the brushy draw an all-but-roofless shed stared listlessly upon the dull February sky. With a man-denying look, the empty reservation landscape round about lay hushed and bluing in the cold.

Raising the flap of the tepee, with its rusty stovepipe thrust through its much-patched canvas, I stooped in a puff of pleasant warmth and entered, placing my last armload of cottonwood chunks behind the sheet-iron stove.

The old man threw back his blankets and sat up cross-legged upon the cowhide robes that served for bed, his gray hair straggling thinly to his shoulders about an aquiline face that had been handsome, surely, before time carved it to the bone.

"Palamo yelo, Kola," he said cheerily, as he fumbled in his long leather tobacco sack; "Thank you, friend. Now we can be warm and smoke together. You shall be my grandson, Wasichu* though you are; for it is no man's fault how he is born, and your heart is as much Lakota† as mine.

"It will be good to remember, as you wish. The story that I have will make me young again a little while, and you shall put it down there in your tongue as I could say it if your tongue were mine. Too many snows are heavy on my back, and when I walk, as you have seen, I am like an old three-legged horse, all bone and hide and always looking for the grass that used to be."

Eagle Voice chuckled at his picture of himself.

"But it is only my body that stoops, remembering the mother ground," he continued, "for I can feel my spirit standing tall above the snows and

* Here the word signifies white man; but see page 36.
† Sioux.

grasses that have been, and seeing much of good and evil days. There are battles to be fought, and ponies to be stolen, and coups to be counted. And there is happy hunting when the bison herds were wide as day, and meat was plenty, and the earth stayed young. That was before the rivers of Wasichus came in flood and made it old and shut us in these barren little islands where we wait and wait for yesterday. And there are visions to be seen again and voices to be heard from beyond the world. And far away on the other side of the great water towards the sunrise where I went when I was young, there are strange things to be remembered, strange ways, strange faces. And yonder there is a woman's face, white and far away; and if it is good or bad I do not know. I remember, and am a boy in the night when the moon makes all the hills and valleys so that he wants to sing; but something afraid is hiding in the shadows."

The old man lit the pipe and his lean cheeks hollowed with a long draw upon the stem. The brooding face went dim behind a slowly emitted cloud of smoke, to emerge presently, shining with a merry light.

"*Washtay!*" he exclaimed, with a look of triumph; "*Lela washtay!*"

"What is very good, Grandfather?" I asked.

"It is what I see clearer than all the rest," he answered, passing the pipe to me; "and that is very strange, for many things were bigger long ago."

He thought awhile, a slow smile spreading until, with a look grotesquely young, he fell to giggling like a mischievous boy. Then his face went sober, and fixing serious eyes upon me he said with great dignity and deliberation:

"It is just a little girl I see, my grandson. I used to be her horse."

His only response to my laughter was a deeper crinkling about the mock-serious eyes.

"Yes, I used to be her horse, and I will tell you how it was."

It might have seemed that he had changed the subject abruptly when he began again, talking eagerly; but I knew that I had only to wait for the connection.

"In the old days, before the hoop of our people was broken, the grandfathers and grandmothers did not just sit and think about the time when things were better, even if they were old as I am. Maybe a man was so bent and stiff that he could not hunt or fight any more and maybe he could hardly chew his meat; but he had happy work to do, because there were always little boys who had to learn how to be good hunters and brave warriors; and he would teach them and tell them stories that were teaching too. When I listened to my grandfather I used to think and think about how tall men were when he was young. I remember the first bow and arrows he made me and how he taught me to grasp the bow—

like this; and put the arrow on the string—like this; and pull with the fingers—like this; and let the arrow fly—so—*whang!* And I remember the day when I came home with my first kill, and he laughed hard and said he could see already that I was going to be a great hunter and a great warrior. I wondered why he laughed, but I thought maybe it was because he was so glad.

"It was just a little bird, but it was a bison bull anyway, and I was more surprised than my grandfather was. For I had been shooting at rabbits in the brush along the creek for a long time, and even when I hit them, they would just wiggle their white rumps at me and hop away. When my grandmother saw the bird, she did not laugh at all. She just said, 'hm-m-m,' high up in her nose, like that; for she was even more surprised than my grandfather. Then she told my mother we would have to make a victory feast for this young man; and it was so, because grandmother said it. She invited some old women and old men to come over and eat; and when they came into our tepee and saw the little bird lying there, they all said, 'hm-m-m,' high up in their noses. And while we were eating they made me stand up and tell just how I did it; and so I did, like a great warrior making a kill-talk after a victory. Then the women all made the tremolo with their hands upon their mouths—so—and the men cried, 'hi-yay-ay.'

"And maybe there was an old grandmother who was getting fat and heavy because she could not chop much wood any more or carry much water; but she could peg down green hides and tan them with ashes, and sit down and beat them until they were very soft. And her hands were never still, for there were always moccasins to make and warm things of deer-hide for the winter, all fine with beads and porcupine quills.

"Or maybe there was meat to be cut in long thin strips and hung on the drying racks—such thin strips that it was just like unwinding a bundle of meat, around and around. The women used to hold their strips up, to see whose was longest; and the strips my grandmother cut were always a little thinner and longer than the others.

"And maybe there was going to be a new baby in a tepee, and it would need a good start in this life; for it is not easy to live on this earth. So the parents would think of two women who were good and wise and nobody could say anything bad about them. They would be grandmothers, for who can be wise and young too? And the parents would ask these old women to come over and help the baby. So they would come when it was the right time. And when the baby was brought forth in this world, the first grandmother would cut and tie the cord. Then she would clean out the baby's mouth with her forefinger, and when she did that her good spirit would get into the baby so that it would be like her.

"Then the second grandmother would take some of the inside bark of the chokecherry that had been soaked and pounded soft, and with this she would wash the baby; and if it was a girl she would say to it: 'I am a good woman; I have worked hard; I have raised a family; and I always tried to get along with everybody. You must always try to do the same way.' After that she would make it dry and rub it all over with grease and red paint, because red is a sacred color. Then she would take some soft powder that she had made by powdering dry buffalo chips and she would put this in a piece of hide that had been tanned very soft and fasten it around the baby's rump, so that it could be kept dry and clean.

"And always there were little girls who had to learn how to be good women; and a grandmother would teach them, because she had been a woman so long that she knew how better than her daughters did; and, anyway, everything was done better when she was young.

"The first thing this grandmother gave to a little girl was a deer-hide pouch with everything in it that a woman needs to make a home—a knife, an awl, a bone needle, and some fine sinew for sewing. And she would say, 'You must always keep this with you whatever happens and never let it go if you want to be a real woman and good for something. With this you can always make a home.' It was the way a grandfather gave a little boy a bow and arrows, a knife, and a rawhide rope for taming horses.

"And when a little girl was still so little that she could not yet do much with a knife or needle, the grandmother would teach her the rolling game. There was a stick about as long as my finger with three short twigs on one end so that it would stand up; and the little girl had to roll a small round stone at this to knock it over. It was very hard to do, and she had to keep on trying and trying, so that she learned to be patient like a good woman.

"Then when the little girl was big enough, her grandmother taught her how to make a tepee cover out of hide, and how to set it up with the tepee poles fixed together at the top just so; and how to set the smoke-flap at the peak to suit the wind and make a fire burn without smoking the people out; and how to take the tepee down quickly and put it on a pony-drag in a hurry, if there should be an attack and the women had to run away with the children and the ponies while the men were fighting.

"The little girls used to get together and play village, with their tepees all set in a circle, just right, with the opening to the place where you are always looking [the south]; and there were buckskin dolls stuffed with

4

grass for children; and the little boys played they were chiefs and councilors and warriors. Of course, there had to be horses."

The old man sat chuckling for a while before he continued.

"I think I was about eight years old that time, and I was getting big fast, for my grandfather would let me have some sharp arrows if I would be careful, and I had killed a rabbit already—maybe two. Many of our people were camped not far from the soldiers' town on Duck River [Fort Laramie]. It was summer, and there was big trouble coming. The old people were all talking about the bad Wasichus and how they were crazy again because they had found gold in our country; and they wanted to make a road through it and scare all the bison away, and then maybe we would all starve. It was the time just before Red Cloud went to war, and the people were camped there waiting to see what would happen.

"We little Oglala boys were playing killing-all-the-soldiers; but we got tired doing that, because nobody wanted to be a soldier, and we had to kill people who were not there at all. And one of the boys said, 'Let us quit killing soldiers. They are all dead anyway, and they are no good. The Miniconjou girls and boys have got a village over there. Let us charge upon them and steal all their horses!' So we all cried, 'hi-yay,' and began to get ready for the charge with our bows and blunt arrows and old sunflower stalks for spears.

"And when we had crawled up on our bellies as close to the village as we could get without being seen by the enemy, we leaped up and cried 'hoka-hey' all together and charged on the village.

"It was a big fight, a big noise. We could have won a victory, because we all said that one Oglala boy was better than two or three Miniconjous; but some of the bigger boys over there got after us, and we had to run.

"And while I was running, I looked back over my shoulder to see how big a boy was chasing me. And it was not a big boy or even a little boy. It was a girl—a pretty little girl—but she looked terrible with her hair all over her head in the wind she made with her running; and she was yelling and swinging a rawhide rope while she ran. I was longer legged than she was, but she caught me around the neck with her rope anyway. Maybe all at once I wanted to be caught. And she said, 'You bad boy! You are just a shonka-'kan [horse], and you are going to pull my tepee.'

"So I let her lead me back to her village; and all the Miniconjou boys poked their fingers at me and yelled and wanted to charge me and coup me; but she picked up a stick and yelled back at them, 'You leave

5

my horse alone or I will hit you.' And, of course, if I was a horse I wasn't a warrior any more.

"So I got down on my hands and knees and she hitched the dragpoles on me and packed her tepee on them. And when I snorted and pranced, she petted me on the rump and sang to me, so that I was as tame as the other little boys who were being horses too and helping to move camp away from the enemy country."

For a while, Eagle Voice seemed to have forgotten me, gazing over my head with a faraway illuminated look. Then he spoke slowly in a low voice as though talking to himself: "Tashina Wan-blee [Her Eagle Robe]. She was a pretty little girl. I liked to play over there; and she said I was the best horse she ever had."

Then, becoming aware of me again, he continued, chuckling: "But one day I got tired of playing horse; so I stood up on my hind legs and I said: 'When I get just a little bigger I am going to marry you, and you are going to be my woman.' And she stuck her tongue out at me and said: 'You are only a *shonka-'kan*. Go and eat grass!'"

The old man's laughter trailed off into silence and the boy look went away.

When the Hundred Died

"—And what became of the little girl, Grandfather?" I asked at length. "Did you marry her when you got a little bigger?"

For some time the old man had seemed unconscious of me as he sat there studying the ground, blowing softly now and then upon an eagle-bone whistle suspended from his neck by a rawhide thong. He fixed a squinting, quizzical gaze upon me and said: "That is a story, Grandson, and so is this whistle. I can hear it crying across many snows and grasses. Why are Wasichus always in a hurry? It is not good."

Then he lapsed into meditation as before, blowing softly now and then upon the wing-bone, polished with the handling of many years.

"*Sheetsha!*" he said at last in an explosive whisper.

"What is bad, Grandfather?" I asked.

"I was thinking of all that is gone," he answered, the meditative mood still strong upon him. "When I was a boy I heard the old people tell about a great *wichasha wakon* [holy man] who did wonderful things; and his name was Wooden Cup. He had a vision of the Great Mysterious One, and that is how he got this power. He could make fire with his fingers, just by touching the wood; and he could see far off into the days that were going to be when babies that were not yet born would be walking with their canes. He saw it and he said it. A strange people would come from the sunrise, and there would be more of them than the bison. Then the bison would turn to white bones on the prairie. The mother earth would be bound with bands of iron. The sacred hoop of our people would be broken by the evil power of the strangers, and in that time we would live in little square gray houses, and in those houses we would starve. He said it, and we have seen it. I will not live in them, for the Great Mysterious One meant all things to be round—the sky and the prairie, the sun and the moon, the bodies of men and animals, trees and the nests of birds, and the hoop of the people. The days and the seasons come back in a circle, and so do the generations. The young grow old, and from the old the young begin and grow. It is the sacred way.

"My daughter in the little gray house yonder is good, but her heart is half Wasichu. She feeds me of the little that she has, and her man brings me wood. They say it is warmer in there; but I was born a Lakota, and I will die in a tepee. It would be well if my young bones had been scattered on the prairie to show where a warrior fell and to make a story, for it is not good to grow old."

For a while the bone whistle called plaintively to him as from a great distance, and he listened, staring at the ground.

"I think I did not believe what Wooden Cup said," he continued; "for I was young and the world was new. There was strangeness everywhere so that maybe something wonderful was going to happen. I remember, before I had sharp arrows for my bow, the way I would be in a valley all alone, and there would be no sound, and all at once the hills would be wrinkled grandfathers looking down at me and saying something good that I could almost hear.

"When we were camped near the soldiers' town on Duck River that time, I heard the old people talking about the iron road the Wasichus were making all along Shell River [Platte]. And there was a long high dust of Wasichu wagons full of people always going and going to the sunset. It was part of what Wooden Cup saw. Little boys talked about it, and they said afterwhile all the bad Wasichus in the world would be yonder where the sun goes down; or if there were any left when we got big, we would just kill them all, and then everything would be the way it was when our grandfathers were boys.

"I remember there was a big meeting at the soldiers' town [Fort Laramie] the day before we broke camp and went north to fight. It was the day more soldiers came to steal the road up Powder River if our people said, 'no.' I can see Red Cloud talking to the people and the Wasichu chiefs who came from the Great Father in Washington. They came to ask for the road through our hunting country; but the soldiers came to take it. When I remember, Red Cloud is standing on a high place made of wood, and he is taller than a man. I cannot hear his words, but he is very angry at the Wasichu chiefs. The men cry, 'how,' and 'hoka-hey,' and the women make the tremolo. We are going to fight, and I am scared; but I am glad too.

"So our people broke camp and we traveled fast with Red Cloud until we came to the Powder River country. There many others came to us. Much of what I remember about that time is like something I have dreamed, but some of it is clear; and I have heard much that is like remembering. But I can see my father going away with a band of warriors; and I can see them riding on a hill into the sky, until the sky is empty and the hill looks afraid. I can see warriors coming back, and my father is among them. They are driving many mules that they had taken from the soldiers, and some big Wasichu horses. I can see the warriors riding about the circle of the village with Wasichu scalps on their coup sticks. I can see my father making a kill-talk, and I can hear the drums beat between his tellings of brave deeds, while the people cry out to praise him. And while I listen, far away now, I can see Wasichu wagons burning yet and the people in them dying on the road that was not theirs.

"The big sun dance that summer made the hearts of the people strong to fight and die; and my heart was strong too. When I got a little bigger I would be a great warrior like my father. The little boys played killing Wasichus harder than ever; and we had victory dances and made kill-talks about the brave deeds we were going to do.

"Then it is winter. The snow is deep and heaped along the creek. The wind howls in the night, and the smoke whirls round inside the tepee. Maybe it is afraid to go out there. I crawl deep under the buffalo robe, for there are angry spirits crying in the dark.

"Then there are nights when the wind is dead and something big is crawling close outside without making any noise. If I peek out through the tepee flap, the stars are big and sharp, and everything is listening. Trees pop in the cold. It is the Moon of Popping Trees [December].

"That was the time when the hundred soldiers died. Lodge Trail Ridge is steep and narrow where it goes down to Peno Creek. It is near to where the soldiers built their town of logs, and that is where they died. I heard it told so often that when I think about it I must tell myself it was my father who was there and I was just a little boy at home with my mother.

"We had our village where Peno Creek runs into the Tongue, and Big Road was the leader of our band. The day was just coming when our warriors rode away to fight the soldiers and many others rode with them—Cheyennes, Arapahoes. They rode up Peno Creek; and when the sun was halfway up the sky, they stopped where the Wasichu road came down the steep, narrow ridge to the ford.

"It was a good place to fight; so they sent some warriors up the road to coax the soldiers out of their town; and while those were yonder, we hid in the gullies and the brush all along the sides of the ridge. No, I was just a little boy at home, but so our warriors did.

"And when they had waited and waited, there were shots off yonder and the sound of horsebacks riding fast. It is our warriors coming back. I can see them there at the top of the hill, and they have stopped to shoot at the soldiers. Then they turn and gallop down the ridge.

"The road is empty. It is still. We hear iron hoofs yonder. Now the soldiers come out of the sky up there. They stop and look. Now they are riding two together down the ridge, walking their big horses. There is a long blue line of them. Their breaths are white; their horses' breaths are white. They are looking here and looking there, and they are seeing nothing. They are listening and listening. They are hearing their saddles whine. They are hearing iron hoofs on the frozen road. Maybe a horse shakes its head, and they hear the bridle bit.

"It is still. There is no sound in the gullies and the brush. We are holding our ponies' noses so that they cannot cry out to the big Wasichu horses.

"The first soldiers are at the bottom of the ridge."

Eagle Voice paused. Leaning forward tensely, with a hand at his brow, he gazed beyond the tepee wall, listening open-mouthed and breathless.

"What do you see, Grandfather?" I urged.

He threw both hands aloft and in a high excited voice, cried:

"Yonder! He is standing up! He is waving a spear! It is the Cheyenne, Little Horse! *Hoka-hey! Hoka-hey!* It is a good day to die! It is a good day to kill and die! Poof!" He clapped his hands like gunshots. "The brush and the gullies are alive! There is noise everywhere—cries everywhere. We are swarming up along the sides of the ridge. The arrows are a cloud. They are grasshoppers clouding the sun. The soldiers' horses are feathered. They are screaming in the evening that the arrows make. They are crowding back up the hill in the smoke of the guns. Saddles are empty; feathered soldiers are falling. They are fighting hard and falling, full of arrows, and the kicking horses upon them are sprouting feathers.

"They are all dead at the ford. . . . Halfway up the ridge they are dead. . . . They are huddled together fighting at the top with the dead around them—and they are dying. A great cry goes up and they are covered with warriors swarming in.

"It is over."

The old man strove to light his pipe, his bony hands trembling as with palsy. I steadied the bowl and held a lighted match to it. "Thank you, Grandson," he said, in a voice gone thin and quavering on a sudden. For some time he sat studying the ground through the slowly emitted smoke. Then, handing the pipe to me, he continued. His voice had lost its former tone of harsh immediacy and seemed weary with its burden of dead days remembered.

"There was a dog—a soldier-chief's dog. He was tall and thin and long-legged, and he was crying and running towards the soldiers' town. Somebody shouted: 'Let him go and tell the other dogs back there!' But many bow-thongs twanged, and he went down rolling in a cloud of feathers.

"A storm was coming on. The sun was covered, and the wind came very strong and very cold.

"I remember when the warriors came back to the village. The night was old and dark and the wind was howling. There were many voices shouting louder than the wind out there, and the sound of many hoofs. When I 'woke, I thought the soldiers had come to kill us all when our warriors were away, and I was afraid. But my mother said: 'It is our people, and they have killed many enemies. Do you not hear them singing?' She stirred the fire and fed it, so that it would be bright and warm for my father. Then she went out into the dark full of shouting and singing and the wind; and I listened and was afraid again, for I could hear women's high voices mourning.

"But my father was not dead. There was one at his head and one at his feet when they brought him in and laid him on a robe beside the fire. His face looked queer when he smiled at me, and it was not the war paint. He was almost somebody else. His hands and feet were frozen and there was an arrow deep in his hip—a Cheyenne arrow. When they cut it out, he grunted but he did not cry. He shivered and shivered by the hot fire until a *wichasha wakon* came and made sacred medicine. Then it was morning and my mother was still sitting there beside my father, and he was sleeping.

"There was mourning in many of the lodges—high, sharp voices of the women crying for those who died in the battle and the wounded who died coming home. *Oosni! Lela oosni!* It was cold, very cold."

For some time the old man sat with his eyes closed and his chin on his chest. At length he said, as though muttering to himself:

"They all died, a hundred soldiers died in the country that was ours. But the forked-tongued ones who sent them did not die. I think they are living yet."

The New Medicine Power

"We have lost Tashina somewhere, Grandfather," I said.

The remark, dropped into a long-sustained silence, fell like a pebble upon empty air. The old man's eyes remained closed and the sharply cut features expressed nothing but age. At length his face came alive with a slowly spreading smile, and he looked at me with gentle, grandfatherly eyes.

"The pretty little girl is not lost," he said. "There is a long road, and she is yonder. But when we get there she will not be playing with her tepee, and I shall never be her horse again.

"That time when the hundred died, the Miniconjous were camped up the creek from us, and our mothers would not let us leave our village to play. 'If you do not stay at home, and if you are not good,' they would tell us, 'the bad Wasichus will get you.' So I did not see her then; and when the big trouble was over for a little while, her band was far away.

"I think the soldiers who were left in the town they built on Piney Creek were cold and hungry all that winter. If they wanted wood, they had to fight to get it. Our warriors burned their hay, and if they wanted brush to feed the mules and horses, they had to fight and die. If they wanted water from the frozen creek, they had to give some blood for it.

"More soldiers came with oxen pulling their wagons. Then the snow was deeper and deeper on the road, and there were no more wagons. Always there were hungry wolves about the soldiers' town. Our younger men were the wolves.

"Before the snow melted, my father was not sick any more and he could ride a horse and fight. But his hip was not good, and I can see him walking on one side with his hand on the other leg.

"The grass came back. It was summer, and the hearts of our people were strong because they knew the Wasichus could not steal the road to where the yellow metal was—the stuff that always makes them crazy. There was a big sun dance that made our people new again. Then it was the Moon When Cherries Blacken [August], and there was another big fight. We call it the Attacking of the Wagons. It was bad. I saw it from a hill, and I was only nine years old; but after that I think I was never all a boy any more. I saw, and when I sit and think, I see it all again; but I have heard much too, and part of what I see I must have heard.

"There were many camps along the valley of the Tongue, for many more of our own people had come to us, and many more of our friends, Cheyennes, Arapahoes. Everybody was talking about rubbing out the soldiers' towns, the one on the Piney and the one on the Big Horn too; then the buffalo would not go away, and we could be happy again.

"Our band and many others moved up Peno Creek and camped not far from where some Wasichus and soldiers had a camp on the Little Piney. They were sawing trees to make the soldiers' town stronger, and getting wood for winter too. We were going to attack this camp so that the soldiers would come out of their town. Then we would rub them out, as the hundred were rubbed out, and after that we would burn their town.

"It was in the cool dark before daybreak when our warriors began riding away from our village, and my father rode with them. I remember how big and bright the Morning Star was—big and bright and still, just waiting up there for something that it knew would happen. It was going to be a hot day. There was no wind, no cloud. I can hear men singing low as they ride away, and dogs barking. It is still again, and the star is waiting. It makes me a little afraid the way it looks and waits and is so still; but I am glad too and I want to sing.

"Then the star is gone and the sun is big and hot.

"Many of the women began going to a ridge where they could see what would happen, and where they would be close enough to take care of the horses for their men. Many of the older men went with them. Little children stayed with their grandmothers, but I was good with horses already, so I went along with my mother and grandfather. We were waiting on the north side of the ridge where the Wasichus could not see us, and there was a crowd of warriors waiting there too and in the gulches on both sides of us. They were naked and painted for battle, and they were waiting for our warriors over there on the other side of the Wasichu camp to start the attack. That is where my father was. Some of the warriors were lying on the top of the ridge looking over; and some of us little boys sneaked along in the grass on our bellies to see what they were looking at. Nobody noticed us because everybody was excited. I crawled up beside a big man lying on his belly with his chin on his arms so that he could see through the grass. He turned his head and looked hard at me, and he was a Cheyenne. I thought he was angry and was going to make me go back; but he just grinned at me and said: 'How, cousin! Where's your gun?' I showed him the bow and sharp arrows my grandfather made for me, and he said: 'Hm-m-m! Washtay!' Then he went on looking through the grass. I felt big and brave, for it was just like being a warrior already.

"The Big Piney was there below us; then there was a prairie, and beyond that we could see the trees along the Little Piney where the Wasichu camp was; and beyond that were mountains. Down there in the middle of the prairie there was a little ring made of wagon boxes where the Wasichus kept their mules at night, so that our warriors could not drive them off. There were two tents beside the ring, and we could see two or three soldiers walking around. There were some thin smokes rising straight up off yonder where the camp was in the trees. That was all there was to see. The prairie and the hills around and the trees over there and the mountains yonder looked asleep in the bright sun.

"Then there were cries away off yonder and the sound of singing. Some of our warriors over there were galloping in single file down a hill towards the Little Piney where the Wasichu camp was, and I tried hard to see if my father was one of them, but they were too far away. Gun smoke puffed from the brush and it was a cloud before the boom came. Some Wasichus began running out of the trees towards the ring of wagon boxes in the middle of the prairie. They would stop to shoot, and run again. There were not many and they looked very small. The big Cheyenne jumped up and all the others did too, shouting to each other and running back to their horses; and I ran with them.

"The people were all mixed up, and I could not see my mother and grandfather, but I was not afraid. I felt big inside of me and all over me, with horses crowding and squealing, and men mounting and shouting to each other. Then they were swarming over the hill, all singing together, and I sang too as loud as I could sing. Everybody crowded up the hill, and I crawled through the people's legs to see.

"It is still down there now. Some of our warriors are coming up out of the Little Piney. Our men have stopped down there by the Big Piney below us. I wonder what they are waiting for. Away off yonder some of our people are chasing mules. In the little ring of wagon boxes a few Wasichus are standing and looking around. On the hill over towards the sun there are many of our people waiting too. They say that is where Red Cloud was.

"Looking glasses are flashing over by the Little Piney. They are singing again below us. Some of the warriors break away from the crowd and gallop out on the prairie. Over by the Little Piney others are galloping. They circle around the ring of boxes, hanging on the sides of their horses, getting closer and shooting arrows from under the horses' necks. One is very brave and he is closer than the others. There is a puff of smoke from the ring, and his horse turns into a dust cloud before the boom comes.

"Then the singing and the shouting and the sound of horses' hoofs are like a big wind coming up all at once and thunder in the wind. They are coming from over by the sun; they are coming from the Little Piney; our men are swarming up out of the creek valley below us. There is dust, dust, and thunder in it and singing over it like a high wind blowing. The horses and men are floating in it. It is closing in over the prairie, but the ring of boxes looks empty and is still.

"No! It is not empty and still. It puffs smoke all around and goes out in a cloud and a roar. The cloud gets higher and does not go away. The roaring does not stop. It is like a great blanket ripping. There is smoke whirling all around it, and horses' heads and men's heads and war bonnets are flying in it.

"They are trying to ride over the boxes. The horses will not go.

"Now they are all coming out of the smoke and circling away from it towards the creek valley below us and the Little Piney yonder. Many of them are riding double.

"All at once it is still down there again. The smoke spreads and the sun shines in. Many horses are down and some are kicking and trying to get up, and some are dragging themselves along. When one of them screams, it is thin and far away, but it fills the big empty place because it is so still out there.

"Everything is holding its breath and looking.

"Now some warriors are going back with their horses on the run, and you can hear their death-songs. They are riding two and two and hanging low on their horses' necks. They are going back for their dead and wounded brothers out there. A great high sound goes up from the women on the hills. They are making the tremolo and singing, for those are very brave men.

"There is shooting from the ring of boxes. Some horses go down and some are dragging their riders, but others go on at a run. Two and two the riders lean and lift the wounded ones, where arms are held up among the dead horses; two and two they lean and lift the dead, and gallop away. They are very brave, and the voices of the women are one great voice on the hills.

"Looking glasses are flashing over there. The warriors are singing again, and they are coming back. They are coming from the Little Piney and from over by the sun. They are galloping up out of the valley below us, whipping each other's horses and riding fast. *Hoka-hey! Hoka-hey!* This time they will go over and the Wasichus will be rubbed out.

"The ring of boxes is a cloud of smoke with thunder ripping in it. It is the same as before. Dust and smoke and horses whirling in it, and a great noise floating high above it like a kind of cloud.

"They are closer than before. They are going over now and it will be finished.

"No! They cannot go over. They cannot make the horses go, and they are coming out of the smoke, circling back towards the creeks. Many, many are riding double.

"It is still again out there, and the smoke begins to get thin. The women on the hill over by the sun have seen, and you can hear them mourning. It is like a little wind high up in pine trees. Now our own women have seen, and they are crying and mourning. I am crying too—because I want to kill Wasichus and I cannot.

"There are many more horses down now, scattered around the ring of boxes. Some of our men are lying at the top of the creek bank below us, shooting with guns and bows at the Wasichus. Fire arrows are falling in the ring, and the mule dung there begins to burn and smoke.

"There is not much shooting from the boxes when the brave ones ride back to save the wounded that are left out there and to pick up the dead. Maybe the Wasichus are getting tired; maybe they are blinded by the mule dung smoking, I do not know. The women are not making the tremolo now. The hills are sending forth a great voice, but it is a voice of sorrow for their men and boys down there.

"We waited. What could we do if the horses would not go over? The ring was little, the Wasichus were few, we were many; but we could not go over. Our people had never seen anything like it before. The Wasichus did not shoot and then wait to load their guns. They kept on shooting—*br–r–r–r*—just like tearing a big blanket all around the ring. It was some new medicine power they had, and it made their few like many. Afterwards we learned about the new guns that were loaded from behind, and that is why they could shoot so fast. It was the first time they had such guns, and we could not understand.

"The sun was high and hot, and we were waiting. The prairie was asleep. The dung smoke rising from the ring of boxes looked sleepy too, and that was all that moved down there. The dead horses scattered around looked lazy, all stretched out and resting in the hot sun.

"Afterwhile we could see some horsebacks galloping both ways from the hill over towards where the sun comes up. Maybe Red Cloud was telling the warriors what to do. Then, as far as we could see, everything was waiting and sleeping under the high sun."

For some time Eagle Voice waited too, his eyes closed, his chin on his chest. I put a chunk of cottonwood in the sheet-iron stove, and still he sat motionless. It seemed that he had lost interest in his story, or had fallen asleep.

"And then what happened?" I asked at length.

"I was thinking about my father," he said, looking through me and far away. "I was thinking how young he was then. If he could come back now, he would be like my grandson." Then he fell to brooding again with his chin on his chest.

"And did the horses go over at last?" I urged.

He came slowly out of his daydream, as though reluctant to continue.

"It was the new medicine power," he said, "and they were afraid; but our warriors were very brave. They had gone away from the creek valley below us, and only a few were lying along the top of the creek bank, waiting for something.

"Then there was a great wind of singing all at once over to the right towards where the sun goes down. They were coming out of a draw there, all afoot and packed together like a wedge pointed at the ring of boxes; and it was a death-song they were singing all together! I have seen a mountain meadow full of flowers high up in the Pa Sapa [the Black Hills], and their war bonnets were like that meadow walking in a wind, and the wind was a death-song. It was long ago and I am old, but I see it and hear it yet. The high sun stared; the hills listened, the ring of boxes slept in the drowsy dung smoke.

"They did not hurry; but they came and came, swaying together in the wind of singing that they made—a loud wind dying, a low wind rising—loud and low, loud and low.

"Some horsebacks charged from over by the Little Piney, and a great cry went up from the women on the hills. And then—the ring of boxes was a whirling cloud again with that ripping thunder in it.

"They were coming faster now and we could hear their singing high above the thunder. We could see the point go dull and sharpen again, go dull and sharpen, until it was hidden in the whirling smoke. Then there was nothing to hear but the voices of the women like one great voice.

17

"Now our warriors would go over, and it would be finished. They had given themselves to death, and what could stop them? They would go over now, and it would be finished at last."

The old man sat tense and breathless for a moment, peering narrow-eyed through and beyond the tent wall. Then the look of battle left his face and his eyes returned to mine. "It was the new medicine power," he said wearily, "and it was stronger than ours. When they came out of the smoke, fleeing back towards the draw, they were like that blooming meadow in a hailstorm. Many, many were carrying their comrades on their backs, the wounded and the dead."

Wandering to Mourn

"We all went away from the hill back to our camp on the Peno," the old man continued, "and I heard them say the soldiers were coming from their town. But they did not follow us. Maybe if they had followed we could have rubbed them out like the hundred on the ridge, for the anger of our people was as strong as their sorrow, and the village was full of mourning.

"When they carried my father into our lodge and laid him on a buffalo robe, his face was a stranger's and it made me afraid. His war paint was all smeared with the sweat and dust of the battle. His eyes were empty and his mouth was still open for the song he was singing to death when it took him, and the blood was black on his chest.

"My grandmother and grandfather came to mourn with my mother and me; and two good old women came also. It was the way they would come to help a baby get started right to live in this world, and now they came to help him go away to the world of spirit. They washed him all clean and rubbed his body with sacred red paint. Then they unbraided his hair and combed it, and when it was all clean and shiny, they braided it again very carefully and tied an eagle feather in it for spirit power. And when this was done, they painted his face, with a young moon on his forehead, blue for the west where it would lead him. There all the days of men have gone, and the black road of trouble ends. The grass is green forever there and the sky is always blue and men and animals are happy together. There nothing is afraid and no one is old. Then they dressed him in a fine buckskin dress that my grandmother had made for him; tanned very soft, it was, and beautiful with beadwork and porcupine quills. And when I looked at him I was not afraid any more; but I cried hard when they wrapped him in a buffalo robe and tied it tight about him with thongs until he was only a bundle, for I would never see his face again in this world, and the land of spirit was very far away.

"It made me cry harder to hear my mother and grandmother mourning. I can hear my mother saying like a song: 'He was so good to us and he always brought us plenty of meat and always gave to the old people too. And now we are all alone.' And I can hear my grandmother singing a low sleepy song to him now and then, as though he were a baby, and I can hear her saying: 'I fed you at these breasts when I was young and you were little. Now my breasts are dry and you have gone away, my son, and I want to go too.' I can see my grandfather with tears shining on his cheeks in the firelight, and I can hear him singing a low song for courage over and over, so that his son would still be brave.

"Afterwhile I cried myself to sleep; and it was morning.

"Then some people came and my grandfather told them he wanted to give everything away. So the criers went about the village calling out to all the people:

" 'Gray Bear's son is going on a long journey and will not come back. His mother will not see him again in this world, and his woman is left alone. Let the needy come to Gray Bear, for now he has no son and he wants to give away the little he has left.'

"So people came to our lodge, mourning with us; and when they went away, we had nothing but sorrow. Only one horse we kept, my father's buffalo-runner, and that was for him to ride on his long journey.

"Then when the day was going to the spirit land, some friends came leading a pony with a drag. When they had placed my father on the poles we started away towards the hills. Behind the drag was my grandfather leading the buffalo-runner; then my grandmother, then my mother, and I followed her; and behind us were relatives and those who had the gifts that made us poor. And as we walked we wept.

"I remember how a big flock of crows saw us coming up a little valley, and rose with many voices of mourning and fled from us, still crying far off; and how the hills looked down at us, all listening and sorry.

"Then we came up out of the valley where the shadows were growing, and in the low sunlight on a hilltop was a new scaffold that our friends had made that day. The four standing poles were stripped of bark, and the story of my father's deeds was painted on them, to tell how brave he was.

"They unhitched the pony and leaned the drag against the scaffold. Then two men climbed up and pulled the bundle to the top and tied it down with thongs against the winds. And when this was done, they led the buffalo-runner under the scaffold, with his face towards the setting sun; and just before they shot him, he lifted up his head and sent forth a great, shrill neigh, as though he were calling to my father away off yonder.

"The people all went away in the twilight, and the night up there was big and still and starry; so big and still that it did not seem to know about my father and our weeping and moaning there by the scaffold. Only the coyotes heard us; and when they raised their high sharp song of sorrow and ceased, the night was bigger and stiller than before, and nothing cared.

"I remember my grandfather standing still and dim and tall against the stars, facing the end of earthly days with his hands held high. Sometimes I could hear him praying aloud to Wakon Tonka, then for a long while he would just stand there holding up his hands. When I heard him asking for 'the strength to understand and the eyes to see,' I forgot to cry with wondering how strong I'd have to be. Maybe the buffalo-runner could understand because he was so strong; maybe he had the eyes to see; and maybe that was why he called so loud towards where the sun goes down. Maybe a buffalo bull, a very big one, could understand everything. Then I got to wondering what it would be like if I were strong as a big buffalo bull and had the eyes to see into the land of spirit. How blue would the sky be and how green the grass? If there were never any clouds, how could it rain and keep the grass from getting yellow? What was my father doing now, and had he caught his buffalo-runner yet?

"Then all at once I wasn't there on the hill any more, and I could see.

"It was a wide land, wider than many looks could reach across, and yet I saw it all together; and what was far away was near too, because of the clear light that lived everywhere. Many smokes rose straight like slender trees from many hoops of people living in green valleys by bright streams. And while I looked and looked, there was a kind of singing everywhere, although everything was still. Then all at once a great happy neighing filled the world, and there was a horseback coming on a green, green hill that lived high up in the blue, blue sky; and I saw it was the buffalo-runner that came prancing and nickering, and on his back was my father smiling down at me, and his face was all shining. Then he leaned to hold a hand for my foot, and I mounted behind him, light as a feather, and the buffalo horse leaped into a run that was like floating, and when he neighed it was laughter. Buffalo beyond counting raised their noses from the glowing grass and lowed softly as we passed, and the elk were glad to see us and the deer and antelope danced with joy.

"Then when we had come to the high green hilltop living in the happy blue, the horse stood floating, and I heard my father saying: 'You must go back to your mother now and take care of her and tell her not to cry any more. Always be good to old people and bring them tender meat that they can chew. And never be afraid of anything.' And when I put my arms around his waist, trying to hold on a little longer, there was nothing in my arms, and the hill went dark; and I awoke, lying beside the scaffold in the cold starlight.

"My grandfather lay sound asleep there where he had been praying; and my mother and grandmother were sleeping too, worn out with weeping. There was a low streak of day far off, and the big morning star was looking down at me, very kind with something that it knew, for what it knew was good.

"I was glad the old ones were resting, and I did not feel alone or afraid, because my father was just a little sleep away. And while I sat there looking at the star, I thought of many great deeds that I would do, for I would be as brave as my father and as good to all the old people. I was almost a chief already in my thinking before the streak of day had widened and the star died. Then all the hills around stood up to stare upon the scaffold with sad looks, and I began to cry again.

"Some relatives came with the sun to take us back to the village, and there was a sweat bath ready for my grandfather and me. And while we were being cleansed and rubbed with sacred sage, some women were taking care of my mother and grandmother, washing the tears from their faces and combing and braiding their hair. Then they fed us, and we ate.

"And when we had eaten, there were two good old men and two good old women who came to teach us, the men for the men and the women for the women. And they taught us, being wise, for they had lived much and wanted nothing any more. It was a good time to become better people, they said, for now we had nothing left but the spirit. We should stay there four days after the village moved away, and those four days we should lament and pray. But there were others who had lost everything, and they were mourning too. We should remember to be kind to them and to try to help them in their sorrow, and that would make our spirits stronger. Then after four days, we could leave that place and wander alone, the four of us; and while we wandered we should mourn less and less, but keep on praying. And always we should be up to see the morning star, for that would give us wisdom.

"So the village moved away from that place of death, and only those who mourned were left; and we were all kind to each other, sharing much sorrow and a little meat.

22

"And when the fifth day came, we caught one of the old horses that had been left behind, a lame old grandfather horse who was always looking at the ground. And we made a drag for him and on it we put a smoke-blackened piece of an old tepee that was left behind because it was no good any more. Then we began wandering alone out into the hills towards where the sun comes up, because there were no soldiers over there.

"We had no gun, but I had my bow with the sharp arrows. It was my second bow and it was still a little too strong for me. My grandfather had said it would make me grow faster so; but that was why I had never killed anything bigger than a rabbit. I could not pull it far enough to kill.

"My grandfather felt bad when we began to wander, and he got sicker until he could hardly walk. So we camped by a water hole and made a shelter with the old piece of a tepee, so that he could rest and get well. Of course, my mother and grandfather could not talk to each other, because he was her man's father, but my mother was good to him anyway. She would hunt turnips and berries, and when she had cooked these, she would put them where he could get them. If they wanted to say something to each other, they would tell my grandmother and she would say it. The little dried meat we had was gone, and we got very hungry eating wild turnips and buffalo berries.

"We did not forget to pray, but it seemed Wakon Tonka did not hear us. I roamed far from our camp looking for a rabbit that I could kill; but I could not find one sitting; and when I would came back with nothing, my mother and grandmother would be crying, because they were thinking how it was before my father went away.

"Then one day when I was far from camp looking for meat, I came to a water hole with deer tracks all around it; and all at once my heart grew strong, for there was a clump of brush just a little way from the hole, and I knew what I would do. I did not say anything about this at home, and I think I hardly slept at all that night.

"Something 'woke me when it was still dark. The morning star was just beginning to look over the world, and I asked it to help me. The others were still asleep, and I started for the water hole where the deer tracks were. There was a long valley, and afterwhile there was a gulch to the right. Up that gulch and over a ridge there was another valley. To the left a long way up that valley was the hole with the deer tracks, over at the bottom of a ridge to the right, and close by was the brush. I was running fast before I knew it; but I made myself go slower because

I could not shoot straight out of breath. It was hard to keep from running, but I came to the place when there was just a little streak of day far off. The star looked happy, waiting for something good to happen.

"It was very still, because the wind was waiting for the sun; but when I wet my finger in my mouth and held it up, I could feel the air breathing a little towards the water hole; and that was good. Then I went into the brush, standing so that I could see the hole, and began to pray hard, just whispering so that only Wakon Tonka could hear me, and I said: 'Grandfather, send me a deer and make me strong to pull this bow and guide my arrow when I shoot. You see that we are poor, for we have given everything to the needy. My mother is crying, and the old people are crying, and we are all hungry. I have been a little boy long enough, and you must make me strong. You can do anything.'

"When I had said this over and over, I got to thinking of my dream there by the scaffold, and how he told me to take care of my mother and be good to old people. While I thought about this, I could feel myself growing stronger and stronger. And when it was just getting daylight, all at once there was a deer with a fawn coming down to the water hole.

"I held my breath and waited until they put their noses in the water. The smaller one had its side towards me, and it was the one I wanted, because maybe I could drag it home, and also the meat would be very tender for my sick grandfather.

"Maybe it was the dream that made me strong. I took a big breath and pulled quick and hard. Maybe Wakon Tonka pulled a little too. The string came back almost to my shoulder. *Whang!*

"I ran out of the brush and danced and yelled and yelled, until the hills across the valley yelled back, cheering me for what I had done. The arrow went deep just behind the shoulder. I had a deer! I had a deer!

"Then I quit yelling, because the fawn began to look so big I wondered how I was going to get it all the way home. I had my knife yet, because I was so proud of it that I kept it hidden when we were giving to the needy. I could cut off a hindquarter and carry that; but I wanted to show the whole deer all at once. So I began dragging it down the valley by the heels. But it was getting bigger and bigger, and when the sun looked over at me, I was all out of breath and had to sit down on it and pant. Then when I had my breath back, I began dragging again. But the sun was getting hotter and the deer was getting bigger. Pretty soon it would be as big as a buffalo, and I could never get it all over the ridge into the next valley.

"I looked around with a forked mind, wondering what to do, and there were some stunted trees standing low down on the side of the

24

ridge I had to cross. I would cut the deer up and put the pieces in a tree, all but one hindquarter, where my mother and I could find them. So that is what I did.

"The sun was getting high when I sneaked up to the camp through some brush because I wanted to surprise my people. And when my mother and grandmother saw me there, panting and all bloody with the meat on my shoulder, they just stared awhile with their mouths open. Then my grandmother began jumping up and down like a little girl, crying: 'O see what our grandson has brought us! O see what our big grandson has brought us!' Then my grandfather sat up; and when he saw, he clapped his hands, crying, 'hiyay! hiyay!' And my mother laughed with joy. It was the first time since my father went away.

"So my mother sliced the meat and roasted it over a low fire, and we feasted. But before we ate, my grandfather raised his hands towards where the sun goes down, and made an offering, like this: 'Grandfather, Great Mysterious One, behold me! You have sent our boy a deer and made us happy. Remembering all living things that are in need, this I offer to you that my people may live and the children grow up with plenty.' Then each of us cut off a little piece of meat and tossed it over the shoulder. It was the first bite to the Spirit that gave. I did not make mine very big, for I could feel teeth inside of me, I was so hungry. While we ate I had to tell how I did it, and I told everything but the dream; for if I told that, maybe I would lose my new medicine power.

"When my mother and I brought the rest of the meat home, we feasted again; and when we were full, we sang. Then my grandfather blew a big breath and said: 'I think this is going to make me well again.' And so it was.

"I did not sleep for a long while that night, thinking about what I had done and all I was going to do. Sometimes I could hear my mother crying a little so as not to waken anybody, and my grandmother moaning in her sleep. It made me feel stronger than ever to hear this.

"It is a long way back to where we have been, and I am weary. You will come again tomorrow."

Was the Great Voice Angry?

It was apparent from a distance that Eagle Voice was up and waiting. A thin stem of smoke from a well-established fire stood tall and straight above the tepee, blooming flatly aloft in the glittering, knife-edged air of the clear morning.

As I stooped through the flap, the sudden friendly warmth seemed to radiate from the old man's happy face. "*How*, my grandson," he said merrily. "The Grandfather has sent us a good day, and I am glad to see you."

The pipe was ready and we smoked awhile in silence.

"That was very tender meat we had yesterday," he said at length, with a mock-serious crinkling about his eyes. "I think it was the best meat I ever ate. It sent me a good dream last night, and I think I am getting younger. If only I had enough of it, maybe I could turn into a boy!

"Yes, it made my grandfather well again, and after that we did not lack meat, for he was a better hunter than I was, even with my new medicine power! In those days I thought he was almost as old as the hills, but I can see now that he would have to be my younger son if he came back.

"So we wandered while the young moon came and grew and died, praying much and mourning less and less; and always we were up to see the morning star. Who sees the morning star shall see more, for he shall be wise. The people were still good in those days before the sacred hoop was broken; but the time of wandering alone with the spirit, mourning and praying, made them better. It was like dying with the dear one and coming back all new again and stronger to live. Now, when somebody dies, we don't go anywhere. We just sit where we are and feel bad, and we don't get along with each other any more, for we have forgotten how to learn.

"Afterwhile it was getting to be the time to make winter meat, and we wanted to be ready for the big buffalo hunt; so we went back to our village in the valley of the Tongue.

"Everybody was happy to see us again. The people sang welcoming songs when we entered the hoop and circled the village from left to right, as young men ride after a victory. My grandfather walked first, leading the horse with the drag, and behind the drag was grandmother, then my mother, and I was last. The old grandfather horse was very tired, but he lifted his head and nickered to the singers, for he was happy too.

"When my mother and grandmother had set up the old smoke-blackened piece of a tepee for a shelter, many people came to us with food, and we feasted together. And while we feasted, there was a big giving of gifts until we were not poor at all. There was a tepee of buffalo hide made double against the coldest winter and the hottest summer, and the deeds of my father were painted on it. Our new horses were staked all around us, whinnying with joy, and none of them was old. We all had new buckskin dresses; my grandfather had a good gun with plenty of powder and lead; and there was nothing lacking in the tepee that women need to make a home. But the best gift of all was the horse I got for myself. He was not too young, not too old either, and I called him Whirlwind because he could run so fast. It was Looks Twice who gave the gift with a speech that made me proud, for he was my father's brother-friend, and he carried my father dead out of the battle. Brother-friends do not have the same mother and father, but they are closer than common brothers, because they are just like one man, and if one of them is in trouble, the other must help, even if he knows he will die. Maybe that horse had some spirit power from my father, for sometimes when I was riding alone, all at once I would be back in the dream that came to me by the scaffold, and Whirlwind would be the buffalo-runner floating."

The animated expression suddenly left the old man's face, and for some time he sat looking at the ground, blowing softly on his eagle-bone whistle. A chuckle signaled his return from the remoteness of the inner world.

"I was thinking," he said with the crinkled look, "about stealing my grandfather's pipe that time; and this is how it was. I knew I had to be a great warrior and a great hunter so that everyone would praise me, and I had a good start already with the fawn. I thought and thought about it. Maybe in the big hunt we were going to have I could sneak out among the hunters when everybody was excited, and nobody would notice; and maybe there would be a lame cow and I could kill her. Or it would be a calf anyway, maybe one that had lost its mother in the dust. I was not very sure about the cow; but the more I thought, the more I knew I had to have that calf; and it came to me that I'd better get Wakon Tonka to help me. I would dedicate a pipe to the Great Mysterious One and make a sacred vow the way I had heard them tell real warriors did. Then maybe I would get that calf. I was already feeding enough old people for ten calves when it came to me that I had no pipe.

"That was when I made a mistake. I said to myself: 'It will be all right to take grandfather's pipe, because I am doing this for *very* old people who have hardly any teeth at all; and anyway he has two pipes now.' I did not ask for the pipe, because I knew he would not let me have it. So I just took it when nobody was looking, and rode far out to where there was a tall, pointed hill, standing all alone above the little hills that sat around it.

"When I tied Whirlwind to some brush and climbed to the top, I saw that some black clouds were coming up over towards where the sun goes down, and it was that way I had to look when I made my offering. I did not know just how to do it, but maybe it would be all right anyway. So I held the pipe up and cried out in a loud voice: '*Tonka schla*, Wakon Tonka! You see me here and you know I must get a calf for the old people, because they can hardly chew. I give you this pipe, and if you send me a calf, I will dance the sun dance, just as soon as I get big enough.'

"When I said this, all at once there was a big thunder off there— *boom-m-m how-ow-ow oom-m-m ow-ow!*

"I dropped the pipe and ran as fast as I could down the hill. Some of me almost got there before I did, because I stumbled and rolled part of the way. Then I rode home as fast as Whirlwind could go, because the big voice sounded angry, and I was frightened.

"When I got home I did not say anything to anybody. And afterwhile grandmother said: 'I wonder what is wrong with our boy. He looks queer.' And my mother said: 'He does look queer. Maybe he ate too much.' Then my grandfather looked hard at me and said: 'Maybe he has been smoking my pipe, for I see it is not here.' And when he kept on looking hard at me for a while, I had to tell him; but I did not tell everything. I just said I took it because I had to make a vow so that we would get plenty of meat in the hunt.

"I thought he was getting ready to be angry, he looked so hard at me. Then he said, '*hm-m-m*,' high up in his nose, and his eyes looked as though he might be going to laugh; but he didn't. My mother and grandmother didn't say anything. They just tried to look sad down their noses."

After chuckling awhile over the memory, the old man continued:

"If I had been a Wasichu boy, I think they would have whipped me; but Lakotas never hurt a child. They were good in those days before the sacred hoop was broken. It was the sacred way they lived in the hoop that made them good and taught the children; and I will tell you how that was.

"There were seven *teoshpaiay* [bands], seven council fires, and one of them was my people, the Oglala. They were all Lakota and had the same tongue, but they did not all say things in the same way, and when we got together, sometimes we boys would mock each other, because our way of speaking was the best. Each *teoshpaiay* was a hoop by itself, and could go anywhere it pleased, for it had its own tepee *okige*, the highest tepee where its chief lived, and its own tepee *iyokihe*, the next highest tepee, where its councilors made the laws for the people.

"When all the seven *teoshpaiay*, or most of them, came to live together, they would camp in a great hoop, which was more sacred than any of the smaller hoops that made it. And if there were laws to be made for all the hoops to obey or something to decide for all of them, then each *teoshpaiay* would bring its council tepee to the center of the great hoop; and with all these tepees they would make a big place for all the councils and chiefs to meet as one, and this they called tepee-thrown-over-together. It had no roof, only walls, because it was not needed very long.

"And it was here that four were chosen to be chiefs above all others— one *wichashita nacha*, who is highest, and three *nacha*, who were next.

"Also each hoop had its own *akichita*, and they were the keepers of all the laws. They were like relatives of the thunder beings, and theirs was the power of lightning. Nothing could stop them; and if any man broke a law, they took care of him, even a brother or a father. If the chief himself broke a law, the *akichita* could throw him out of the tepee *okige*, and a better man would be chosen. If any should go on a war party or a hunt when the council said, 'no,' the *akichita* could whip them and cut their tepees in pieces. And if any fought the *akichita*, they would be killed. If you broke a law, it was like breaking the sacred hoop a little; and that was a very bad thing, for the hoop was the life of the people all together.

"If an *akichita* did some bad thing or did not do what he ought to do, then the *wichasha yatapika* could throw him out before all the people; and it was better to die than to see shame in every face. Even little boys could mock such a man and no one would stop them. For the *wichasha yatapika* [men whom all praise] were stronger at last than all others except Wakon Tonka; and yet they did not make the laws. They chose the chiefs and the councilors and the *akichita* from among themselves; and any man could become one of them, but it was not easy, and it took a long time.

"It was like this. Maybe I am a young man and I think to myself that I want to be a chief sometime. I don't say anything to anybody about this, but I know what I must do. First, I must be very brave. I have to kill an enemy, I have to count coup so many times, and I have to get a scalp. Nobody can say I was ever afraid. But that is only the beginning I must never break any laws, I must be good to everybody in the hoop, so that afterwhile people notice this and talk about it until everybody is saying it. And that too is only the beginning, although it takes a long time. I must be very generous and always see that old people and the needy have meat. I do not do this once or twice. I keep on doing it until everybody notices and talks about it, and then I keep on doing it.

"Maybe some old men and women are sitting around under a sunshade made of boughs. They are talking about the old days when everything was better. And, afterwhile, one of them, who can see a little better than the others, squints at a hilltop, and says: 'A horseback is coming over there, and he is bringing something. I wonder who it is.' Then they all squint at the horseback coming, and when he is closer, another one says: 'Why, that is Gray Bear's son, Eagle Voice, and I think he is bringing some meat.' Then they all cry out together, *'hi-yay!'* Because people have been talking about me, and the old ones know I will come to them first with the tenderest pieces. But if I am somebody else, and a stingy fellow, then the old people will say, *'heh-heh-heh,'* and look down their noses. And if that is what old people say about me, I am never going to be a *wichasha yatapika,* even if I have killed a hundred enemies.

"After people have noticed these things for a long time, even the *wichasha yatapika* begin to talk about me in their meetings, and at last they say: 'This young Eagle Voice ought to be one of us.' So they have a big feast and a ceremony at the center of the hoop, with all the people sitting around. And before they take me to be one of them, the people are asked to say any evil thing they may know about me. But all the people cry out together, *'hi-yay, hi-yay,'* and not even a jealous one can say anything bad at all. So they make me a man whom all praise, and before all the people they teach me what I must do, and they say I do not belong to myself any more, but to the people. Then I take the pipe they offer and smoke it; and that is a sacred vow.

"Now I am a *wichasha yatapika,* and I can be an *akichita,* or a councilor, or even a chief, if I keep on being brave enough and generous enough and good enough. It is hard to be any of these, but it is hardest of all to be a chief, because he must be *wachin tonka* [great minded] standing above himself, as he stands above others.

"When they make him a chief, they will say: 'Maybe your favorite dog will come home with an arrow in him. You will not be angry, but hold fast to your pipe and remember the laws. Maybe some mangy dog will water your tepee in the dark [malicious gossip]. You will have neither eyes nor ears, but you will look into your heart, and go ahead. If anything you have is better for another than for you, it will be his. You do not belong to yourself.'

"I will tell you a little story to show how it was in the old days before the sacred hoop was broken. Once there was a great chief, a *wichashita nacha,* and although he was still strong like a bear, he was not young any more; and the people listened to his words for he was wise. This old chief had taken a young woman who was very good to see, and he was so fond of her that people talked about it and smiled behind their hands; but they felt kind when they smiled. And I think the young woman liked the chief because he was so good to her, but maybe she was only proud because his power was so great. And afterwhile there was a young warrior who was very brave, and also very good to see; and these two looked upon each other until they could see nothing else at all. So they ran away together far from the village; and the people talked and talked, wondering what the chief would do. And this is what he did.

"When he had called an *akichita,* he said: 'Go find this man and woman wherever they are and bring them here to me.' It was done as he had spoken. And when at last the two stood before him in the tepee *okige,* for they had hidden far away to be alone together, they were so afraid that they could hardly stand. But the old chief smiled at them and said: 'Sit down beside me here, and do not be afraid. No law is made against your being young, and, if there were, I broke it long ago.'

"So the young woman sat upon his left, and on his right the other. And when the three had sat thus very still for a long while, just looking at the ground, the old chief spoke to the *akichita:* 'Bring here to me my best buffalo runner, the young sorrel with the morning star on his forehead.' And when this was done, he took the end of the horse's lariat and placed it in the hands of the young man on his right. Then he said: 'Give me my bow and arrows yonder'; and these also he placed in the young man's hands.

"Then he turned to where the young woman sat weeping with her face in her hands, and what he did then was very hard for him to do.

"They tell it he was very gentle while he undid the long braids of the young woman, who was weeping harder now. And when her hair was hanging all loose down her back and she was just a girl again, he took a comb and combed it gently. Over and over he combed it, until it was all smooth and shining like the bend of a crow's wing in the sun. Then with great care he parted it and braided it again, doing this very slowly. And when the braids were tied, he took the woman's hand and placed it in the hand of him who sat upon the right. 'Go now,' he said, 'and be good people.' Some tell it there were tears upon his face, but others that he kept them in his breast. I do not know.

"All this was many snows ago, before the sacred hoop was broken, and when people still were good."

Chased by a Cow

The old man chuckled after one of his long silences. "Yes," he said, "I wondered if the great voice was angry when it called to me on the pointed hill. But my grandfather was not angry about the pipe, and maybe the great voice was not either. I thought and thought about this. Maybe that was the only voice Wakon Tonka had, and it only sounded angry because it was so big. Maybe it was cheering me for making the offering.

"Everybody was getting ready for the big hunt, and something wonderful was going to happen. I might even get a cow, a lame one; and then everybody would praise me. Anyway, it would be a calf—one that got lost, maybe in a draw to one side away from the herd. When I had killed it, I would find my mother and grandmother, and they would come and butcher it. Then we would pack the meat on Whirlwind, and when we came into the village with the meat, people would notice and my grandmother would tell the other old women: 'See what my grandson did, and he is going to give it all to the old people.'

"The scouts had gone out to look for a bison herd over towards where the sun comes up, and one day the criers went about the village, calling: 'Make moccasins for your children! Look after the children's moccasins!' And that meant to be ready, for we were going to move. Then early next morning the criers went around, calling: 'Councilors, come to the center! Councilors, come to the center and bring your fires!' They did this because in the old days a long time ago, the people had no matches or flint and steel. They could make fire another way in dry rotten wood by rubbing sticks together, but that was hard and could not always be done. Fire was sacred then, and had to be kept alive when the people moved. Then when they camped again, everybody came to the center and got fire for their own tepees. They did not have to do it this time, but it was part of living in a sacred manner, and that was good for the people.

"When the councilors had brought their fires to the center, the criers shouted to the people: 'Take it down! Take it down!' And the women all began taking down the tepees and packing everything on pony-drags. Then when everything was ready we began moving towards where the sun comes up, for that way the scouts had gone. First were the six councilors on foot; then came the chiefs with the criers behind them, then the *akichita,* and after them were the people with the loaded pony-drags. If there were enemies to be feared, there would be riders out there on our flanks and some ahead and behind; but there was no enemy to fear the way we were going; and we were so many that no band of Crows would attack us moving.

"There were four *teoshpaiay* going together on this hunt, one after the other in a long line; and it makes me feel good to remember how it looked. The *akichita* were not very strict before we came near the bison, and the children could play along the way. Maybe the girls would pick pretty flowers or dig up some wild turnips, or there might be a clump of rabbit berry bushes looking smoky with the berries getting red in them, like sparks; or, if it was late enough, plums might be getting good to eat, and the children would pick them while the people were passing. The bigger boys could play 'throwing them off their horses.' That was a rough game, but it was good for boys because it helped them to be brave warriors later on. They would divide up into little bands and charge each other, wrestling from the horses' backs, and sometimes a boy would get hurt. I was not big enough yet for that game, but I had a good time on Whirlwind, and sometimes I would get on a high place and see all the people traveling in a sacred manner. They were happy, and you could hear them singing here and there along the line. Maybe a drag pony would lift his head and neigh because the singing of the people made him want to sing too; and then the other ponies would lift their heads and sing down along the line.

"That was the next time I saw Tashina. I was riding up and down the line with some other boys; and when we came to where the Miniconjou were, I heard somebody cry out: 'Shonka 'kan! Shonka 'kan! Come and pull my tepee!' And it was Tashina looking up at me. I was getting to be a big boy, for I had mourned and wandered, and I had killed a deer. Also I was going to kill a bison cow pretty soon, or anyway a calf. So I was too big to play with girls any more, and I did not say anything back. I wanted to talk to her, because I liked her; but I just made Whirlwind prance and rear. And when I rode away, I could see her sticking her tongue out at me and I heard her cry: 'Yah! Yah! Go and eat grass! Go and eat grass, Shonka 'kan sheetsha [bad horse]!' "

With a chuckle the old man went into one of his reveries, gazing at me with eyes that saw what wasn't there. "She *was* a pretty little girl," he said, more to himself than to me; "a very pretty little girl." Then the focus of his gaze shortened to include me, and he continued:

"It was a time for the people to be happy, so we traveled slowly. And when the sun stood high above us, it would be time to rest awhile and let the ponies graze. The councilors would choose a place where there was water and good grass. Then the criers would call out to the people: 'Take off your loads and rest your horses! Take them off and rest your horses.' And if wild turnips were growing there, they would say: 'Take your sticks and dig some turnips for yourselves!' And the women would do this while the ponies drank and grazed and the councilors sat on a hillside watching the people. And when they had smoked together maybe two or three pipes, it would be time to move again, and the criers would call: 'Now put on your loads! Put them on!' And we would move, as before, until the sun was getting low.

"By that time the councilors would know a good place to camp for the night where there was plenty of wood, water, and grass, and the criers would tell the people to make camp.

"We were all camped the sacred way, in a big hoop of four hoops with the opening towards where you are always facing [the south], and the tepee-thrown-over-together was in the center. The drags were all outside the circle, and, all around, the horses were grazing with the horse guards watching them. Smokes were standing above the tepees, for it was morning and the people were eating.

"Then there was a crier shouting: 'They are returning! The scouts I have seen. They are returning!' And all the people came out of the tepees to look. Three horsebacks were coming over the hill towards where the sun comes up, and they had something good to tell, for as they galloped down the hillside we could hear them singing together.

"When they had entered the hoop where you are always facing, they turned to the left and rode single file about the circle from left to right, looking straight ahead and saying nothing; and the people waited and were still. And when they had come again to the opening, they turned to the right and rode towards the center where the councilors and chiefs were waiting in the tepee-thrown-over-together. And as the riders came near, a crier spoke for the scouts, calling to the chiefs and councilors: 'Come forth and make haste! I have protected you, and you shall give to me in return.'

"Then the chiefs and councilors came forth, and the scouts sat down in front of them, facing the tepee, and all the people crowded around to see and hear.

35

"Then the chief filled a pipe and lit it; and when he had presented it to the Six Powers, first to the four quarters of the earth, then to the Great Mystery above, and last to the ground, which is the mother of all living things, he placed it on a buffalo chip in front of him, with the stem towards the scouts. There was bison hide on the mouthpiece of the pipe, and it was sacred; for it was through the bison that Earth, the mother of all, fed the people, and whoever smoked the pipe was nursing at his mother's breast like a little child. The chip was sacred too, for it meant the bison. They were the life and shelter of the people's hoop, and when they died, the sacred hoop was broken.

"Then the chief spoke to the scouts: 'The nation has depended upon you. Whatever you have seen, maybe it is for the good of the people you have seen it.' And when he had said this, he offered the pipe to the scouts. They took it, smoking in turn, and that was a sacred vow that what they told would be the truth.

"Then the chief spoke again, and said: 'At what place have you stood and seen the good? Report it to me and I shall be glad. You have been raised on this earth, and every corner of it you know. So tell me the truth.'

"The first scout was so anxious to tell that he forgot the sacred rules and held up his thumb to the Great Mysterious One. But before he spoke, the chief shook his head and said: 'Hunh unh! The first finger! The first finger for the truth!' So the first scout raised his first finger and said: 'You know where we started from. We came to a hill yonder, and there in the next valley we saw some bison.'

"The chief stood up when he heard this, and said: 'Maybe you have seen more farther on. Report it to me and I shall be glad.' And the second scout raised his first finger, saying: 'Beyond this hill there is another, and there we saw a small herd grazing in a valley.' And the chief spoke again: 'I shall be thankful if you will tell me more of the good that you have seen.' And the third scout said: 'From still another hill farther on, there we saw a big herd grazing in a valley and on the hillsides.'

"Then the chief spoke again, saying: 'Maybe you have not told me all the good that you have seen. Tell it now, and all the people will be glad.' When he had said this, the scouts forgot the rules and all began talking together: 'There is still another hill! *Wasichu! Wasichu!* There was nothing but bison all over the prairie! More than many looks could see! *Wasichu! Wasichu!*'

"When they said that, they did not mean white men. They meant very, very much of something, more than could be told or counted, like a great fatness. Then the chief cried out: 'Hetchetu aloh! [So be it].' And all the people shouted, 'hi-yay, hi-yay,' and the grazing horses out yonder, hearing the people, sent forth voices, neighing for gladness; and dogs raised their snouts and howled.

"Then the criers went forth and the people were still to hear them: 'Many bison I have heard! Many bison I have heard! Your knives you must sharpen! Your arrows make sharp. Make ready, make haste, your horses make ready! We shall go forth with arrows. Plenty of meat we shall make!'

"I had already sharpened my arrows so often that if I sharpened them much more, I wouldn't have any left. While the people were all getting ready for the big killing of meat, the council sent for certain young men who were being noticed by the people, and to these the chief said: 'Good young warriors, my relatives, your work I know is good. What you do is good always. So today you will feed the helpless and the old and feeble. Maybe there is an old woman or an old man who has no son. Or there may be a woman who has little children but no man. You will know these and hunt only for them. Today you belong to the needy.' This made the young men very proud, for it was a great honor.

"Then as the people were taking their places for going to the hunt, the criers shouted: 'Your children, take care of them! Your children, take care of them!' After that the children must stay close to their parents and not run around, for they might scare the bison; also, they might get hurt.

"Then we started off towards the big herd. First went the three scouts, riding abreast to show the way. Then came the councilors and the chiefs with the criers; and after them came all the *akichita* riding twenty abreast, and next were all the hunters, four or five abreast. If any hunter rode ahead of the *akichita,* he would be knocked off his horse and he would get no meat that day. Also, he would see shame in all eyes. The killing was for the nation, and everyone must have the same chance to kill. After the hunters were the women and older men, who would follow up and butcher the kill. Each hunter knew his arrows by the marks, and so he claimed his meat. And if two should claim a kill, then an *akichita* could decide between them or have the meat divided.

"We did not stop to rest that day, and when the sun was getting high, we began to see bison. Sometimes they were scattered out and sometimes there were small herds, but nobody was allowed to shoot at them or to cry out in a loud voice. They might get frightened, and the running fear might spread like fire in dry grass, until the big herd yonder caught the fear and started running. It was hard for the younger hunters riding behind the *akichita* up there; but no one pulled a bow or raised a voice; and all the children kept close to their mothers with the drags in the rear.

"The sun was high and had started down a little, when we saw that those ahead up yonder had stopped on a ridge to look. And while they were looking, voices came running all along the line down to us: 'Many bison they have seen! Make ready, make haste! Make ready to follow with your knives! They are going to charge!'

"Then just when the voices had come running back to us, we could see the hunters and *akichita* up yonder splitting into two big bands; one to the right and one to the left."

With a hand at his brow the old man peered narrow-eyed at the head of the column on the ridge that was a lifetime away. Then, clapping his hands high above his head, he cried: "They are charging over the hill! They are all charging! The hunters and *akichita* are charging! *Hoka-hey! hoka-hey!*

"Everybody was excited, and the people were hurrying towards the hunt, except the very old ones and the women who stayed back to take care of the drag ponies and the children and to set up the tepees; for that was a good place to camp and there would soon be plenty of meat to dry and many hides to tan.

"Nobody was noticing me, and there were no *akichita* around there, so when I saw the hunters charge I charged too—not towards where the hunters had gone, but away from the people to the right where there was a big patch of buffalo berry bushes to help me. When Whirlwind and I got behind them, we started on the run towards where there was a break in the ridge ahead, to the right of where the hunters went over. While we were crossing the valley, my calf grew so fast that when I rode into the ravine, it wasn't a calf at all any more, but a big fat cow, and maybe even two cows.

"The ravine was full of thunder that was coming from a rolling storm of dust ahead. And when we got close over there and stopped to look down, we were a little scared. Whirlwind snorted and wanted to go back, but I had made an offering and I had to do something.

"Dust and thunder, dust and steady thunder with bull voices roaring in it! And wherever the dust blew thinner in the wind or lifted a little, there were backs, backs, backs of galloping bison bobbing up and down; bison beyond counting and more and more. And here and there over to the left I could see horsebacks charging in and out along the flanks of the herd, killing and killing, lost in the dust and appearing, lost and appearing. And while I looked, a big man on a big Wasichu horse that he must have taken from the soldiers came charging out of the dust. He was after a big bull with only a spear. Just as he was coming in front of me, he rode close and leaned far over. Then I saw him drive the spear with both hands in behind the bull's front leg. I forgot that I should not be where I was, and I yelled and yelled; but the man did not know I was there. I could see that his mouth was wide open and I knew he was shouting for a kill, but he did not make any sound in the steady thunder. Then the bull stopped and turned and charged the horseback; but the man did not run away. He was very brave. Also he knew how to handle his horse, and the horse was wise too. They dodged and reared and circled until the man got hold of his spear again. Then with both hands he drove it deeper and pried it back and forth. The bull's mouth gushed blood, and when he started running again, he wabbled; and I could see the man prying the spear back and forth until the dust hid them.

"Just then, right down there not far away, a cow came loping with my calf! I did not wait. I charged. It is not easy to put an arrow where you want it from a galloping horse's back and the horse all excited. I was yelling, 'yu-hoo,' already, because I had one arrow sticking in the calf's hump and was pulling the bow for another try at the right place behind the front leg, when Whirlwind squealed and reared and wheeled away. For a long time after that it made me feel a little better when I blamed him for running away with me just as I was really getting my calf. But I was as scared as he was when I saw the cow charging us, and I did not look around until we were far up the side of the ridge. By that time the cow was loping back to find her calf.

"When I got Whirlwind to stand still, I was a little scared yet, and I was ashamed too. Nobody but the cow saw me running away, but Wakon Tonka could see everything, and I had made an offering. So I thought, there are plenty of calves, and when Whirlwind is not afraid any more I will charge again. Maybe it will be better next time.

"But that part of the herd was getting thinner as it passed to the right, and I could see more and more hunters among them, killing and killing. Sometimes I could even hear their cries above the rumbling sound when they killed: 'Ohee! Yuhoo!' Then I said to myself, 'If I go down there now they will see me and the akichita will get me.' So I did not go down. Anyway, it was good to watch the hunters killing, and that is what I did. Afterwhile, when the dust and rumbling had passed, I could see the people yonder scattered in spots all over the prairie butchering the kill. That made me very hungry, so I galloped down there where the grass was beaten to dust; and wherever I came to a butchering they would give me something to eat—a chunk of liver, maybe with gall poured over it, or a piece of the strip of fat that runs along the backbone. It is good raw, but it is even better roasted a little. By the time I found my grandmother and grandfather, they had a fat cow all cut up on the stretched-out hide. They told me to ride over to a draw and to get some dry brush; and when I got back, my grandmother made a little fire. Then she roasted pieces of fat hump meat, and some old people came over to help us eat it.

"When the sun was getting low people were going back to camp with their horse-loads and drag-loads of meat and hides; and they kept on coming in with their loads long after it was dark. Before the feasting began, all the councilors and chiefs went into the tepee-thrown-over-together, and people came from all over the village with gifts of the best meat. This is how they gave thanks for good leading. Then the councilors cried, 'hiya-hiya,' and sang all together to the bringers of food. And when the councilors had eaten awhile, the criers went about the village again, calling: 'All come home, for it is more than we can eat. Come home! There is plenty for all!' Then the people came with their cups and crowded about the tepee-thrown-over-together that all might have some of the councilors' meat; and after that the feasting began— feasting and dancing all night long. I can see the circle of the village yet with all the fires and the happy people feasting and singing. It makes me want to sing, too, for that is the way the Grandfather meant we should live. It was the sacred way and it kept the people good.

"That was near the Rosebud River, and it was a big killing; for we stayed there and killed until there was plenty for all. We had no hunter in our tepee, but the chosen young men offered us more than we could use, and my father's brother-friend, Looks Twice, took care of us. He brought the meat to my grandparents; but I know now that he was thinking most of my mother, because he wanted to be my father; and afterwhile he was.

"Next day there were drying racks all over the village, and I can see the stripped red meat turning brown in the bright sunlight, and the brown turning black. And I can see the happy women sitting in little circles with their sharp knives, unwinding the chunks of meat in their laps. They are joking and laughing and holding up their strips of meat to see whose is thinnest and longest. And outside the village raw hides are pegged out everywhere, and the old women are scraping and beating them for the soft tanning that made them good to wear and to sleep in on the coldest night.

"But I kept thinking and thinking about the calf I did not kill and of the way I got chased by the cow. If it had only been a bull I might have felt better. It helped a little to blame Whirlwind for running away; but then I would remember the big voice that called to me on the pointed hill when I offered my grandfather's pipe, and I began to feel sure the voice was angry at me.

"Some of us boys made a war-game of sneaking up to the racks at night and stealing meat without getting caught. It was like going on the warpath for enemy horses. We had war councils out in the brush before we went and kill-talks around the fire if we got back safe with the meat. That was fun; but I kept thinking and thinking about the angry voice, and I was not quite happy. I wanted to try for a calf again, but I was afraid to try because I kept hearing the great voice scolding me for stealing the pipe from my grandfather.

"When my grandmother noticed how I was acting, she said: 'I wonder what is the matter with our grandson. He looks queer and he does not say anything.' Then my mother looked at me and said: 'I think he has been eating too much again. He is always eating.'"

Going on Vision Quest

After putting a chunk of cottonwood in the sheet-iron stove, I sat waiting for the old man to emerge from a reverie that he seemed to be in-
ducing with faint, dreamlike tones from his eagle-bone whistle. Finally,
as he had given no indication of emerging, I broke the silence: "Are you
sure now that the great voice was not scolding you?"

He peered squintingly at me for a while, and said: "I am very old,
and I have learned so many things that I do not know much any more.
Maybe I was wiser before my ears were troubled with so many forked
words.

"In the old days, it was from the seven tepees and the seven council
fires that our teaching came. It was older than the oldest grandfather
could remember his grandfather telling him; and more and more grandfathers before that until it was old as hills, old as stars.

"The wisdom of the teaching was from vision and the vision was from
Wakon Tonka: The people could not do anything right unless the Great
Mysterious One helped them; and for this they prayed and made sacred
songs and dances, and had a sacred way for doing everything. When a
boy was just beginning to be a man, he had to go on vision quest; for
what he saw would show him the good road and give him power, so
that his life might be a story good to tell. I was thinking of my vision
when you bothered me."

He was silent again while he filled his pipe and lit it. Then, drawing
hollow-cheeked upon the stem, he smoked awhile and brooded in the
little cloud he made.

"*Dho!*" he said at length, uttering with explosive force the syllable of
emphasis on something said or thought. "*Dho!*" Passing the pipe to me,
he resumed aloud the tenor of his brooding. "It is so! Are the people
good. and do they get along together any more? The hoop is broken and
the people have forgotten. There is no voice on any hill to tell them,
and they have no ears to hear.

"The hoop was breaking even then when I was happy and a boy; but then I did not know it, for the world was still as big as day, and Wakon Tonka could be found on any hill, and something wonderful could happen.

"After the Attacking of the Wagons the soldiers went away and our warriors burned their towns. And when the grass was new again there was a treaty with the Father in Washington. He said our land would be ours and no Wasichu could ever come there. You can see his tongue was forked. Red Cloud was not with us any more. The Great Father made an Agency for him on the North Platte. And that was bad; for many of our people went down there to eat Wasichu food, and take the many presents the Great Father gave them. And these they traded for the *minne sheetsha* [bad water, whiskey] that made them crazy, so that they forgot the Mother of all and the bison and the sacred hoop.

"But our Bad Face band that had been Red Cloud's people would not go. Big Road was with us, and Little Hawk and Black Twin. Also Crazy Horse was ours; and now I see that he was greatest of them all. Sometimes some of our young men would go down there to get new guns and lead and powder, and what they told, the people talked and talked about it, and some of it I heard; but it was like a story. I think there were fifty lodges of us, and we lived the old way in the bison country of the Tongue and the Powder and the Rosebud; and with us were the Miniconjous and the Sans Arcs. I remember how they said the loafers and Wasichus at the Agency made fun of us and called us the wild Lakota; but they were the foolish ones. The hoop we lived in had grown smaller, but it was not broken yet, and the voices of the seven tepees were not still.

"I was getting stronger fast and I think it was about the time when Red Cloud made the treaty that I got my first calf. The treaty was just something people said, a little thing a long way off that maybe was not so; but the calf was very big. I gave the meat to old people, and they praised me, so that my grandmother and my grandfather and my mother were proud of me.

"There were more snows and grasses and I was getting tall when I heard Looks Twice telling my mother about Red Cloud's long journey to see the Great Father and of the strange things that he saw in the world of the Wasichus where the sun comes from. Looks Twice was my father then, and my grandparents did not live with us, but he took care of them, and he was good to me and taught me many things about hunting and war.

"What he told about Red Cloud was like an *ohunka* story the old folk tell only at night, and it is wonderful to stay awake and listen, but only little children must believe it. There were so many Wasichu towns yonder where the Great Father lived and the sun comes from that they could not be counted; and so big they were that a horseback could ride and ride and always stay in the town. And in those towns the Wasichus were as many as the bison when they follow the grass all together. And the tepees were made of stone, tepee on top of tepee, so that if you would see the top, you must look far up and then look again, and sometimes after that, again. And there was more and more about the great medicine power of the Wasichus. There were big iron horses breathing smoke and fire, and there was a gun so long and heavy that maybe a hundred men could not lift it, and when it shot, there was a great thunder cloud full of lightning, and the whole sky was full of thunder. And the story got bigger, the more it was told; for on the other side of a great water that was like all the prairie without grass, there were more and more Wasichus, more and more towns of stone.

"I could look around and see the world was just as it always was. Maybe Red Cloud was getting to be a Wasichu with a forked tongue like all the others. People said he had worn Wasichu clothes yonder and looked foolish. He was not ours any more and we did not like him.

"I think I was about thirteen winters old, and I was a big boy. You can see that I was tall before so many snows bent me down, and then I was almost a man. I could swim farther under water than most boys, and when we played throwing-them-off-their-horses, only an older boy could throw me off. I liked to fight, and I wanted to go to war; but Looks Twice, who was my second father, said I would be ready after another snow and that I ought to go on vision quest first. It made me feel bad when he went with a war party against the Shoshonis and told me to stay at home and look after the horses. And I felt worse when he came back with a scalp on his coup-stick and some more good horses. He always took me hunting with him, and I could kill a cow, but it was not easy for me yet, and he would come and finish killing one that was getting away from me. Sometimes he could shoot an arrow clear through a cow if the point did not strike a bone.

"Of course, I played all the games with the other boys, but we all wanted to go to war, and we would get tired playing. In the winter before the deep snow had covered the ice, we would play *chun-wachee-kyapi* [make-the-wood-dance]. We had short round pieces of wood with sharp points on them [tops], and when we wrapped them with a long piece of sinew and threw them, they would spin on the ice, and we tried to break the dancing woods of the other boys by making ours dance against theirs. Or we would get tired doing that and maybe play ice-mark. We would fasten pieces of hard rawhide on our moccasins, then run and slide to see who could slide farthest. Or we would make little sleds with two buffalo ribs fastened together, with two feathers to guide them; and these we would throw on the ice to see whose would go farthest. We called this *huta-nachuta*, but I never knew why. Then maybe if we got tired doing that we would have a war, dividing up and fighting with blunt arrows; or maybe we would put mud balls on willow sticks and throw them at each other. Sometimes we would have very hard fights, and boys would get hurt; but they did not care.

"There was another game that showed how brave we were. It could be played with dry sunflower seeds or pieces of dry rotten wood that would keep on burning without a flame. A boy would hold out his hand and they would put the burning piece on the back of it. If his hand shook or he made a face or brushed the piece off, he lost the game and some other boy tried it. Sometimes when a boy was very brave this made a big sore, and he was very proud of it.

"When the snow was deep and it was very cold, it was good to lie back against the tepee wall with the wind outside sending forth a voice like a bull, and listen to the men telling stories about war and hunting and brave deeds. They would come over to eat and smoke, and sometimes they would stay so long I did not know when they went. If they got to arguing about something, I would just roll up—and go to sleep; then it would be morning and they would not be there. I was hungry for the stories, but they made me want to go out and do something that would make a story with me in it.

"We had been camping on the Greasy Grass. The tender grasses had appeared and were a handbreadth high in the valley; and the tops of the hills were greening a little. Then my grandfather came over and talked about me with my new father; and they said it was time for me to seek a vision. So my new father caught a couple of his best horses—both of them young—and took them as a gift to an old *wichasha wakon* [holy man], whose name was Blue Spotted Horse. When the old man had accepted the gift for what he was going to do, my father and grandfather took me over to his tepee. He could not see very well, and he was so old that he had something like new moons in his eyes. He looked at me a long while, and it made me feel queer, because I thought it might be a ghost behind me that he was seeing. Afterwhile he said: 'Let a sweat-lodge be prepared for this young man, and when he has been cleansed, bring him here, and I will teach him.'

"So there were two friends who made a sweat-lodge for me with willow boughs bent over like a cup upside down, and over this they fastened rawhide. At the opening of the lodge they set a stick with a piece of red cloth at the top for a sacred offering to the Spirit. Then they heated rocks in a fire, and when they had put these in the center of the little lodge, they poured water on them, and I had to go into the steam and close the flap tight. I felt like crying when I was in there again, because the other time was when my father went away and I saw him in my dream under the scaffold. Afterwhile they told me to come out. Then they rubbed me with sacred sage until I was dry and felt good all over. After that they gave me a buffalo robe to put around me and took me back to Blue Spotted Horse, and went away.

"I felt queer again and a little scared while I sat there all alone with the old man in his tepee, and maybe a ghost behind me that he was seeing. When he had looked at me that way for a long time and I wanted to get up and run away, he said: 'This is a sacred thing you are doing, and if the heart is not good something very bad will happen. But do not be afraid, for I have seen into your heart. Already you have fed old people, and you want to be a man they all praise. While you were in the sweat-lodge your father came to me, and he will help you on the hill. So do not be afraid, and I will teach you.'

"Then he filled a pipe and lit it; and after he had presented the stem to the four quarters of the world and the Great Mysterious One above and Maka, the mother earth, he held the stem to me and I touched it with my mouth. When I did that, I could feel a power running all through me and up my backbone into my hair.

"Then he taught me what I must know to go on vision quest. I did not learn it all then, but I heard it again when I was older, and this is what he told me.

"There is a great hoop; and so big it is that everything is in it, for it is the hoop of the universe, and all that live in it are relatives. When you stand on a high hill and look all around, you can see its shape and know that it is so. This hoop has four quarters, and each is sacred, for each has a mysterious power of its own, and it is by those powers that we live. Also each quarter has its sacred objects and a color, and these stand for its power.

"First is the place where the sun goes down. Its color is blue like the thunder clouds, and it has the power to make live and to destroy. The bow is for the lightning that destroys, and the wooden cup is for the rain that makes live.

"Next is the place where the great white giant lives, and its color is white like the snows. It has the power of healing, for thence come the cleansing winds of the winter. The white wing of the goose stands for that wind of cleansing and a sacred white herb for the healing.

"Next is the place whence comes the light, where all the days of men are born; and its color is red like the sunrise. It has the power of wisdom and the power of peace. The morning star stands for wisdom, for it brings the light that we may see and understand; and the pipe is for the peace that understanding gives.

"Next is the place of the summer, and the color of it is yellow like the sun. Thence comes the power to grow and flourish. The sacred staff of six branches is for the power to grow, and the little hoop is for the life of the people who flourish as one.

"Then at the place whence comes the power to grow, a road begins, the good red road of spirit that all men should know; and it runs straight across the hoop of the world to the place whence comes the power of cleansing and healing, to the place of white hairs and the cold and the cleansing of old age.

"And then there is a second road, the hard black road of difficulties that all men must travel. It begins at the place whence come the days of men, and it runs straight across the hoop of this world to the place where the sun goes down and all the days of men have gone and all their days shall go; far beyond is the other world, the world of spirit. It is a hard road to travel, a road of trouble and need. But where this black road of difficulties crosses the good red road of spirit at the center of the hoop of the world, that place is very holy, and there springs the Tree of Life. For those who look upon the Tree, it shall fill with leaves and bloom and singing birds; and it shall shield them as a *sheo* [prairie hen] shields her chickens.

"While Blue Spotted Horse was telling me this, he drew the hoop and the roads with his finger in the ashes by the fire, and I could see it all as from a high place, like a picture.

"Then he told me how I must pray on the hill. Always before I pray I must lift both hands high with my pipe in the right, and send forth a voice four times—'*hey-a-hey, hey-a-hey, hey-a-hey, hey-a-hey!*' First I should pray at the place where the sun goes down; then at the place whence come the cleansing and healing; next where the light comes from and the days of men begin; and after that where lives the power to grow; and I should ask each power in turn to help me.

"Then I must walk the red road of spirit to the center of the hoop of the world, and there I must present my pipe and pray for help to Wakon Tonka. And when I have done this, I must remember the ground, the mother of all, who has shown mercy to her children; I must

47

lean low and present my pipe to Maka, the earth, the only mother, and ask her to help me; for my body is hers and I am her son.

"When I have done all this, I have only begun; for after I have rested awhile, I must do it all over again. I must walk the black road to the sundown and pray; then back to the holiest place in the center; then up the red road to the quarter of cleansing, and pray; then back again to the center and over the black road to the light and the beginning of days. I must pray there, and return; and last, I must walk the red road to the place where lives the power to grow. And when I have returned to the holiest place at the center and prayed, I can rest awhile and think hard about what I am doing.

"I cannot eat anything while I am on the hill, but I can have some water; and I must stay awake as long as I am able. Afterwhile I shall be crying, but I must keep right on, for that is when the praying begins to have power.

"Then Blue Spotted Horse taught me a prayer that I must offer to Wakon Tonka at the center of the hoop, and I said it after him six times. There is great power in that prayer, and I could feel it even then when I was a boy. Maybe you will learn it, Grandson, Wasichu though you are, and it will help you to find the good red road and to do what you must do in this world. But when I had said it six times, all at once I was afraid; for what would happen if I could not remember it all!

"I did not say anything about this, but Blue Spotted Horse looked hard at me awhile; and then he smiled, just like my own grandfather, and he said: 'Do not be afraid, Grandson, for Wakon Tonka will remember all that you forget. There is one, there is no other, and all things are in Wakon Tonka. The powers are only the ways the one makes all things live. Take this pipe; hold fast to it and never let it go, for on this will you depend. Now you will go forth to the hill, and do as I have taught you. I will be with you there unseen; and when your prayers are heard, I will send the friends to bring you here. To me alone the vision shall be told.'

"He looked so kind when I took the pipe that I was not afraid of him at all. So I said: 'Palamo yelo, tonka schla—thank you, Grandfather.' And as I got up and went forth into the slanting day I felt lighter on my feet than I had ever felt before."

"Hold Fast; There Is More!"

"Dho!" said Eagle Voice musingly, as he came slowly out of his inner solitude; "I felt queer and light when I left the *wakon's* tepee, and wherever I looked there was a strangeness like dreaming; and the sun was getting low.

"The two friends were waiting there with a sorrel horse all saddled and painted in a sacred manner for me. On his forehead was a thin new moon, because he was facing the world of spirit where the new moons lead; on his rump was the morning star to shine from behind me upon the dark road ahead; on his left flank was the sacred hoop; and on his right flank was the white wing of the goose.

"The friends did not say anything. They just took hold of me and set me in the saddle; and then we started for the hill of vision. The one who walked ahead to show the way was carrying the offerings for where the sun goes down—the bow and wooden cup—, and for the place of cleansing—the white wing and the herb. The other walked behind me with a morning star made of rawhide for where the light and the days of men are born; the hoop and staff for where the growing power lives. I held the pipe; and I was holding it very tight with both hands in front of me, for on that must I depend. It was a sacred, fearful thing that I was doing, and although my legs were getting long there was still a little boy inside me. I did not look where we were going. I just looked hard at the pipe, and held it tight. There were four painted strips of skin hanging from the stem, blue, white, red, and yellow for the quarters and the powers. Also from the stem a long wing feather of an eagle hung, and that was for the Great Mysterious One. Last, upon the mouthpiece was the bison hide, and that was for the breast of Maka where all that live, with legs or wings or roots or fins, are little children nursing. I did not understand it all till I was older, but I could feel the power in the pipe.

"The sun was shining bright and level across the world, getting ready to go under, when we came to the hill standing high and alone, with shadows gathered around it like a blanket and the last of day upon its head. I felt an aching in my breast, for it was like the time we took my father to the scaffold on the hill.

"When we came to the top I could see that the friends had prepared the place for me. It was flat, and they had dug a hole there as deep as to my waist, and round about it sacred sage was scattered. Then, with the hole for center, they had made a circle, maybe fifteen steps across, and at each quarter a stick was set, each with the proper color on it—blue, white, red, yellow. There were strips of painted rawhide for the black road and the red; and where these crossed at the holiest place in the center the two friends put me down. Then when they had placed the offerings at the proper quarters, they left a skin-bag full of water, and went away down the hill leading the horse. They did not say anything to me, and they did not look back. It was the way they would have done if I were dead up there and lying on a scaffold.

"With my robe about my shoulders, I stood in the hole up to my hips, holding the pipe in front of me. I watched the round red sun slip under. A thin new moon appeared low down and like a ghost. It looked lost and lonely yonder going to the spirit world. Some wolves mourned. I remembered I had heard the criers calling to the people that the village would move next day. The stars got brighter. The night was big and empty when the wolves were still. The thin new moon touched the edge of the world and sank. All at once I wanted to get out of the hole and run and run back to my people before they went away. Then I remembered my pipe. I must hold fast to it. On it must I depend. So I held it as tight as I could, and right away I could feel the power running all through me again, up my back and into my hair. I remembered the *wakon* said he would be with me, and that my father would help me on the hill. I could almost hear him saying, 'Never be afraid of anything.'

"Then all at once everything was different, and I felt like praying. So I threw back my robe and started naked for the quarter of the sunset where the bow and cup were hanging; and as I went, the world was a great shining bubble and in the midst of it the pipe and I were floating. At the blue quarter I raised both hands with the pipe in my right and cried out to the power that makes live and destroys, the power of the rain and the lightning. Four times I cried, '*hey-a-hey.*' Between the cries I waited and listened, but it was so far out yonder that no voice came back. And when I cried, 'Lean close and hear and help me,' there was nothing.

"I walked backward to the center and waited there awhile with my face to the white quarter, where the goose's wing and the white herb hung. Then I went there, and, as before, I raised my hands and the pipe, crying out four times and asking the power of cleansing and healing to hear and help me. But the world was a big, empty bubble, and no voice came back. At the red quarter of the morning star and the sunrise, where the light is born and the days of men begin, I cried out four times and asked for help; but there was nothing. At the yellow quarter, where the sacred hoop and tree were set, I called upon the growing power for help. The voice I sent forth went far, so far it could never return, and there was stillness. When I stood in the hole at the most sacred place in the center and raised my face and my hands and the pipe, and prayed the prayer Blue Spotted Horse had taught me, there was nothing. And there was nothing when I leaned with my face and my hands and the pipe on Maka's breast and asked the mother of all to help me.

"I prayed around the hoop again and again, but still there was nothing. So I stood in the hole for a while and thought hard about what I was doing. It was not easy to find a vision, and I must try and try until I found it—like getting the first deer or the first bison calf, only harder, maybe. Pretty soon I was not thinking about the vision at all. I was in the brush by the waterhole and the deer was coming down with the fawn to drink. The cow was chasing Whirlwind and me up the hillside. I was coming into the camp with the haunch of the fawn on my shoulder. My grandmother was jumping up and down crying: 'Oh, see the vision our grandson has brought us!' Only it was not my grandmother, but the *wakon* looking that queer way at me. 'If the heart is not good something very bad will happen.'

"My head jerked, and at first I did not know where I was. Then I remembered my pipe and held it tight and began my praying all over again. I did that all night long, advancing to each of the quarters in turn and back to the center. I did not rest long there, because I had to stay awake as long as I was able. I got so tired and sleepy that sometimes I would forget what I was saying; then I would remember the old *wakon's* eyes with the new moons upside down in them and the queer look, and then I would hold my pipe as tight as I could, and go ahead. Sometimes the coyotes would mock me when I waited and listened between cries, but that is all there was.

"The night was like always, until all at once there was the morning star out yonder and a pale streak of day beneath it. It was looking at me the way it did when I 'woke beside my father's scaffold. I remembered how I tried to hold him fast in the dream, but he melted away and the buffalo-runner too.

"When I got back to the center that time I was crying a little, and when I put my hands and my pipe and my face on Maka's breast and asked for help, I cried harder, because I was sad for my father, and the grass on my face was soft like my own mother's breast when I was little.

"When I looked again the sun was shining. Something was happening away off yonder. There was a big whirling cloud of dust, and things were flying around in it. Then I saw that the cloud was full of coup-sticks with scalps on them, and they were flying about in the cloud and the cloud was the whirling dust of many hoofs in a battle.

"I looked until it was not there any more. Then there was a voice above and behind me that said, 'Hold fast to your pipe, for there is more.' When I turned to see whose voice that was, it was an eagle soaring low and looking back at me until it was not there.

"The sun was shining almost level. I had gone to sleep kneeling in the hole with my face and hands on the grass, and I thought it was still morning. But the blue stick, with the bow and cup, was where the red stick should be! The sun was shining low out of the blue quarter, and it was getting ready to go under! I had slept dead all day, and it made me feel good; but there were teeth in my belly, I was so hungry; for I had not eaten the day before.

"I filled up on the warm water in the skin and thought about what I had seen. Maybe all those coup-sticks and scalps meant I would be a great warrior. But if they meant that, what more could there be, and what did the eagle mean?

"I began to pray again as soon as the sun went under and the thin moon appeared going to the spirit land. I prayed harder than ever because of what the eagle said, and I could feel power getting stronger and stronger in me every time I came back to the center. When I advanced to the quarters, it was like floating with the pipe in the midst of a great starry bubble. And afterwhile, whenever I began to say the prayer to Wakon Tonka at the most sacred place, the prayer the *wakon* taught me, it made me cry. And this is the prayer:

" 'Grandfather, Great Mysterious One! You have been always, and before you nothing has been. There is nothing to pray to but you. The star nations all over the heavens are yours, and yours are the grasses of the earth. You are older than all need, older than all pain and prayer. Day in, day out, you are the life of things.

" 'Grandfather, all over the world the faces of living ones are alike. In tenderness have they come up out of the ground. Look upon your children, with children in their arms, that they may face the winds and walk the good road to the day of quiet.

" 'Teach me to walk the soft earth, a relative to all that live. Give me the strength to understand and the eyes to see. Help me, for without you I am nothing.' *

"That is the prayer, Grandson. Maybe it will help you, Wasichu though you are, to walk the black road and to find the flowering tree.

"The lean moon was gone and the night must have been getting old when a great sudden voice roared from the quarter of the sundown where I was facing. I had not seen it coming; but all at once it was there—a heaped-up cloud coming fast towards me, with swift blue lightning on its front and giants shouting in it. And in between the shouts that shook the hill I could hear the deep voices of the rain singing all together, like many warriors charging.

"I was not afraid. I felt very big and strong, and I cried back to the thunder beings as loud as I could, 'hey-a-hey, hey-a-hey,' and they answered. Then the lightning and the voices were all about me, so that I could not hear the cries I sent forth, and the rain was a roaring between thunders. I stood there, holding my pipe high in both hands, but not a drop of rain touched me. And when the swift storm had past and the stars were bright again, I could hear the giant voices cheering far away.

"I knew my praying had been heard and I would see. The power was mighty in me as I prayed around the hoop and back to the most sacred place at the center.

"I was standing in the hole with my face and hands and pipe raised to the Great Mysterious One, and I was crying hard while I prayed, but I was happy and my heart sang. I was saying, 'All over the world the faces of living ones are alike.' But all at once I was not saying; I was seeing!

"I was standing on the highest hill in the center of the world. There was no sun, but so clear was the light that what was far was near. The circle of the world was a great hoop with the two roads crossing where I stood, the black one and the red. And all around the hoop more peoples than I could count were sitting together in a sacred manner. The smokes of all the peoples' little fires stood tall and straight and still around the circle; and by the murmur of the voices of the peoples, they were happy. And while I looked and wondered, there was a tree that sprang at my feet from where the two roads crossed. It grew so fast that, while I watched, it reached the sky and spread, filling the heavens with blooms and singing leaves.

"Then I felt dizzy, and all at once I was sitting in the hole with my head on the grassy edge of it. When I looked about me, the circle of the

* This prayer was given to me by my old friend and teacher, Black Elk, the Oglala Sioux holy man.

world was empty and the sun was high above. While I sat there looking around me at the empty world, I felt homesick for what I had seen without my eyes, and there was an aching in my breast.

"Afterwhile I knew I was very hungry and thirsty. So I filled myself with water from the skin; and when I looked around me again, far off down a valley I could see the friends returning with the horse."

The old man fell into one of his prolonged silences which I finally broke with a question: "And the *wakon*? What did he say when you told him?"

"I was alone with him in his tepee," Eagle Voice replied, "and a little fire made the light. He looked hard at me for a long time when I had spoken, then he said: 'You have seen in a sacred manner and your praying has come alive. By the lightning and the thunder and the rain that fell about you, the power to make live and to destroy will protect you to the end of the black road, and the road will be long. You shall breathe the dust of battles, counting many coups, and shall not be hurt. You shall travel far and see strange peoples; but the sacred hoop of all the peoples under the flowering tree, you shall not see by the light of the sun. It was your father talking through the eagle. Hold fast to the vision Wakon Tonka has sent you, and pray for the strength to understand it. *Hetchetu aloh!*'

"Then he waved his hand, and I went out into the low day. I was very hungry."

The Old Bull's Last Fight

Dry snow had fallen in the night, and it was scurrying drearily under a dull sky when I reached the old man's tepee the next morning. He sat smoking serenely with his blanket tucked about his waist and legs. "I thought you might not come, Grandson," he said; "but you are here, and it is good." When we had smoked awhile together, he began:

"We are going on my first war party today, and it is very bad weather for fighting; but no snow has fallen in my story. The grass is getting strong; the animals are making fat; there is a warm wind blowing; and I am just a boy with long legs.

"After my vision quest people noticed me more than before, and they did not treat me like a little boy. So when it was time for a war party to start out, I went along on Whirlwind. There were thirty-seven of us, and we were not all Oglalas. Some of us were Miniconjous and Sans Arcs, and a few were Cheyennes, for we had camped together along the valley of the Greasy Grass that winter. Some of us were only boys getting started to be men; some had been in many fights and had scars to show; and there were a few who almost could have been the grandfathers of the boys.

"Crazy Horse was leading the party, and he was already getting a big name then, for he had a mysterious power. People talked about him, and told stories of his deeds in fights with the Crows and Shoshonis. Also he had fought the soldiers when the hundred were killed on the ridge, and that was a story too. He was not a big man, for I was even then almost as tall as he; and he was not a little man either; just above a little man, and he was not fat at all. He was slender and very strong; and his face was lean too. It looked sharpened like an arrowhead. They said he never wanted anything for himself but a good horse and weapons to fight for his people, and that he always gave everything away.

"His hair was not so dark as most other Lakotas' hair, but was a little brown; and his skin was not so dark either. He always braided his hair with one braid down each side of his head, and he wore a braided buckskin with his medicine in a little bag at the end of it, also an eagle-bone whistle, like mine, tied on. This he always had with him.

"Just before the beginning of a battle, when they were ready to charge, he would get off his horse and take a handful of earth from a mole hill or an ant hill or a prairie dog's house. This he would put between the horse's ears and then on the hips of the horse. After that he would stand in front of the horse and throw the earth back over him. Then he would stand behind and throw some towards the horse's head. Last, he would rub some of the earth from the horse and put it on his own head. He never wore a war bonnet in battle and he did not paint his face. He wore only one spotted-eagle feather tied in his hair and hanging down the back of his head. It was Chips, the *wakon,* who taught him to do this, and always advised him. He would be ahead in a fight, and when he killed an enemy he did not count coup. He would call others to take the honors. I think he had so many honors he did not want any more, but helped others to get them.

"He had a society of his own; not a feast and dance society, but just followers. They were called *Ho-ksi-ha-ka-ta* [The Last Child]. The last child in a family is not thought of as much as the others, and so he chose the last child to follow him. They were very brave warriors because they had to do great deeds and be honored even more than the first child. They were always trying to make themselves greater, and so they were not afraid to do anything.

"They say the ponies Crazy Horse rode never lasted very long. They wore out fast because of the great power that was in him. It was from a vision that he had. When he rode into a battle, he would remember his vision and be in it again, so that nothing in this world could hurt him. I do not know this, but so the people all put it out. They did not say it about other brave men, and I think it was so. When the Wasichus murdered him, they had to do it from behind when he was not ready for battle.

"I had seen him around the village as long as I could remember. People thought he was queer because he did not talk often, and sometimes he would not notice anybody. But he would stop to play with little children, and he liked to tease and joke them till they laughed. When he was on a war party, he was different. Then he would joke with the warriors, and tell funny stories. It kept them feeling good, so that they could fight better. They all liked him, and whatever he said, they would do that.

"We rode towards where the sun comes up when the summer days are long. The world was young and wide as day, and we were going almost to the end of it beyond Mini Shoshay [the Missouri]. We crossed the Rosebud and the Tongue and the Powder, and there were no enemies. The young grass was getting strong for our horses, and there were deer and elk in plenty, so that, man and horse, we feasted every night.

"There was story-telling around the fire when we had feasted; and there was always one I did not hear the end of, being over-full of meat and heavy sleep. When I had to take my turn along with older horse-guards, it was like a wonderful story with no one to tell it out there under the stars, listening to the horses chewing and blowing, and watching every shadow all around. It made me feel tall and brave, and something was always about to happen all at once, so I did not feel like sleeping.

"In the daytime we were often merry; and if someone started singing, we would all sing together. That made the horses feel good, and maybe one would neigh and start the others neighing.

"Where we could not see far, there would be riders out ahead of us and off on both sides to watch for enemies. Sometimes when we were walking the horses slowly to rest them, somebody would start a funny story, and others would crowd close to take it from him and go on with it. There was one about the young woman bear who saw a handsome young hunter; and right away she loved him so much that she made up her mind to have him for her man. This was very hard on the young hunter, and it got harder and harder the longer the story became. He did not want to shoot anybody who loved him so much, but he did not want to be her man either. Sometimes he would think he had lost her at last; but just at the wrong time she would show up again.

"Maybe there was a pretty girl and he had been sneaking around a long while, trying to make her talk to him. And at last he would catch her down by the creek when she was getting water for her mother, and they would be talking. Then that woman bear would rush out of the brush groaning and with tears running down her face, because she loved him so much. And when the girl screamed and ran and he turned and ran too, the bear would chase him—maybe up a tree.

"Then maybe the handsome young hunter had the girl for his woman at last, and the bear would sneak into his tepee in the night just at the wrong time, and there would be a big woman fight in there, and all the people would come yelling to see who might be killing somebody.

"The bear always got away and there never was an end to that story. I think it is still getting longer somewhere. Anybody could tell about another time the woman bear did something, and he could make it up if he could not remember any. This story had to be told like something very sad and without seeming to know it was funny. I would laugh so hard to hear the story and see how sad and worried the story-tellers looked, that I could hardly stay on my horse. Maybe at night the bear story would begin again; and when they got it going it was hard to stop."

Eagle Voice chuckled awhile, evidently enjoying remembered fragments of the bear yarn.

"Yes," he continued at length, "High Horse and I would roll and hold our bellies with laughing. High Horse was a Miniconjou boy as old as I was. I knew him when we were small and I used to play over there being Tashina's horse, and he was a girl's horse too. It was on this war party that we began to be brother-friends. We were always together; and we liked each other so much that we decided we had been twins over in Twin Land and had got parted because we did not happen to find the same mother over here. We had heard the old *ohunka* story from our grandmothers, and maybe we did not quite believe it; but we wanted to, because the story made it more wonderful for us to be together.

"Twins are not like other people, and there is something *wakon* about them. They come from Twin Land where they have lived together always; and when they come into this world looking for a mother, they ride around on jack rabbits. Nobody can see them; but they ride around anyway, looking and looking for a good and pretty young woman. Maybe she is getting water from a spring or a creek and the twins have followed her on their jack rabbits. They are hiding in the brush, and when the good and pretty young woman leans over, they hurry and get inside of her. If only one gets inside, then the other must find himself another mother, and all their lives each will be hunting the other one.

"So we had found each other, and we said we were never going to be parted any more. If the story wasn't so, why did everybody know it?

"Beyond the Powder we came to a great flat land where many antelope were feeding. Some high buttes were there standing all alone, and when High Horse and I climbed one of them, far off towards where you are always looking [south] we could see the tops of Pa Sapa [the Black Hills] low down in the sky like a black thundercloud just beginning to come up.

"We crossed the Slim Buttes, where our people had a big fight with the soldiers a long while afterwards, and then we turned left towards where the White Giant lives. Afterwhile we came to a stream that ran the same way [the little Missouri] until it turned towards where the sun comes up and ran into Mini Shoshay [the Missouri]. But before we got there, we had to go through a strange land that was not like this world, and sometimes it was hard to travel and we had to go around [badlands]. There would be flat grassland with many buttes scattered in it, all staring at us like strangers that maybe never saw men and horses before. And there would be places where the land was all tangled with buttes and gullies; and sometimes these were burning and smoking. High Horse and I said maybe it was always like that when you were getting near the end of the world. Sometimes when I would look around, and everything was still and strange and there were only the ponies' hoofs to hear, it would make me feel like getting out of breath.

"Afterwhile we came to where they said it was not far to Mini Shoshay, and we would have to make boats. We were on the right side of the little river that we were following, and our scouts had seen bison on the other side. The river was not very deep or wide, so we crossed over to kill some bison and to get hides for the boats.

"There was a steep hill, almost too steep for the horses; and we rode up there to look. Bison were grazing all over the flat green valley in among little hills down there, and they could not smell us or see us. It was good to look at them, and we lay down along the rim of the hill to rest and see awhile before we started killing. Right below us the hill was very steep, and we could see almost straight down. One Horn, the oldest in our band, was lying beside High Horse and me with his chin on his arms, just looking; and afterwhile he said: 'Watch that old bull right down there. He is eloping with that young cow. See him? When they do that, the cow is always a nice fat one. She will make good eating, and I want a bite out of her hump.'

"We looked down, and there was an old grandfather bull with a young cow following close after him. I think he was the biggest bull I ever saw, and he looked proud and handsome like a great chief who lived a long while ago in some great-grandfather's story. He walked slowly with the cow at his tail and did not notice the other bison at all.

"Then somebody said: 'Look over there! We're going to see a big bull fight!' We looked, and there were four fine young bulls all in a row walking slowly towards the grandfather and the cow. When they were not very far apart, they all stopped and looked at each other awhile. Then the first young bull began to roll and tear the earth up with his horns, throwing the dirt over his back and bellowing. When the old bull saw this, he began doing the same thing, rooting up big chunks of sod and tossing them over his back. His voice was deep like thunder rumbling. Then they stopped and looked at each other a little while with their muzzles near the ground.

"All at once they both charged, and when their skulls came together it was like a gunshot. There was so much dust for a little while after they came together that we could not see what was happening in there. The cow just stood looking, and so did the three other young bulls. Then all at once we saw one of the bulls up in the air. When the dust cleared away, the grandfather was wiping his horns on the grass. Then he walked over to the cow and licked her face, while the young bull was getting up and staggering away with his insides dragging and his hind feet tangled in them.

"In a little while the second young bull began rolling and bellowing and tearing the earth with his horns. The old bull did the same; and when they came together the dust rose in a cloud. They fought so hard that we could hear them panting and grunting. Then the dust thinned in the wind and we saw one rise into the air and the other horn him coming down. Again the grandfather wiped his horns on the grass and went back to lick the cow. The other one was trying to get up, but he would always fall down again, and his belly was all torn open.

"Then the third young bull did as the others had done, and there was a longer fight in the dust and more panting and grunting. It ended the same as before, with the young bull staggering away dragging his insides. But we could see that the old grandfather was bleeding hard and wobbling. This time he just stood there and did not go back to the cow. High Horse and I were sorry, because we were on his side; and we wanted One Horn to shoot the last young bull with his gun. But he just laughed at us.

"Right away the fourth young bull rolled and tossed earth and bellowed, and the two came together with a loud sound. High Horse and I yelled, 'hi-yay, hi-yay,' cheering the old one; but One Horn told us to stop; and, anyway, maybe the young one would think we were cheering him. This last fight was the longest of all. We could see big bodies getting tossed in the dust, and the panting and grunting were louder than ever. Afterwhile the cloud cleared away. The young one was trying to get up, but, the way it looked, one of his shoulders was ripped nearly off and he was open underneath. The old one was still on his legs, bleeding hard from his nose and his belly, and we could see it was hard for him to steady himself. Then he staggered back to the cow without trying to wipe off his horns first. He just stood there trying to steady himself and bleeding hard.

"And what do you think the cow did? She went over to the last young bull that was trying to get up, and nudged him and pushed him, trying to help. She was right under us, and One Horn shot her with the gun he got at Red Cloud's agency.

"When we went down there, the five bulls were dead, and they were all so torn up and full of holes that we could not use their hides for boats. Also, the old men said we should not eat any of their meat, because they had murdered each other. But the young cow was fat and tender; and when we had killed and skinned enough bison for the boats, we had a big feast."

The Boys Who Had Sister Trouble

When I had returned from the woodpile and fed the stove, Eagle Voice continued eagerly:

"There is no meat like that any more, and I can taste it now. It is hard to chew the meat they have these days; but sometimes I get a tender piece from a calf, and it always makes me think of a story I heard for the first time while we were eating that cow. Also, whenever I think of the story, it makes me hungry like a boy, although it is not about eating.

"We feasted and listened to stories most of the night, while the horse-guards took turns. Sometimes I would fall asleep, being stuffed with meat, then I would be wide awake again and everybody would be laughing at some funny tale, or saying, 'how! how!' around the circle, cheering a good story just ended. Then I would eat some more, and listen to the next one.

"Charger told this one, and I can see him yet, although he fed the wolves somewhere, I do not know how many snows ago. I thought he was an old man then, but now I think that he was almost young. He was always joking, but I cannot remember him laughing, for he had a face that made him look always sorry and surprised. He could never tell a story sitting down, because he could not tell it all with his mouth. He told it mostly with his face and his hands and his whole body; so he had to tell it on his feet, and if you did not see the story he was telling, you could not hear it all. Sometimes when he got a tale started he would go right on telling it without a word for a while, and everybody would look and look and not move. There was one about a wild young fellow who played ghost, and people would coax him to tell it again, although they knew it as well as he did. They wanted to see him telling it with looks and motions.

"This wild young fellow liked tobacco very much and he never had enough of it. He was always wondering how he could get some more. So one day he was traveling with his father and his mother, his grandfather and his grandmother. They had been away somewhere and they were going back to camp. There was some fresh meat on the pony-drag so that they could eat on the way, and with the meat there was a fresh cow's bladder packed full of *wasna*, made of meat and tallow and buffalo berries pounded up together.

"They were all traveling along on their horses with the pony-drag; and they got to talking about tobacco. Maybe the wild young man started it. There was none at all in their *iglaka* [a family outfit on the move]—only red willow bark; and when they camped that night there would be nothing to mix with it for a good smoke.

"When the sun was getting low they saw an *iglaka* coming towards them. It was an old man and an old woman, and they were mourning. So when the two *iglakas* met they stopped to talk awhile and tell each other what they had heard. Then the grandfather of the first *iglaka* asked the old man of the second *iglaka* for some tobacco. And the second old man said he had not any; but his son was lying dead in a tepee back there, and in the tepee was an offering of five plugs of tobacco. These old people had stayed all night with their dead son and now they had started to wander and mourn. The old woman was crying all the time they were talking. And the old man said: 'He was a very generous son, and now he is dead back there. I think if you ask him for one of the plugs he will let you have it. He always liked to give to old people.' When he said this, they both wept hard.

"While the old people were all feeling bad together, the wild young man had a big thought, and what he thought, he did. First he sneaked the fresh cow's bladder from the drag and hid it under his blanket. Then he remembered something he had lost back on the trail, and told the old people he would have to ride back and find it.

"So that is what he did; only he did not ride back very far. He dodged into a side draw and came around some hills until he was far ahead of his people; and there was the tepee with the dead man in it.

"He did not go in there right away, because that was not the way it was in his big thought. He went down to the creek and tied his horse in the brush. Then he stripped naked and covered himself all over with mud, and made streaks in the mud with his finger. After that he painted his face with the mud to make it look terrible. Last of all, he emptied out the fresh cow's bladder and pulled it over his hair and his head and his ears, right down to his eyes. He almost scared himself when he looked into the water.

"By now the sun was going down, and he went into the tepee where the dead man was lying all dressed up with five big plugs of tobacco be-

63

side him. The wild young man wanted to smoke right away; but he knew if he did that, the old people would come and he would not get all the tobacco for himself. So he hid under his blanket over against the tepee wall and waited.

"Afterwhile when the day was just getting half-dark, he could hear the four old people coming. Then he heard his grandfather say: 'Soon our grandson will be coming back, and while we are waiting we may as well make an offering and get the tobacco.' So they came into the tepee and sat down at the feet of the dead young man. The grandfather then filled his pipe with red willow bark and made an offering to the spirit. 'Young man,' he said, 'whoever you are and wherever your spirit is now, here is an offering. We ask the favor of you that no harm shall come to us for taking your tobacco. We will always remember you when our days are ripe.'

"Just then the wild young man put his head out from under the blanket and yelled: 'How!'

"When Charger got to this place he always quit talking awhile; but you could see the story going on. You could see how terrible the ghost looked, the way grandmother waddled as she ran, the way grandfather hopped with a lame leg, how mother covered her head with her blanket, running and falling, getting up and running some more. And you could see the father away out ahead going like a man in a foot race with his braids standing flat out behind his head because he was getting out of there so fast. You could see grandmother look back at the ghost and faint because it was so terrible. Then grandfather looked and fainted. Then mother looked and fainted. And then there was a big foot race between father and the ghost. You could watch Charger and see it— father puffing and grunting with his eyes almost popping out of his head, the ghost puffing and grunting and looking terrible. By the time the ghost caught up and father fainted, everybody was laughing so hard that Charger would have to wait before he could finish his story. And it was not easy to quit laughing, because Charger kept on looking so sorry and surprised, as though he thought it wasn't funny to be chased by a ghost like that.

"Then the wild young man went back to the creek and washed himself all clean, and threw the cow's bladder away. And when he was dressed, he got on his horse and rode around so that he could come galloping from where he said he had lost something and had to go back for it.

"So he did that, and when he came to where the four old people were huddled together waiting for him, he heard all about it, and he was so

64

brave that his father and mother and his grandfather and grandmother were very proud of him. He said: 'I will go and get that tobacco, and if the ghost tries to chase me I will fight him.' They begged him not to do that because the ghost was so terrible. But he said: 'Make a fire here and I will get the tobacco and bring the drag and the ponies so that we can eat and smoke. Maybe that ghost can chase old people; but if he tries to chase me, there is going to be a dead ghost around here.'

"They tried to hold him, but he went anyway; and afterwhile he came back with the tobacco and the horses and the drag. Then grandmother said: 'We are safe now, for I think the ghost is afraid of our brave young grandson.' But when they had eaten, the old people would not even touch the tobacco.

"So the wild young man had enough for once."

Eagle Voice chuckled for a while, enjoying the boyhood memory; and then—

"Charger could tell sad stories too," he said. "And when he told one, the people would be looking down their noses, feeling very bad. And he could tell the kind of stories that made a boy feel cold on the back of his neck and keep looking behind in the dark, because something that was not there, was there anyway, and it might grab you all at once. —Like the one about the evil *wakon* who got his power from eating dead peoples' tongues. In the night he would sprout great wings like a giant buzzard's; and when somebody was sick and about to die, the people would hear him flapping, flapping, flapping, with a queer whisking sound above the tepee in the dark. Maybe somebody coming back late in the night would pass a new scaffold, and that man-buzzard would be sitting up there in the moonlight, and maybe the moon would be old and broken and just about to go down. Then the man-buzzard would lift slowly and fly away, and you could see him cross the moon and hear him going—flap, flap, flap, with a queer whistling sound. In the morning when relatives went to look, there would be another tongue missing! It took a long while to tell that story, because it took the people a long while to find out who was the evil *wakon*. They had to try this and try that and look here and look there. And when they did find out, everybody was surprised and you could hardly believe it.

"But the story that always makes me hungry is the one Charger told that night about the Two Boys Who Had Sister-Trouble. I want to tell it because what I eat these days does not do me much good, and I want to be hungry like a boy again.

"So this is the way it was with the two boys who had sister-trouble.

"A long while ago before the hoop was broken and the people still were good, there was a right way and a wrong way to do everything, and something bad would happen if you did the wrong way. I have told you how a man could not speak to his daughter-in-law and she could not speak to him, even when they lived in the same tepee. If they had to say something to each other, they said it to the son's mother and she said it to the other one. Neither could the two eat together. It was the same way with a brother and sister when they were no longer little children. They respected each other so much that if they had to say something to each other they would say it to their mother and she would tell it. These ways were good for the people, but now there is nothing good at all. In those days a young man wanted his sisters to be proud of him, and they might make beaded clothing for him to show how proud they were, but they would be so ashamed to say it to him that they would rather die.

"Now there was a young Shyela [Cheyenne] and his name was Thunder Sounds. His father was a chief and people looked up to him. Also the family had many ponies and a fine tepee. Thunder Sounds was a very good-looking young man and his clothes were fine because his mother and his sisters thought so much of him. He wore a shield of otter skin across his breast. His quiver was full of arrows and covered with porcupine quills; and even his blanket was beautifully quilled. Also he had two fine spotted ponies that looked just alike. But I think he was prouder of his two older sisters than he was of the ponies, because they were very good to see and already they could do any woman's work a little better than any of the other girls could.

"This happened in the spring when the people were moving camp, and Thunder Sounds, not being a man yet, did something just for fun that would bother his sisters at their work. They were so bothered that they forgot all about the right way to do, and scolded him. And that was how it began.

"When the camp moved, Thunder Sounds did not go along. He stayed right there, sitting on the ground in his fine clothes with his head hanging and his two spotted ponies looking at him with their heads hanging too; for it made them sad to feel how sad he was. It was morning when the camp moved, and when the sun was getting low, he still sat there thinking and thinking about his sisters and about death. Not only had they spoken to him and thus shown they did not respect him; they had even scolded him the way you scold a dog for stealing your meat. He knew that he just could not live any more; but how could he find death?

"About that time a young man came back from the camp and stood

66

beside Thunder Sounds and said: 'Your sisters have sent me. They are sorry and they are crying for you to come back. Also they are cooking some tender meat just for you.' But Thunder Sounds did not lift his head and the ponies did not lift their heads either, and the young man heard nothing but his own words. So afterwhile he got tired standing there, and went away. And the sun went down and there were stars and it was still.

"Then Thunder Sounds stood up and began singing a death-song there in the big empty night, and the ponies neighed shrill. When he had sung, he mounted and the other pony followed and the three went away in the still starlight, looking for death.

"As he rode, Thunder Sounds thought: Surely tomorrow or the next day or the next I shall meet an enemy who will kill me, and then all the shame will be gone. All night long he rode, and when the morning star looked out across the world where it was no longer night nor yet quite day, and he could hardly keep the saddle any more, and the ponies stumbled with weariness, he lay down on the prairie, thinking: Maybe an enemy will find me while I sleep and the sun will never see my shame again.

"But when he awoke, the sun was high and staring hard at him; so he got upon a pony and rode away, and the other pony followed. And as he rode he lifted up his voice and sang a death-song. Some wrinkled old hills mocked him, and a flock of crows jeered, fleeing from his shame.

"Now the sun was getting low again, and as Thunder Sounds rode, there grew a gnawing in his belly even sharper than the shame that gnawed his breast; and he said to himself: Am I a sick old woman to die by starving? It is no way for a brave man to meet death. I will eat and be strong to meet death like a man. So he found a water hole and let the ponies drink. Then he hobbled them and left them where the grass was deep along the slough. And having done these things, he hid with his bow and arrows near the water hole and waited, with that gnawing getting sharper in his belly. It was not long before some fat deer came there to drink in the cool evening. So that night he feasted long beside his lonely fire; but when the gnawing in his belly had grown dull and ceased, the gnawing in his breast grew sharp again for all the heaviness of sleep that was upon him, and he thought: This meat and a good sleep will make me strong to die tomorrow like a man. And he slept.

"Then all at once the sun was staring hard at him again and the hobbled ponies were looking down at him and nickering. So Thunder Sounds filled his belly again against the gnawing, and, having done so, he said to himself: Here is much good meat left. I cannot be always stopping to hunt food when I am looking for death; and if I do not eat, how can I be strong to die like a man? So he made a drying rack from bushes that grew along the slough, and stripped the meat and hung it on the rack to dry in the hot sun. It was the third evening at that camp before the meat was light and dry and he could start again in search of death.

"Now it happened the next evening that Thunder Sounds came to a deep narrow valley where trees grew and a little stream flowed among the trees and the grass was deep and green beside the running water. There was growling, jolting thunder just beyond the valley, and yonder clouds were piling up above the treetops, and surely there was going to be much rain. So Thunder Sounds thought: I have no tepee; it is nearly night already, and the rain will be cold. It is no way for a brave man to get sick and shiver until he dies. Maybe there is a cave to shelter me so that I may be strong to die like a man when I meet an enemy.

"And so there was a cave but not just one. There were many caves, one above the other up the steep side of the valley. The thin flat stone top of one was the flat stone floor of the next one higher up. So Thunder Sounds hobbled the ponies and left them where the grass was deep and green. Then he took his bundle of *papa* [dried meat] and crawled into one of these caves a little way up the steep side of the valley where he would not be far from his ponies.

"Thunder roared, lightning flashed, the wind howled, the rain came down like a river; but Thunder Sounds was dry and warm, and being weary and full of dried meat, he slept a dead sleep.

"When he awoke, the storm was gone, the night was still and there were stars out yonder above the dark treetops. He held his breath and listened. There was a sound just beneath him—a low regular sound like breathing; then it was louder like the snoring of a heavy sleeper; then it changed into snorts for a while, and again it was like steady breathing.

"Thunder Sounds lay there awhile wondering if it might be a bear there below him; but while he wondered, the breather snorted again and began muttering queer words. And although the words had no meaning at all, he knew that no bear could have said them. And he thought: It is no bear, but a man. So he reached down into the cave below; and hardly had he done this when a hand seized his and held it with a strong grip. There was no sound of breathing now, and it seemed a long while before anything happened. Then the grip loosened, and he could feel the man's fingers making sign talk upon his: 'Who are you?' Then Thunder Sounds made the signs for Shyela, and asked in the same way: 'Who are you?' And the other, with a rubbing of finger across

68

finger, like two trees scraping each other in a wind, made answer; and Thunder Sounds thought: This is a Chickasaw and maybe the enemy I have been looking for. But as he thought this, the other made a sign that seemed to mean, 'let us sleep.' Then the hand went limp and dropped away, and the deep breathing began again.

"Right away after that, it seemed to Thunder Sounds, the sun leaped up above the trees and stared hard upon his face, for he had fallen into a heavy sleep. His first thought was of the enemy there beneath him. So he sprang out of his cave, and at the same time the other sprang out of his cave, and there the two stood silent for a while just looking at each other so surprised they hardly breathed at all.

"Surely they were very handsome young men, and they looked so much alike that they could have been twins. Each wore an otter skin shield upon his breast. Their quivers were beautiful with porcupine quills and full of arrows, and the blanket that each held with one hand about his waist was very finely quilled. Only the sun saw them, but if anyone else had been looking he would have said: 'These handsome young men have fathers the people praise, and their mothers and sisters love them very much.'

"After they had looked hard into each other's eyes for a while, the Chickasaw began sign-talking and the other answered, sign-talking, and I will tell you in words what passed between them. The stranger said: 'If you are a Shyela, where are you going and what are you looking for?' And Thunder Sounds said: 'I am riding far looking for death. If you are a Chickasaw, where are you going and what are you looking for?' And the other answered: 'I am looking for the same thing! Why do you want to die?' And Thunder Sounds replied: 'I have two older sisters more beautiful than all other girls in the world and they have scolded me, so I cannot live any more.' The Chickasaw looked hard at Thunder Sounds for a while with his mouth wide open and no sound or breath in it, he was so surprised. Then he said, sign-talking: 'You lie, Shyela! They are not more beautiful than my two older sisters who have scolded me too, and that is why I am riding far looking for death.'

"Now Thunder Sounds sprang back from the other, sign-talking fast: 'You are looking for death. I am looking for death. It is right here!' He dropped his blanket and grasped his knife and crouched, ready to spring upon his enemy; and as he did so the Chickasaw did the same thing. But each seemed waiting for the other, and when they had looked hard at each other for a long while, Thunder Sounds dropped his knife and sign-talked again: 'It is still early and we have not eaten. I have much meat. Let us eat first, and we shall be the stronger to kill each other.' Then the Chickasaw also dropped his knife and sign-talked back: 'It is well. Let us eat first.'

"So the two sat down with the dried meat between them, like two brothers who are twins, and when the meat was all gone, the Chickasaw said: 'I will go to the creek for a drink, then I will give you what you are looking for.' And Thunder Sounds replied: 'I too will drink before I give you what you want.' So, side by side, they went to the creek and, side by side, they stooped and drank, and as they did so, Thunder Sounds' two spotted ponies came stumbling close and nickered; and the Chickasaw's two piebald ponies, that were just alike, came stumbling close and nickered. And when the two young men stood up full of sweet, cool water and drew long breaths, they looked at each other again; and all at once the Chickasaw grinned, maybe because his belly felt so good. And when Thunder Sounds saw the grin, he grinned also, for was his belly not as full as the other's?

"When the two had walked back to where they had left their knives on the ground, each stood waiting for the other to pick his up. But neither would stoop first. So afterwhile the Chickasaw said, sign-talking: 'Let us play the hand-game before we die. If you win all I have, you will kill me. If I win all you have, I will kill you.' And Thunder Sounds replied: 'Let us play the hand-game.' So they did.

"First they cut two small sticks that could be held in a closed hand, one with the bark left on and the other peeled. Then they cut twelve larger sticks for each, to be used as counters. And when this was done, the Chickasaw said: 'My ponies against your ponies.' And the game began. First the Chickasaw sang, 'Hi-yay, hi-yay—hi-ee-hi-yay,' while Thunder Sounds swung his hands about him in time with the song, changing the little sticks from one hand to the other as he did so. When the singing stopped suddenly, the swinging stopped too, and Thunder Sounds held his closed fists up in front of him that the other might guess which held the unpeeled stick. The guess was wrong, and so the Shyela had thirteen counters. The game went on, the Chickasaw singing and Thunder Sounds swinging. Sometimes one had nearly all the counters, then the other had nearly all the counters; but afterwhile the Chickasaw had them all, and the ponies were his.

"Then Thunder Sounds said in sign-talk: 'My otter shield, my blanket, my breech clout, my leggings, my moccasins, my bow and arrows, everything but my knife, against yours.' So they each stripped and placed these things in a pile. Then Thunder Sounds began singing, the Chickasaw began swinging, and after each had nearly won many times, Thunder Sounds, at last, had all the counters and the Chickasaw had no clothes and no bow and arrows—only the four ponies, his knife and his gleaming long hair. And the Chickasaw, being angry, said: 'My hair against your hair.' And he took the sticks, swinging while the other sang. It took a long while, but this time Thunder Sounds lost. Then the Chickasaw gave a war whoop, and, seizing one of the counters for a coup-stick, he struck his enemy, crying, 'An-ho.' And when he had counted coup, he cut off the gleaming long hair of Thunder Sounds close up to the scalp and danced a few steps of the victory dance.

"This made the Shyela angry, and he said: 'All that I have but my knife against your hair.' And after much singing and swinging and guessing, Thunder Sounds had all the counters. Then with a war whoop he seized a counter for a coup-stick and struck the other, crying, 'an-ho.' And having counted coup on his enemy, he cut off the long gleaming hair of the Chickasaw close up to the scalp and danced a few steps of the victory dance.

"When this was done, each stepped back to where his knife was lying on the ground; but neither stooped. And as they stood there looking at each other, the Chickasaw began to grin again—a grin that broadened until his whole face was puckered. Seeing this, the Shyela also began to grin—a grin that broadened until it touched his eyes and set them dancing. And seeing this, the Chickasaw snickered. Then Thunder Sounds snickered; and all at once both began to laugh so loud that the steeps along the narrow valley roared with mirth, and the four ponies yonder in the deep green grass lifted up their voices all together in screaming laughter. If there had been anyone there to see, he might have said: 'These young men are dying of the bellyache the way they hold their bellies and howl. Naked and hairless!—ho ho ho, ha ha ha, he he he hi-ya-hi-o!' They looked so funny to each other, that it was a long while before they could stop laughing; and when they stopped at last, they were standing with their arms about each other to keep from falling down, for the very weakness of mirth. With the tears running down their faces, they were like twins long parted who had found each other again—but the tears were tears of laughter.

"And after a while, they staggered apart, and the Chickasaw said, sign-talking: 'You are too funny to kill.' Then he held his belly again and howled, and Thunder Sounds sign-talked, saying: 'You are as funny as I am.' Then he held his belly and howled awhile.

"And when the laughing-fit was over, the Chickasaw said: 'Let us not kill each other at all. We will be brother-friends. I will give you all that was mine along with my hair. You will give me all that was yours along with your hair. Then we will both go home and tell our people to meet here when two moons have come and gone and the next new moon is low above the sunset. There shall be a big feast and our people shall be as one people forever.'

"And Thunder Sounds replied: 'It is good; let it be as you say, my brother.'

"So when they had held each other close for a while, each dressed in the other's clothes, and with the other's hair and weapons rode away towards his home, the Chickasaw upon a spotted pony exactly like the one that followed, and Thunder Sounds upon a fine piebald pony followed by its twin.

"The narrow valley, where the grass was deep and green beside the running water and the trees made pleasant shade, lay waiting there until two moons had grown and died above it. And when the thin third moon hung low above the sunset, the place was filled with happy voices. On one side of the sweet running water the Chickasaws had pitched their tepees, and on the other side, Shyelas; and their ponies knew each other, feasting together, muzzle deep, as the peoples feasted. And the steep sides of the valley laughed and sang. And because all hearts were strong with kindness, there was a big giving-away until no one had anything left at all that had been his or hers; but everyone had plenty. Even the little children gave their playthings to each other. Men who had been strangers gave themselves and were brother-friends. And their sisters became sisters, and the father of each became the other's uncle, and the mother of one the other's aunt. From that day to this no Shyela has ever harmed a Chickasaw, no Chickasaw a Shyela.

"And this was all because two boys had trouble with their sisters!"

Helping a Brother-Friend

When I arrived next morning, the fifing of wagon tires in the subzero hush of the creek bottom yonder proclaimed a family fuel shortage belatedly acknowledged. Not only was the son-in-law up and doing with the blanketed sun; but the old man himself, bent to the horizontal from the hips, his thin hair whiter than the snow, his sharp face frosted with his breath, plied an ax among the gnarled remainders of the woodpile.

"*Lela oosni!*" he remarked, smiling brightly up at me and panting. "You see I can get my own wood." Yielding the ax to me with some reluctance, he shuffled towards the tepee, apparently unaware of the ragged moccasins that gave no protection to his heels and toes against the searing snow.

When the fire was going merrily and the tepee was snug with heat, I said: "Grandfather, I have brought you a present." With something boyish shining in his face, he made a high prolonged nasal sound of pleasure and surprise as he watched me unwrap the sheepskin slippers I had brought him; and when he held them in his hands, he giggled like a youngster. The business of getting the slippers on the old man's feet became something like a catch-as-catch-can wrestling match, for in choosing the size, I had not allowed for the cozy fur inside. He lay in his bed chuckling while I held a long skinny leg under my arm and wrestled with the foot. When the business was finished, he sat up, placed an arm about my shoulder, and pulled me close. Then, as though he were making an announcement to the universe in general, he said: "This is my grandson! *Dho!* This is my grandson!"

When we had smoked awhile in silence, I asked: "And did the story of the two boys make you hungry?"

"*Dho,*" he said, regarding me with the crinkled, quizzical look; "but the meat is not the same. It has no strength in it." He meditated awhile, gazing at the ground. Then his face brightened. "That was the time

73

when High Horse and I killed our first bison bull," he began, catching up the loose thread of yesterday's narrative; "Also a young cow—fat—tender—strong meat to make a man of a boy. Thirteen winters made a man those days. It must have been the meat.

"We had plenty of bull-hides to make the *watah* [boats] we needed for crossing Mini Shoshay [the Missouri]. Also there were willows in plenty for making the frames. We tied these together with green rawhide thongs, and over the frames we stretched the green bull-skins tight, sewing them with strips of hide. Then we hung them up to dry in the wind and sun; and while they dried and shrank tight we rested and feasted three more days. *Washtay!* Good boats! Kick them—they sound like big drums! Float high in the water! *Washtay!*

"We put all our belongings in the boats and most of us swam, pulling them with rawhide thongs that we held in our teeth. The ponies did not give us any trouble after we got the first ones into the water; and some of us swam with our horses, so that we could catch the others when we got across.

"Our scouts had gone out while we were making boats, and they came back to our first camp beyond Mini Shoshay. They had been watching a big war party of Flatheads, Nez Percé and Absoraka [Crows] not far away, and they said we must attack as soon as we could that day and not wait for night, because the bands had not yet made camp together and were still coming up. If we waited, there would be too many for us. This was in the morning, and the sun was about straight up when we made the attack. There was a big butte close by, something like Bear Butte near Pa Sapa [the Black Hills], and we sneaked around that until we were close enough to charge. I think they did not know we were in the country, and it was a big surprise. Women were putting up tepees, children were playing anywhere, and the men were scattered around, not thinking of trouble because it was the middle of the day, and the ponies were grazing without guards. It was not much. There was no fight. We did not kill one man or count a coup. We just charged in there, waving blankets and yelling, and it was funny to see the people running here and running there all mixed up. The ponies had not had time to scatter far, and right away we got about a hundred started south on the run. When we reached the top of a ridge and looked back, we could see that we'd better hurry, because the warriors of the bands that were still coming in to camp back there were after us, and there were many.

"The sun was halfway down when we came into some hills with trees on them here and there. So we stopped to let the ponies rest; and if the enemy wanted to come and fight, we would fight right there with the trees and gullies to help us. They did come, but it was not much. Maybe they thought we had a big party waiting for us there and we meant to trap them. It was hard to see us among the brush and gullies, and they did not charge; but now and then they would see somebody and shoot, and we would shoot back. It was lazy war, and I guess they were tired too.

"High Horse and I were up in a tree with old Maza Ska [White Metal], or anyway he seemed old to us. He had a gun, but we had only bows and arrows. Sometimes we could see an enemy's head and we would shoot at it. White Metal would make fun of our shooting, but I think he did not hit anybody either. He only made the others know where we were, so that they could shoot back; but nobody got hurt.

"Afterwhile I could feel my belly gnawing, and over beyond a low ridge I had seen some stray bison cows. So I said to High Horse: 'Let us go over there and kill some meat, for there are no enemies that way.' Our three ponies were tied to some brush under the tree. White Metal's was a mare with a big colt at her side, and that is what I want to tell you about. When we got on our ponies we had to ride fast and swing low under their necks, because several of the enemy began shooting at us. We could hear old White Metal bang away up there. Even if he did make fun of us, we knew he liked us and wanted to help by keeping the enemy down. When we got over just under the low ridge, we stopped, and High Horse said: 'Let us smoke before we kill a cow; it may help us.' I had brought my pipe with me because it would protect me and give me power. So we sat down and smoked. When we had passed the pipe awhile, all at once there was big yelling over there beyond the low ridge, and we got up to see if the enemies were coming; and this is what we saw.

"Old White Metal's big colt was bucking and squealing and running in circles there on the open hillside, and White Metal was riding belly-down on its back; but he was not riding the way the colt was going. He was riding backwards, holding on with his legs, and with both hands around the root of the tail. His mouth was close to where the colt was breaking wind every time it bucked, and with every jolt White Metal yelled, 'hown hown.' It seemed that he was arguing with whatever the colt was saying under its tail. We could hear yelling and laughing down in the brushy draw where enemies were standing up waving their arms and cheering White Metal. Our own people were standing up too, laughing and cheering: 'Hi-ya! hoka-hey! Hold him, Kola! Bite his bottom! Don't eat it all! Give me a piece! Hoka-hey!'

75

"It was not much like war.

"This is what had happened. When High Horse and I were over the ridge, White Metal thought: I will go and help the boys kill some meat, for I too am hungry. But when he started to climb down out of the tree, some enemies shot at him—bang! bang! bang!—and he was so excited that he let go and tumbled. The loose colt was right under him ready to go, and so they went together in opposite directions.

"When White Metal was right in front of us, the colt stopped short, went straight up in the air, hump-backed, and whirled as it came down stiff-legged. That was the end of the ride, and the colt made off for its mother, still bucking and squealing. White Metal came limping up to High Horse and me, and when he had wiped the blood and dust from his mouth, he began poking us in the ribs, saying: 'That's right! Laugh! Laugh! It's funny! Don't be serious! Why don't you laugh?' And we did not quit laughing, for the rib-tickling and the fun of it, until the enemies began shooting at us again from the brush down there.

"We did get a fat cow before the sun went down, and late in the night we started for Mini Shoshay with the ponies. When the morning star was up and day was just beginning, we came to a small round valley with steep sides and only one easy way to get in. So we drove the herd in there, and Crazy Horse told us all to get a good sleep. He would watch at the opening to the valley, and if the enemy came he would waken us and we would stay right there and fight, no matter how many there might be. But no enemy came; and when it was dark we started again for the river where we had left our boats hanging in some brush.

"There was no victory dance when we got home, because we had no scalps and had not counted coup. Nobody said much about our war party. We lost about half the captured ponies on the way back; and that was not enough for thirty-seven warriors to sing about. High Horse and I each got a pony—not very young ones.

"No, it was not much, but we boys had a good time, and we learned. After that we could not talk about anything but going to war. We did go to war after High Horse went crazy."

"Did he really go crazy?" I asked.

"It is a story," the old man answered, chuckling; "and I will tell you how it was with him, and why we made war against the Crows that time.

"I was often at the Miniconjou village with my brother-friend, and sometimes I would see Tashina Wanblee over there. She was getting to be a big girl, and she was very pretty. I could see that she still liked me and that she wanted me to talk to her; but High Horse and I were going to be great warriors and we did not want to be bothered with girls. Once I came upon her down by the creek when she was getting water for her mother. She looked up at me quickly, and I can see her eyes yet; but I was older before I knew what I saw there. It was not the way it used to be when I was her horse. I thought I had scared her because she did not know I was there. When she had looked that way at me, she would not look any more. She just stood still with her hands clasped in front of her and her head bent. I talked to her, but she did not answer. Only once she said, hardly louder than a whisper: 'Shonka 'kan, Shonka 'kan.'

"I knew she was pretty, with her long hair combed smooth and shining like a blackbird, and I think she was waiting for me to throw my blanket over us and whisper to her in the dark. But my head was full of horse-stealing and war and the great deeds High Horse and I were going to do before very long; and it was such things that I told her, bragging like the boy I was, for I think I wanted her to be proud of me.

"There was a band of Shyelas [Cheyennes] camped up the creek that time. High Horse and I would go up there to play throwing-them-off-their-horses or maybe hoop-and-spear with the boys our age; for the Shyelas were friends and almost like our own people come to visit us.

"One day when we were up there having a good time, I noticed that High Horse was not with us any more, and I wondered if he had gone home. So afterwhile I rode off down the creek towards the Miniconjou village. There was some brush around a spring, and High Horse was in there. He was talking to a Shyela girl, and he did not see me. First I thought I would yell at him; but I did not, for all at once I felt sad and ashamed. So I turned back and rode home another way.

"The next time I saw him, I thought he was sick because he was queer with me, but he said he was not sick. Afterwhile he began talking without looking at me, and he said that maybe when we were great warriors we would have women too just like other men. Crazy Horse had a woman, didn't he? And all the other great warriors had too, didn't they? And so maybe it would be the same way with us. And I said we were not great warriors yet, and we did not have to think about that now. And he said, 'I know you talk to Tashina, because I have seen you doing it. Maybe you will have her for your woman sometime; and maybe I will see a girl I want too.'

"Then I laughed and said I talked to Tashina because I used to be her horse, and she wasn't like other girls anyway. I was just telling her about the things we were going to do. And he *yah-yahed*, making forked fingers at me. Then I was angry, and I said: 'You have been sneaking around in the brush after that Shyela girl again, haven't you?' Then he was angry too, and left me, and I rode home.

"All the rest of that day I was angry at High Horse; but when I awoke in the morning, I thought of him the first thing, and I was not angry any more at all. I was sad, and I got sadder and sadder all that day. So I rode out on a high hill and sat there thinking about how we had said we were twins, and we had found each other at last and we would never be apart again, and we would be brother-friends and do great deeds and everybody would praise us. And when I looked around at the sky and the prairie, it was big and empty, and I was all alone in it and nothing cared about me. So I sat there and wept a long time.

"Next day I was sadder than the day before, and I thought I would go and see High Horse again. Maybe he was sad too and would not be angry at me any more. So I started towards the Miniconjou village, riding slowly because my mind was still forked; and all at once there was a horseback coming slowly out of the brush up there. When I saw it was High Horse, my heart drummed; but when he came close I could see that it was bad with him. 'How, Kola,' he said; and his voice was low and weak, as though he might be getting ready to die pretty soon. And I said, 'What is wrong with you, brother-friend? Are you sick in your belly?' And he groaned and said, 'I am sick all over, brother-friend, and you must help me, for if nobody helps me I think I shall die.' Then he groaned some more; and I said, 'You know I will help you, for we are twins and brother-friends, and if you die then I must die too.'

"So we got off our horses and sat together in a clump of brush where nobody would see us, and High Horse said, 'My brother, it is true. I have been talking to a Shyela girl and her name is Wacin Hin Washtay Win [Good Plume].' When he had said that he muttered the name to himself for a while—like singing to yourself under your breath. Then the sickness went out of his face, and it was all shining when he looked at me and began telling me about Good Plume and how beautiful she was. It made me sad again to hear him, for I thought he was going crazy the way he told it, all out of breath. Then all at once the sickness came back in his face again, and he said, 'Brother-friend, I want her so much that I cannot eat and I cannot sleep, and if I do not get her, maybe I shall just starve to death.' 'I will think,' I said, 'and we shall see what we can do.'

"Then I thought awhile. If my brother was about to die, would I not have to go and help him even if I died too? If he was going crazy, then would I not have to help him, even if I had to go crazy too? So I said, 'You must take some horses to her father and tell him how much you want the girl. Maybe then he will give her to you.' But High Horse shook his head and groaned. 'Her father is a man of many horses,' he said, 'and I have only my buffalo-runner and the old horse we got from the Nez Percés and Absorakas.' And I said: 'If you are not man enough to try, how can I help you?' 'You will see that I am man enough to try anything,' he said, 'and I will do just what you tell me.' When he said that, he looked like a warrior charging. Then he jumped on his horse and galloped away towards his village.

"I waited and waited, and after that I still waited a long while. It was getting dark when High Horse came riding back slowly with his chin on his chest. When he had got off his horse and sat down beside me, he just held his head in his hands for a while. Then he said, 'The old man laughed at me. He just laughed and waved his hand for me to go away from there.'

"After I had thought awhile, I said, 'Brother-friend, it is harder than I thought. This is something that will take a little more time. You will sleep with me tonight, and tomorrow I shall have a better plan.'

"So after we had slept, and it was morning, I said: 'Hold fast to your pipe, brother-friend, and do not lose courage. I have a plan. The old man will not take two horses. You will offer him four horses, for I will give you Whirlwind and the horse I got from the Nez Percés and Absorakas. You will go to the old man with these. You will say how much you want the girl and that you have two good buffalo-runners, also a horse just beginning to get old and another one hardly old at all. Maybe he will not laugh at you this time. If he takes the horses, you will have the girl and we shall have only our four legs to ride. But that will be good, for we will go on the war-path *maka mani* [earth-walking, on foot], and when we get back we shall have many, many ponies and be great warriors, and everybody will praise us and the old man will be proud of you.'

"So High Horse did as I told him. But before the sun was overhead, he came back looking even sicker than ever, and he had to groan awhile before he could tell me how the old man laughed harder than before and waved his hand to say go away and quit talking foolishness.

"So I thought awhile, and then I said: 'The old man will not take four good horses for the girl, and that is all we have. Maybe she will run away with you, and then when you come back she will be your woman and you will have your horses too.' But that was no good either, because High Horse said he asked her when they were talking under the blanket, and she did not want to run away. She wanted to be bought like a fine woman.

"So I thought awhile, and then I said: 'I have the right plan at last, brother-friend; and if you quit groaning and have a strong heart, you will get her this time.' And High Horse said, 'My heart is strong enough to do anything anybody can think up, if I can only have Good Plume.' Then I said: 'The old man will not take two horses. He will not take four horses either. The girl will not run away with you. Then you will just steal her, and I will tell you how to do it. Maybe she wants you to steal her anyway. This is going to be the biggest thing we ever did.'

"So this is how it was.

"When it was dark High Horse and I rode up the creek to the Shyela village and hid in the brush until we thought everyone was asleep. Then I tied my horse and we sneaked up to the old man's tepee, leading the other horse and being very careful not to make any noise. Once a dog barked and a man came out of a tepee and looked around in the starlight. We were flat on our bellies by then, and when the man saw it was only a horse grazing, he kicked the dog and went back into his tepee.

"I would be holding the horse outside until High Horse could pull up a couple of stakes, crawl inside, gag the girl and drag her out. Then we would put her on the horse in front of him and he would get away from there fast and be happy all his life. The old people might start yelling, but everybody would be too excited to do anything, and I could run to my horse and get away. When High Horse came back, Good Plume would be his woman, and the old man would get used to it.

"When High Horse pulled the first stake, he waited awhile to see if the snoring would stop inside. It did not stop, so he pulled another stake, and still the snoring went on. Then I could see him crawling under. The snoring still went on, and that is all I could hear for a while. Pretty soon something popped, and the old man snorted.

"This is how it was. The old people had only this one girl, and they liked her so much that they had made a fine bed out of rawhide thongs for her to sleep on. Then when they saw how pretty she was getting to be, they were afraid some foolish young man might steal her in the night; so they always tied her with thongs to this bed.

"High Horse was in there feeling around for a good way to grab the girl, and when he knew she was tied, he took his knife and began cutting thongs. When the first one popped and the old man snorted, he was so scared that he dropped on his belly and quit breathing awhile. Then he began cutting thongs again. His heart drummed so hard that he was afraid it would waken the girl; but she just went on breathing quietly until he got down around her thighs. Of course he was getting more and more excited by now, and all at once the knife slipped and stuck the girl."

At this point Eagle Voice fell to chuckling; and he did not resume the tale until he had filled his pipe, lit it, and passed it to me. Then, gazing at me with his mock-serious, crinkled, quizzical look, he shook his head slowly and continued.

"Grandson, it was bad. It was very bad. The girl shrieked, the old man began yelling, the old woman began screaming, and High Horse was getting out of there so fast he nearly knocked the tepee down. By the time we were both on the horse, people were rushing out of their tepees shouting to each other and all the dogs were barking. It was dim starlight, and everybody was so excited that nobody knew what anybody was yelling about; so we got away.

"Next day High Horse was feeling sicker than ever, and even I was feeling a little sick. But I said, 'Brother, we nearly got her that time, and if you are man enough and your knife does not slip, next time we will get her, for I will think up a better plan.' And High Horse groaned and said, 'Maybe they will kill me next time, but I am going to die anyway if I don't get Good Plume, and I am man enough to fight the whole Shyela village if they catch me.' 'Then quit groaning,' I said, 'and have a strong heart, for I have a plan already; only we must wait until the people up there are not excited any more.'

"So we counted ten days and waited; and while we waited we talked about my plan. Maybe I got it from Charger's story about the wild young man who liked tobacco so much he could never get enough of it; but it was different too.

"So this is the way it was. When we had counted ten days, we rode far around the Shyela village and came to the creek above it when the sun was low. Then High Horse stripped naked and I began painting him with mud all over. When I was through, he was all crooked stripes and spots, and he looked like some animal nobody ever saw. When he saw himself in the water he said, 'I look so terrible that I scare myself.' And I said, 'You look so terrible you scare even me a little, and I made you. If you get caught, people will think you are some bad spirit and they will all run away; so you must not be afraid of anything; and don't let your knife slip this time.'

"When the night was getting old and no dogs barked, we crawled into the Shyela village leading the horse. We did this so slowly that no dog noticed us. There was snoring in the girl's tepee. So High Horse pulled a stake. The snoring went on. He pulled another stake. The snoring still went on. Then he crawled in. Pretty soon a thong popped and I heard the old woman say, 'Wake up! Wake up! There is somebody in this tepee!' And the old man said, 'Of course there is somebody in this tepee. I am in this tepee. Go to sleep and don't bother me.' Pretty soon there was snoring again.

"I listened hard for another pop, but there was only snoring—more than before, like two men snoring back and forth at each other. And this is how it was in there.

"When the old woman and old man talked, High Horse lay flat on his belly and stopped breathing for a while. But he was very tired and very weak because he had not slept or eaten much for a long time, he was so sick about the girl. So all at once he was snoring as hard as the old man was.

"I waited and waited. The morning star came up. I waited and waited. There was a thin streak of day. I could not call to High Horse, so I waited. The hills were beginning to stare. Then I got out of there with the horse and hid up the creek in the brush where I had tied Whirlwind.

"Pretty soon all at once there was a big noise—screaming and yelling and barking down there in the village. It was even worse than the other time. Then I could hear somebody running hard, and it was High Horse, coming like an antelope. He was coming up the creek towards me, and he surely looked terrible in the daylight. All at once he dodged into a big hollow tree by the creek, and I could not go to him or call to him because I could hear people coming. It was a party of men with axes and knives and spears and guns. They were looking here and looking there and being very careful because of the terrible thing they had seen running. They stopped close to the hollow tree, and when they could not see any tracks, one said, 'It was a bad spirit that has gone back into the water.' Then they went away, for I think they were glad not to catch what they had chased.

"This is how it happened in the tepee. When the day began to come in through the flap, the girl awoke and looked around. The first thing she saw was that terrible animal sleeping there beside her bed. And that was when the big noise began and High Horse started running.

"I was lying there in the brush now listening, and afterwhile the big noise stopped and I could hear tepee poles coming down. The people were moving camp because of the bad spirit in that place; and when I had waited some more, there was no sound to hear at all, and I knew the people were all gone. So I went to High Horse; and when he came out of his tree he looked so sick and sad and terrible all at once that I had to laugh. Anyway, they had not caught us, and that was good. But High

Horse did not laugh any; he just groaned. So I quit laughing, and said, 'Have a strong heart, brother-friend, and when I have washed the mud off, I will think up a better plan.' So we went into the water and I washed him. And when he was dressed, he said, 'I know now I can never have Good Plume, so I shall have to die. I will go on the war-path alone, and somebody will kill me.' And I said, 'I am your brother-friend and you will not go to war alone, because I am going with you. We shall see if the old man laughs when we get back with a hundred ponies and I do not know how many scalps.'"

The Mysterious Mother-Power

When Eagle Voice had ceased chuckling, the look of boyish merriment left his face, and for some time he sat motionless with closed eyes and bowed head, his hands upon his knees. He seemed very far away, as though the drifted wastes of many winters stretched between us. When I had fed the stove again, I said, only meaning to arouse him: "And did you get the hundred ponies and the scalps, and did High Horse get the girl at last?"

He lifted his head, gazing through me and beyond. Then the far look shortened slowly, and he smiled. "It is a story, Grandson," he said, "and you are in a hurry again, Wasichu that you are. There is a road, and what you ask is yonder. We are going on the war-path."

"'But before we go, Grandfather,' I said, 'tell me why Lakotas sold their women. Wasichus sell their horses, but their women they give away. Was a Lakota woman only an animal that a man should buy her?'

"Your heart is Lakota, Grandson," the old man answered, smiling indulgently as upon a child, "but you ask a foolish question like a Wasichu. In the old days we did not buy and sell the way Wasichus do. We stole our horses from our enemies, daring much, for we were brave men. If we gave them to a father and asked him for his daughter, who should have a woman but a brave man good for something?

"Before the sacred hoop was broken it was made of men and women, and from each there was a power that kept it strong. I think, before we go to war, I will tell you an *ohunka* story about the power of women. Old people used to tell it in the night; and their grandchildren after them, grown old themselves; and their grandchildren too, and theirs, and theirs, the story is so old. Now all of those are gone and many more, and I will tell it, being old myself. Old people used to say that if *ohunka* stories were told by daylight, something bad would happen to the teller. Maybe he would get sick and die, or his grandson would be

84

killed, or his old woman would fall and break her hip. And I have even heard them say—" Here the old man paused to chuckle. "I have even heard them say he might grow long curly hair all over his backside; but maybe they were joking. Sometimes if somebody who wanted to hear made a gift, an *ohunka* story could be told on a dark day. You have made a gift, Grandson, and the day is dark, so I can tell it; and this is the story about the power of women.

"Many snows ago there were two young Lakota warriors. One was named Good Voice Hawk, and he was a very good-looking fellow. The other was called Brave Eagle, and he was not good-looking at all.

"There was a girl, too, and she was very beautiful. Also her father was a *wichasha yatapika* [a man they praise], because he had counted many coups, had given much meat to the old people, and nobody could say anything but good of him. Of such men chieftains were made. The girl's name was Red Hail, which is a sacred name; for hail and rain and lightning come together with the power to make live and to destroy; and red is a holy color.

"The people had camped in a pleasant place with plenty of wood, water, and grass; and the councilors had announced that it was a good time for war parties to go forth.

"Now these two young men had been talking to the girl whenever either could find her alone, for both wanted her very much. Good Voice Hawk, the handsome one, would talk much about himself and say little evil things about Brave Eagle; but Brave Eagle, the homely one, would just look at the girl for the most part, making few words and saying nothing bad about anybody.

"A big war party was about to set forth the next day, and the two young men would be going with it. Maybe Red Hail liked them both and could not choose between them. Anyway, that evening when it was dark, she stole up to the big tepee where Good Voice Hawk lived, and peeked in through a little hole. Everything was fine in there. The young man was sitting on his braided rawhide bed, and his mother, sitting on his left side, was gently combing his long hair and preparing it for braiding. On his right side sat the father, busy making new wraps on arrowheads for his son. A younger brother was at the fireplace in the center, keeping a bright flame alive so that there might be plenty of light. And while Red Hail watched, the younger sister of Good Voice Hawk came with a bowl of *wasna* and held it in front of her handsome brother, so that he might eat and enjoy himself before he went to war.

"Then Red Hail stole away in the darkness to a much smaller tepee where the other young man lived, and peeped in through the side of the flap. She saw nothing fine in there. Brave Eagle was sitting by the fire and he was busy wrapping arrows. The mother was sitting on her side of the tepee, the father on his, and the little brother was watching the young warrior. That was all she saw.

"Then Red Hail stole back to her own tepee, and what she thought the story does not tell.

"In the morning the war party started, passing the tepee of the girl, who stood there watching. Among the first came Good Voice Hawk, and surely he was very handsome on his fine horse that danced about as he paused to smile at Red Hail and let her see how handsome he was. And as he went, he often turned to look back at her again, until he passed out of sight over a hill. Last of all came Brave Eagle riding a mule, and he did not look at Red Hail at all, but just rode on and out of sight. Maybe there were no mules in the old days, but stories change like people, and this is how it came to me.

"When Red Hail's father came back, the girl was crying, and she said, 'Father, I want to be where the boys are. I want to go wherever they go.' The father knew how it was with the girl, and after he had thought awhile he said, 'My daughter, we will go together.'

"So when he had caught two good horses and everything was ready, they started after the party; and when they overtook it, camp was being made for the night.

"Now as the war party moved on, the people noticed Red Hail, because everyone knew about the two young warriors; and there was much talk of how Good Voice Hawk would bring her tender pieces of cooked meat when they camped in the evenings; but Brave Eagle did not bring her anything. Now and then the girl would ride ahead to sit upon a hill and sing when the two young men were passing; and there were some who said they heard a difference in the singing, and that it did not favor homely boys who rode on mules.

"One day when the war party was getting near to enemy country, the *blotan hunka,* who were the leaders of such parties, held council and decided to send out two scouts. Brave Eagle and Good Voice Hawk were chosen to go, maybe because everybody had been talking so much about them. So after they had been told just what to do, and it was growing dark, the two young men rode forth together, the one on his fine horse and the other on his mule. All night they rode towards the country of the enemy, and just as the day was beginning to break, they came to the sloping side of a bluff, sprinkled with stunted pines.

"Maybe there were people on the other side; so they tied the mule and the horse in a brushy place, and began crawling up the slope. It was not very far to the top, but daybreak had brightened when they reached it, and there below them was a village with many smokes rising, and already the people were moving about.

"As the two scouts gazed, they heard hoofs coming, and out of the brush not very far away a band of horses came trotting, and after them rode a man who was driving them to a good feeding place for the day.

"Then Good Voice Hawk whispered to Brave Eagle, lying there beside him, 'Cousin, let us kill the man and scalp him and drive the horses home.' And Brave Eagle answered, 'No, cousin, I think that would be wrong, for we are only scouts. We should tell the *blotan hunka* what we have seen, and they will know what is best to do.' But Good Voice Hawk would not listen. 'If you are afraid,' he said, 'of course I will do it myself.'

"He started crawling back and then got up and ran to where the mule and horse were tied. So what could Brave Eagle do but follow him? Should a warrior let his comrade fight alone, even if he is wrong?

"Now when they had ridden back to the top of the slope, there not very far away was the man with the band of horses. So Good Voice Hawk charged upon him, crying, *'hoka-hey,'* in a loud voice; and Brave Eagle followed on his mule. The man had time to draw his bow and let an arrow fly, but he was so excited that he missed; and just as Good Voice Hawk came near, the man's horse shied, and Good Voice Hawk charged by and did not touch him.

"Then Brave Eagle, who was close behind, with one swing of his war club struck the man from his horse; and already he had taken the scalp when the other circled back, crying, 'Cousin, they are coming!'

"By now it looked very bad down there in the valley, for the people were boiling out of the village like a swarm of bumblebees, and over them a roar of voices grew. 'Let us get out of here!' cried Good Voice Hawk; and, without stopping to coup the enemy, he headed down the slope at a run; and after him went the homely warrior pounding on his mule.

"They were not very far out in the open country when, looking back, they saw many mounted warriors coming out of the pines back yonder, and they were coming very fast, because their horses were fresh and strong with plenty of grass. They were coming too fast for the mule, and it was beginning to look bad for those who fled, when Good Voice Hawk stopped his horse and cried out to his comrade, 'Cousin, give me the scalp.' And the other, who thought only of the scalp and that it might be taken from him, gave it to his comrade; for it was not his way to think bad things of people.

"Then Brave Eagle was all alone, kicking his mule along; and Good Voice Hawk grew smaller, fleeing yonder, and the sound of many hoofs behind grew louder.

"Well, that night the handsome young warrior rode into the camp of his people with a scalp to show and a brave story to tell. There were many, many enemies, too many for even the whole party to fight; but it was good to hear how Good Voice Hawk had fought until his friend was killed. Then he had fled, and only the Great Spirit and a fast horse had saved him.

"That night the people heard the sound of mourning in Red Hail's tepee—weeping and mourning far into the night; and when the sound ceased, those who still listened thought, 'The girl has cried herself to sleep at last!'

"But Red Hail had not slept; and when the morning came, she was not there. Wherever the people looked, she was not there either. She had just vanished like a spirit in the night, and her horse was grazing with the others near the camp.

"Now this is what had happened. While she was weeping in her tepee, Red Hail thought more and more, 'I must go to see where he died'; and the thought was so big by the time her father fell off to sleep, that she went, creeping away into the darkness so that not even the horse-guards saw her.

"She was far away when the sun came, and when she had hidden in a clump of brush, she prayed that she might be led to where Brave Eagle had died; and then she fell asleep. And as she slept, a sacred power from her praying and her sorrow came upon her, and in a dream Brave Eagle came to her, alive as ever, and looked at her awhile the way he used to do. But there was such a light about him that he was not homely any more; and when she awoke, the sun was low and her heart was very strong.

"So when she had eaten of some roots and rabbit-berries that were growing there beside a creek, she started out again and walked all night. Again she slept and walked; and the sacred power must have led her, for she came at last to where the hoofs of many horses made a trail. It led her up a slope sprinkled with stunted pines, and when she reached the top it was beginning to get dark. There just below her in the valley was the village of the enemy, and the sound of drums and singing came to her; for in the center of the village was a fire and there the people danced as for a victory.

"And now the sacred power came upon Red Hail stronger than ever, and it told her that Brave Eagle was yonder in the village waiting to be tortured. So when the dark had come, she crawled down the bluff to a creek that ran close to the village, and there she sat in the brush awhile, praying that she might know what to do. And as she sat she began to sing a little song, very low, the way mothers sing to fretful children in the night. And while she sang, she took a piece of clay and shaped it to the singing until it was like a little baby that she swayed and comforted. And as she sang, the woman-power to make live and to destroy grew stronger all around her, spreading far. And the singing of the victors in the village slowly died away, and the drums were still, and even the bugs in the grasses made no sound.

"Then Red Hail placed the baby in a soft bed of grass and arose and went into the village. The fire was burning low as though it slept, and round about it in a circle lay the dancers, sleeping soundly; and no dog barked. The very ponies that had come from grazing in the dark to look upon the singing people in the light stood still as stones with noses to the ground.

"There was a tepee yonder, bigger than the others, and Red Hail's power led her to it. And when she raised the flap and looked inside, there beyond the little sleeping fire in the center she saw Brave Eagle sitting, bound with thongs and sleeping soundly with his chin upon his breast. And, all around, the tepee guards were sitting, sleeping soundly with their chins upon their breasts.

"Then Red Hail stepped across the sleeping fire and touched Brave Eagle, and he awoke and looked at her the way he used to do, and the light upon his face was the same the dream had shown her.

"'I have come for you,' she said, 'and we are going home.' And that was the first time she had ever seen him smile. So when she had cut the thongs that bound him, Brave Eagle killed the guards with their own war clubs and took their scalps with their own knives.

"Then the two went about among the tepees, finding robes well tanned and soft, and pretty dresses finely made of elkskin, and moccasins well beaded, and parfleche panniers beautifully painted, and many other things to make a home. And these they packed upon six of the finest horses that slept with drooping heads till Red Hail stroked their noses and told them to awaken.

"Then they rode away and left the village sleeping soundly; and no one knows how long the village slept. All night they rode, Red Hail ahead, and after her the horses with their packs, and after them, Brave Eagle on his mule. And they were far away when daybreak came.

"Now while this was happening, the war party had grown weary of looking for Red Hail and had gone back home. And when at last the two with the horses and the packs came near the village of their people, they camped behind a hill, and peering from the top of it, they saw the people dancing yonder as for a victory.

"It was getting dark, and Brave Eagle said to Red Hail, 'I will go to see my father, and you will watch the horses.' So he crawled down the hill and came to a little tepee standing all alone outside the village. It was made of ragged hides and it was full of mourning. And when he raised the flap, he saw his father and his mother and his younger brother sitting there in ragged clothes, with their hair cut off and nothing in the tepee but their sorrow, for they had given everything away.

"And when Brave Eagle entered, they thought he was a ghost and just stared at him, afraid, until he spoke. And when he had told his story and heard that the people were dancing for Good Voice Hawk, his father said, 'I will go to Red Hail's father and tell him, for he is mourning too and has given everything away. We will say nothing to anyone else about this, and in the morning you will come with Red Hail and the horses and the packs.'

"So Brave Eagle went back to Red Hail there behind the hill. And in the morning when the dancing had begun again, some people saw the string of laden horses coming yonder with a woman leading them and a warrior in the rear. The dancing ceased and all the people stood and stared awhile without a word, for they could not yet believe they really saw. And around the circle of the village, left to right, rode Red Hail clothed in soft elkskin beautifully beaded, and after her the horses followed with their packs, and after them rode Brave Eagle clothed as when he rode away to war.

"Then at last a great cry went up from all the people, and the horses lifted up their heads and neighed, and there was great rejoicing. But Good Voice Hawk had fled.

"Now when the chiefs had called Brave Eagle and Red Hail into the great lodge and heard the story, they summoned the *akichitas*, who are the keepers of the law and have the power of thunder beings. And the head chief said to them, 'Find Good Voice Hawk wherever he has fled, but do not bring him back.'

"Then there was feasting in the village and all the people gave gifts to those who had mourned, until they had more than plenty of all good things.

"And when he was still young, Brave Eagle became a *wichasha yatapika* and then a chieftain. And when the two were bent beneath the snows of many winters, Red Hail and Brave Eagle were still happy together, for all their daughters were like their mother and all their sons were brave."

Four Against the Crows

Dry snow whined to the footstep in the hush of the blue-cold morning, and the tepee smoke stood straight. Before I entered I could hear the old man blowing meditatively upon his eagle-bone whistle—like a sleepy bird questioning the first promise of a summer dawn. "I thought you might not come," he said, "for it is very cold; but it is good that you are here. We are getting closer to that story about this whistle, and I was sitting here thinking about it, and about the quirt too.

"This would be a bad day for going to war," he continued after we had passed the pipe awhile; "going *maka mani* too. I think our feet would freeze before we found Crow horses. And scrawny horses they would be, with pawing snow for little grass and gnawing frozen bark along the creeks. But horses are fat where we are going, for the Moon of Making Fat [June] is nearly full, the grass is good, and cherries are beginning to darken; also, we are young.

"High Horse was not sick any more, because we had talked so much about going to war that it had made him well. Also, he was either going to feed the wolves, or have so many ponies that the girl's father could not laugh at him.

"Looks Twice, my father's brother-friend, was like my father now, for he had come to live with us and my mother was his woman. He was very good to me, and I learned much from him. When our war party came back from across Mini Shoshay, he gave me a good gun that loaded from behind. He got it from somebody who brought it from Red Cloud's camp. High Horse's father gave him a gun too, but it was not as good as mine.

"We did not say anything to anybody about going after Crow horses, because the councilors had not announced that war parties could go forth, and they might not let us go. So when we were ready, we started with the first sunlight on our backs. Somewhere over towards the mountains we would come upon the Crows. We had not eaten yet, so when we were out of sight behind a hill we sat down to eat some *papa* so that we might be strong to walk fast and far. While we were eating, some-body came over the hill, and it was Kicking Bear. He was a Hunkpapa, and a small band of his people had come to visit and camp with us. He was not very much older than we were, but he had come from far away, and he seemed to us like a man who had counted many coups. He said, 'Where are you going, cousins?' And we said, 'We are going to get some Crow ponies, but do not tell anybody.' And he said, 'You are very brave men to do that *maka mani*, and I am going with you.' So that was good; and when we had eaten some *papa*, we started walking towards Crow country. But we had not gone far when two horsebacks came, and they were *akichitas* bearing a pipe from the council. When they had held the pipe out for us to touch, they said, 'Where are you going?' The pipe was sacred and we had to tell, so we did. And they said, 'You are brave young men to do that *maka mani;* but it is not the time for war parties and you must come back. The council has spoken.'

"So we went back.

"That night High Horse and I were sitting outside the village. The moon was bright and we were talking about what we could do next. Afterwhile there were two people coming in the half-dark. It was Kick-ing Bear with a friend called Charging Cat. And Kicking Bear said, '*How*, cousins! We are going after those Crow ponies tonight, for we are men. If you are men too, we will all go together.' And I said, 'You will see that we are men too.' And High Horse said, 'We might as well go now, for if we make a *wakte-agli* [kill-come-back] with horses, there will be a victory dance and nobody will be angry at us for going. This we will do, or else we will feed the wolves yonder, and then nobody will be angry either.'

"So we went, and there were four of us. When the moon was low in front of us and the morning star shone upon our backs, above a streak of daybreak, we were far away, for we had walked fast. There was a place with rocks around it, and a clear creek was flowing there with grass be-side the water. And near the place was a high hill that was not quite a mountain. It was a good place to eat what was left of the *papa* and to sleep awhile. But before we did this, Kicking Bear took a pipe out of a deerskin bag. The stem was wrapped with red porcupine quills and an eagle feather was hanging from it, and there was bison-hide on the mouthpiece. And Kicking Bear said, 'My Brothers, this is one of the hardest things we are doing, and we shall need help, for we are only men. We will go up on the high hill yonder before we rest and eat, and there we will dedicate this pipe to Wakon Tonka and make a sacred vow.'

"So we climbed the high hill, the four of us, and when we stood breathing on the top the day had grown and spread, and the prairie 'rose steep from beneath us to the end of the world. We stood and looked until the sun leaped up and blazed against our eyes. Then Kicking Bear gave me the pipe and I held it high to the place whence comes the light of seeing; and on my left side Charging Cat was standing and on my right stood High Horse, both with their hands upraised palms forward; and behind us Kicking Bear was sending forth a voice. He was asking the Great Mysterious One to behold us and the pipe we offered and to hear the sacred vow we made. We were four young men with strong hearts who wanted to do great deeds that our people might praise us, and by ourselves we could do nothing. So we were dedicating this pipe and asking that we might return as victors to our people. And if this should be, then we four would dance the sun dance, piercing our flesh with thongs; and this we would do for thanks. And when Kicking Bear had finished, we all cried, 'hetchetu aloh!' Then we left the pipe on the hilltop with the mouthpiece pointing towards the sunrise, and went down to the place with rocks around it and a clear stream flowing through, with grass beside the cool water. And there, with hearts made stronger by the prayer upon the hill, we ate what was left of the *papa*, and lay down in the grass to rest.

"And all at once the sun was on the other side and getting low, for we had walked far and fast and our sleep was deep. The first thing we saw when we looked around us was a deer drinking from the creek not far away; and because I had the best gun, the others waited for me to shoot while we were still lying down. I hit it just behind the front leg, and it fell down and did not get up. By this we knew that Wakon Tonka had beheld us on the hill and heard us, and that our offering was received. So we made a little fire and feasted there beside the running water; but the first piece of meat and the tenderest we each gave to the Spirit that helped us; and our hearts were stronger than before.

"When we had eaten, we took some of the best meat and followed the last light of day. All night we walked; and the moon traveled with us and all the star nations, going yonder to the country of the Crows. Then we ate and slept; and two more nights we traveled in the same way, and Wakon Tonka sent us meat. And then when the moon was shining in our faces and the morning star stood up behind us we lay down in some brush to rest, for we thought by now we must be in the country of the enemy. We slept, and when the sun found us there and blazed in upon us, we awoke.

"There was a high hill that was almost a mountain, and on it scattered pine trees grew to the top. And I said, 'From the top of that high hill yonder we can see everything. Let us go up there to look. Maybe there will be a Crow village.' And Kicking Bear said, 'Cousins, that is what we are going to do.' And High Horse said, 'There may be a valley full of horses.' And Charging Cat said, 'We can eat what is left of the meat up there while we are looking.' So we went.

"When we stood breathing hard on the very top, there was a wide empty land to the end of the world—valleys without smoke and hills with pines upon them; and then beyond the hills of pine, the mountains. So we made a little fire where it could not be seen and roasted what we had left of the meat. When we were eating and talking about what we could do next, High Horse said, 'Look, cousins! Something is coming down that valley. See? It is coming this way.' We looked hard where he pointed, and Kicking Bear said, 'Maybe it is some deer or maybe elk coming.' After we had looked awhile longer, I said, 'It is neither elk nor deer. I think it is an *iglaka* coming.' And Kicking Bear said, 'I think it does look like an *iglaka*.' And Charging Cat said, 'It is an *iglaka,* cousins; and there are some loose horses following.' And High Horse said, 'Now we shall have horses to ride, and then it will be easier to get all we want.'

"So we made a plan for attacking the *iglaka*. I would go with Charging Cat down the left side of the hill, Kicking Bear with High Horse down the right side. We did this because High Horse and I had guns that loaded from behind. The *iglaka* was coming from the right side. I would shoot when the man in front came close to me. The others would hear. High Horse and Kicking Bear would shoot then, and all of us would charge, coming from in front and behind the *iglaka*.

"Then we started down the hill. When we were at the bottom, Charging Cat and I hid behind some rocks where we could see the valley in front of us, and afterwhile we could see the *iglaka* coming. There was a man in front, not young but not very old; and when I saw the horse he was riding, I whispered to Charging Cat, 'There is the horse I have been looking for.' And he said, 'I have been looking for the same horse.' It was gray-spotted and taller than Whirlwind, and it held its head high and kept looking all around as it came. Back of the man on the fine horse was an old woman riding on a pony-drag, and she was driving the pony with a long stick. She made me think of my grandmother, and I whispered to Charging Cat, 'Be careful and do not shoot the old woman.' And he said of course he would not shoot her. I thought more about this when I was older. When the man was in front of us, he was close enough for a good bow-shot. I put my gun on top of the rock and took a good aim. I must have hit him in the spine, for he fell back screaming; and while he was falling Charging Cat's arrow stuck in his shoulder. All at once there was shooting over there where Kicking Bear and High Horse were—one shot, and yelling; another shot, and more yelling, and horses squealing and the sound of hoofs. The old woman's pony started running away with her as we came out of the rocks yelling, 'hoka-hey! hoka-hey!' She was bouncing and holding on tight and screaming. When we came to the man on the ground he was not through dying yet. I let Charging Cat count the first coup, because I had killed. When I leaned down to take the man's scalp he looked at me once and then died. I think I did not see that look until I was older. There was more yelling over to the right, and there were horses milling around in the valley, maybe eight or ten. The old woman's pony was running in a big circle off yonder to our left. She was fat and she looked funny bouncing that way, but we did not laugh. Then the drag hit something, maybe a rock, and she rolled over and over on the ground. When she got up, she just stood screaming and shaking her long stick at us. Then there was a horse-back coming fast from over on the right. It was a young Crow, and we shot at him as he passed, and he shot back, but we all missed, and he did not stop to fight. He was going over there to help the old woman. Then High Horse and Kicking Bear came running, and High Horse had a scalp, for there were two driving the Crow horses, and one of them died.

"By now the Crow that rode past us was waiting over there with the old woman behind him. He just sat on his horse and waited. And Charging Cat said, 'When we have caught some horses, we can go over there and kill him.' And I said, 'Maybe that is his grandmother.' And High Horse said, 'Maybe it is; and he is a brave man to wait for four of us.' And Kicking Bear said: 'We will let him go if he does not charge us while we are catching some horses. That is what we are going to do. If he wants to die, he can charge us.'

"So we spread out and began trying to round up the horses. It was not easy, because they were still frightened. They would sniff and snort at us and then start running. But afterwhile we got three of them in some brush up against a steep place, and Kicking Bear caught one. Most of them had thin rawhide lariats looped around their necks for staking out. Kicking Bear tied the lariat around the horse's jaw and rode after some more. When he caught one, I rode and helped him; and in a little while we were all riding. The fine horse the older man was riding got away. I chased him, but he ran like a high wind blowing. I think he was the best horse I never had.

"By that time we could see the old woman was on her drag again and we could hear her mourning. The young Crow was riding beside her pony and leading it. We watched them going and listened until they were out of sight around a bend in the valley. Then Kicking Bear said, 'I think there is a Crow village up yonder and they were going visiting with some horses to give away.' And I said, 'They will have a story to tell, and the village will be looking for us.' And High Horse said, 'If they were going to visit, maybe they came from another village and that is the one we can attack, for they will not hear the story.' And Kicking Bear said, 'That is what we are going to do, cousins.'

"So we started up the back trail of the *iglaka*, and Charging Cat said, 'We ought to take the other horses with us.' And High Horse said, 'There are only four and I have so many cousins that one more horse would not be much.' And I said, 'If there is a village, there will be a herd of horses, and these here will only bother us.' And Kicking Bear said, 'You are right, cousin; we will find the village and drive off the whole herd. The Crow can have his four horses when he comes back for the old man and the other young man yonder.'

"So we rode on up the back trail of the *iglaka*, and we were careful when we came to a bend, for there might be a village. But there was no village, and we rode on; and still there was no village, and the sun was getting low. So Kicking Bear said, 'Cousins, we must find that village before it is dark. Eagle Voice can climb up that hill yonder and High Horse can climb up this one here. Maybe they will see something and they can hurry back and tell us. Charging Cat and I will keep the horses here in the brush.' So we did this, and when I was on the top of my hill, there were smokes yonder below me. There were many smokes in a circle, for the night is not warm in that country and it was getting time to eat. On the other side of the smokes there was a valley sloping up to a big gulch through the hills towards where the sun comes up; and in the valley and up along the slope there were horses, horses. My heart was drumming, and I looked all around to see how we could get in there; and I saw another deep gulch through the hills that stood between the valley of the village and the valley where Kicking Bear and Charging Cat had our horses. When I saw this, I knew again that Wakon Tonka had heard us when we made our vow and dedicated the pipe. We could go in through that gulch and come out right between the village and the herd. Then we could scare the horses and drive them through the other gulch towards our home.

"I ran down the hill and told the others; for High Horse was there by now and he had not seen anything. So we rode on up the valley until we came to the gulch I saw, and there we waited in some brush. The sun was under a hill and there were shadows. We waited, and it was getting dark. We waited, and moonlight was beginning to show over the hill ahead of us. When the moon looked over into our valley, High Horse said, 'Let us go in now.' And Kicking Bear said, 'Cousins, we must wait until the village is asleep and the horse-guards are nodding. That is what we are going to do.' And I said, 'Yes, we will do that.' And Charging Cat said, 'I could eat the hump of a fat bison cow.' And I said, 'The four of us could eat the cow.' And High Horse said, 'We can eat tomorrow when we are far away with all those horses.' And Kicking Bear said, 'We are men, and that is what we can do.'

"The moon was high, and we waited. Sometimes one would fall asleep and the others would wake him. The moon was above us, and we waited. It was starting down, and we waited. It was halfway down, and Kicking Bear said, 'Cousins, they are sleeping hard and the horse-guards will be nodding. Eagle Voice has seen, and he will lead the way. Remember the vow and have strong hearts. Nothing lasts but the hills.' Then High Horse said to me, 'Brother, if you die in there tonight, look back as you are going to the spirit land, for I will be coming.' And I said, 'I will remember to look back, and if you die, look back and wait for me, for I will be coming too.'

"So we rode into the gulch. It was steep at the top and there were some rocks. When one rolled and bounced it made a big noise, for the night was still and cold. Then we would wait and listen awhile. We came to the mouth of the gulch. There were tepees to our left, all asleep in their shadows. To the right there were shadows scattered on the slope and we knew that was the herd. We lay down close to our horses and rode in slowly. If someone saw, we would look like strays from the herd. A dog raised a long howl. And for a while there was barking. We just lay flat on our horses, and let them graze until the dogs were still again. Then we moved ahead slowly, one behind the other, and I was ahead. We would move a little and then stop to let our horses graze. Then we would move ahead a little more and stop to graze, like strays eating their way back to the herd. I looked ahead, and looked, and I saw my horse's shadow. I could hear horses blowing in the grass, and I could see they were grazing towards the gulch that opened to where the sun comes from. That was good.

"I moved slowly and stopped; moved and stopped. There was something ahead a little way. It was like a shadow, with nothing to make a shadow. All at once it stood up, and it was a man. He said something like a question, but I could not understand. I touched my horse's flank with my heel, and he moved ahead quickly. The man yelled. My gun was ready; and I was so close, I could almost touch him with it. When he yelled, I shot. He went down, but my horse reared and leaped and I did not stop to count coup. There were two shots behind me, and I could hear the other three yelling where they were strung out behind the herd. Dogs were barking among the tepees and there was shouting yonder. I heard this, and then I heard only myself yelling. Then my own yelling was not loud, for there was thunder in the moonlight, thunder roaring from the ground and a thin cloud rising with the thunder.

"They were running, the herd was running away. I could see their heads and backs tossing, but they were shadows in the thin, rising cloud that thundered in the moonlight.

"The hills that were yonder came closer and all at once they were standing dark above the thundering cloud with moonlight on their heads. The herd was slowing. Horses were crowding and screaming, crowding and rearing and screaming. By now I was waving my blanket above my head, and I was still yelling. When I looked off to my right I could see blankets waving in the moonlight like great wings flapping, and I knew the others were working as hard as I was. The cloud ahead was thinning a little, and I could see a dark river of horses flowing up the break in the hills that was narrow at the bottom. They flowed and tossed and roared the way a sudden flood in a coulee does. I rode at a run up and down the flank of the crowding herd, waving my blanket and yelling to keep horses from breaking away and heading back towards the village. If they had no horses to ride back there, they could not catch us. When I looked back I could see only dusty moonlight; and if there was yelling yonder, the river of horses was louder.

"Then I knew the herd had narrowed ahead and the rear was crowding into the mouth of the gulch—horses on top of horses, rearing and fighting and screaming. And all at once, the four of us were together again, and Kicking Bear was yelling, 'We have got them, cousins! Drive them hard! We have got them!' So we kept on yelling and waving our blankets. And when we rode into the mouth of the gulch behind the last of the herd, we rode over horses that were down, kicking and squealing, and trying to get up.

"In a little while we were at the top of the gulch, and the herd was a river of shadows roaring in the moonlight ahead of us. They were flowing fast into a wide valley that we could not see across. The gulch widened and we spread out. Charging Cat and High Horse stayed behind the herd to keep them going. Kicking Bear rode up the right side and I up the left, so that they would keep bunched and not stray off.

"When the morning star was up and there was a streak of day on the range of hills ahead of us, the herd was getting harder to keep going, and they would not gallop any more. They would only trot. Sometimes my horse would stop all at once with his four legs spread out, and wobble and pant. I caught a bigger horse, and it was not hard to catch him. Then I turned mine loose with the others.

"We pushed the herd on over the next range of hills, and when the sun came up we let them stop to rest and graze awhile. There was a creek, and they made for it, crazy with thirst. Many of them piled up in a bend of the creek where it was easy to reach the water. Some died there and some died later, from drinking too much I think. Also, we had lost some in the night, but there were many left. We had not slept or eaten and we had been riding hard. Charging Cat said, 'We can kill a yearling and eat the best of it while they are grazing.' And High Horse said, 'Maybe they will be catching strays and following us.' And I said, 'If there were some strays near the village they could catch others fast, and maybe a big party is on our trail now.' And Kicking Bear said, 'We can kill a yearling beyond that next range of hills there. Maybe there will be a deer or a fat cow. We can eat over there. We are men, and that is what we are going to do.' And Charging Cat said, yes, we were men, and we could do that.

"So we filled ourselves with water, and when we had changed horses we began driving the herd again. They were so tired that they did not try to run away, and we had to ride up and down and wave our blankets and yell to make them trot. When the sun was high we were over the next range. Even then we did not stop. Sometimes a horse would just lie down and stay there. If we kicked him, he would not get up. And we said, when we got home there would be only good ones. All the time we kept looking back at the ridge behind us. Maybe there would be a party of Crows coming yonder. But the ridge got lower and the sun blazed there. High hills were ahead of us, and there was a place in the edge of them like the one beyond Mini Shoshay where we kept our horses that time. It was open towards where the sun goes down, and we could rest. So we drove the herd in there and made a little fire where we could see back and watch the horses too. No game was in sight, and we were too tired to hunt. So we cut a yearling's throat. The backbone meat was good when it was roasted, and we ate the liver too.

"When we had eaten, Charging Cat rolled over like dead, and it was hard to hold my head up; but I thought of Crazy Horse and I wanted to be like him. So I said, 'Cousins, go to sleep and I will watch. Then I can 'waken you and sleep too.' And they rolled over and were like dead men.

"The sun was gone. There were stars, and the tops of the hills saw the moon coming far away, but it was dark around me yet, and the herd was only shadow. I kept staggering around to stay awake. It was not easy to be like Crazy Horse. I thought hard about the victory dance they would have for us. So I made myself dance the way I would be doing then, and sang to myself. All at once I would be down on my hands and knees, and it would be hard to get on my feet again. The moon looked over a hill at me, and it was trying to dance. The stars danced too. I tried to 'waken somebody.

"All at once it was not the moon looking over the hill. It was the sun blazing on us and I was lying on the grass. I looked around, and when I did not see any horses, I yelled. The others jumped up, excited and ready to fight. But there was nothing to see. The place in the hills was empty.

"When we had looked awhile, Kicking Bear said, 'We are not dead, so it was not enemies that did this.' And I said, 'Maybe they went looking for water.' And Charging Cat said, 'That is what they did, and we can find them.' And High Horse said, 'If we do not find them, we can go back maka mani the way we started and find another village.' And we all said, yes, we could do that.

"But it was easy to track the horses, for they were all going one way down along the edge of the hills. And after a while we saw them. They were scattered out in a valley below us. The hills opened up there and a creek was running through towards where the sun comes up, and the grass along the creek was deep. It was not hard to catch the horses we had been riding, because their lariats were looped around their necks, and they were tired; but this time we tied them to bushes. It was a good place to rest the horses and get them full of grass; and it was a good place for us to eat and sleep.

"There were deer in the valley, and some of them were grazing with the horses at the edge of the herd. I think they had not learned to be afraid of men. So I got on my horse with my gun ready and rode slowly among the grazing herd towards where the deer were. I was lying close to the horse's neck, and a little wind was blowing towards me. I got a fat one. When I shot, the horses nearby started milling and crowding, but they were so tired they stopped soon and began grazing again.

"We ate plenty. Then before we slept, High Horse and I prepared the two scalps we had taken. There were four of us, so we cut the scalps in two; and when we had soaked them in water awhile, we scraped them thin and stretched them on hooped sticks to dry. Also, we had to have drums for the victory; so we scraped enough of the deer-hide to make four and stretched it on hoops. When we had done this, sitting by a little fire, we slept; but this time two slept while two watched.

"When the morning star looked over the edge of the world, we ate again. And when we had bunched the horses and started driving down the valley of the creek, a streak of day was growing away off yonder towards our home. We drove all that day, but sometimes we stopped a little while to let the herd rest and drink and graze. There were many lame ones, and it was hard to keep them going with the others, for we were in a hurry yet. Maybe the enemy had caught enough strays by now to follow with a large party. Maybe they thought there were many of us, and so they waited until they could find enough horses. We talked about this, and we said if they came we would fight them; it was not good to grow old; nothing remained but the hills; we were men and we could die. But all day, whenever we came to a ridge and looked behind us, the back trail was empty. I think the pipe helped us, the pipe and the vow we made on the high hill."

The old man fell silent, and for some time he sat with closed eyes, head bowed, his hands on his knees.

"It was many snows ago," he said at length, emerging slowly from his reverie. "That was my first victory. Before it was dark that day, we began to know our own country again, and we sang to see all the good horses we had, for we began to feel safer. There were about seventy-five of them, and they were the good ones. We had done great deeds; the people would praise us; and we would not be boys any more, but men.

"There was a ridge that looked down on our village, and there next day, when the sun was high above us, the people saw us coming with the horses. They were getting ready for the sun dance, and the other bands had come to camp with the Oglalas in one big circle, because it was a good place for the dance. Some rode out to meet us, singing as they came. These took care of the horses and went back with them to the village, telling the people to prepare for a kill-come-back and a victory.

"We had to get ready; so we made a fire back under the ridge; and when there was charred wood, we blackened our faces with it. If any of our party had been killed, we could not have blackened our faces, and the people seeing would have known, and there would have been mourning with the rejoicing. If I had been killed, maybe, and was feeding the coyotes, then the people would sing to my spirit as the others rode in the victory, 'Aah hey! Aah hey! Eagle Voice, it is so! We have heard about you, and it is good to hear! Aah hey, aah hey, aah hey! Aah hey!' They would sing that song because any old man would tell you it was an honor to die on the prairie when you were young, and it was not good to grow old. But we were all alive, and so we blackened our faces. Then we tied the scalps to coup-sticks, and each had one. The deer-hide drums we made had dried tight in the hot sun, and we were ready. While we were waiting, we danced around the fire and sang the way we would do before all the people. And afterwhile two came to tell us the people were waiting for us; and when they had gone away, we got on our horses, and we had chosen the best and strongest ones for this. Then we charged over the ridge single file. I was first because I had killed first, and after me was High Horse, for he had killed after me. Then came Charging Cat who had counted the first coup, and last rode Kicking Bear, who had counted coup also. We went galloping down the hill, crying, 'hown, hown, hown,' all together, as though we were going into battle; and when we were near the village we all yelled, 'hokahey' and shot the guns in the air. With our horses on the run, we swung low on the off-side and charged around the circle of tepees, left to right. And as we rode, the people raised one great voice, 'hiyay, hiyay'; and we could hear the women all making the tremolo high above the voices of the men.

"When we had circled the village outside and come to the opening towards where you are always facing, we stopped in a line and the people sang a welcoming song. Then, because High Horse and I had killed, we rode first around the circle inside the village, left to right, which is the sacred manner, while the two others waited. Our relatives had all blackened their faces and they were all together watching and feeling proud of us. Our horses were tired, but we made them prance around, and they were excited too. As I rode, I looked straight ahead, singing to my drum, 'Eagle Voice, you have said, I have met an enemy and killed him.' And when I had sung this four times, High Horse sang the same about himself, and all the men cried, 'hiyay hiyay,' and the women raised the tremolo all around the big circle.

"When we were at the opening again, the women came, with blackened faces, to walk ahead of us around the circle inside the big village, and we four rode abreast behind them with the scalps held high on our coup-sticks. And as they walked, the women sang about the enemies we had killed and the many horses we had brought them.

"Then when we came again to the opening, the four of us rode to the center of the big village circle where they had made a tepee-thrown-over-together, and there the chiefs and the councilors sat waiting to welcome us. When we had got off our horses and sat down in a row before the head chief, he prepared a pipe and offered it to the six powers. And when we had smoked after him, he spoke to us and praised us. I think he forgot about us running away, because of the horses and the scalps. And all the people cried out with one voice.

"Then the victory dance began, and the feasting and the giving away; and the night was old when it was over. Kicking Bear told the story of our going to war *maka mani* and of the vow we made on the hill. Charging Cat made the tale longer with the taking of horses. High Horse and I made kill talks, telling how it was. And all the people, hearing, cheered each of us in turn, and the drums beat and the victory song was loud. And after the men, the women danced in their best buckskin dresses, beautiful with beads and colored porcupine quills.

"There was much giving away. It was time for the sun dance, and the hearts of the people were strong. Our relatives gave horses to many, showing their gladness for our safe return; and the four of us gave and gave, until we had left only the horses we had before. If there had been more, we would have given them too; for the heart grows stronger with giving. I gave most of mine to old people, and some to old women who were my grandmother's friends. Maybe I was remembering the old woman bouncing on her pony-drag, and the pony running away."

"Am I Greater Than the People?"

When I had fed the fire again, the old man came slowly out of his reverie and began fumbling for tobacco in his long buckskin sack. I waited until the pipe was lit, and having drawn a few puffs, I expressed surprise that High Horse had not saved any horses for Good Plume's father. Was not that the reason for his going to war? And did he not get the girl after all?

Eagle Voice chuckled, and said: "I think when we got back he was not sick any more. Our heads were full of great deeds and the victory and the people's praise and the sun dance. Maybe that made him well. Also, the Shyela band went away after the sun dance. Maybe the girl got another man. I do not know."

"And I was surprised," I remarked, "that you seemed a little sorry for the old Crow woman bouncing on the drag when her son was killed and her pony ran away. Also, you could have killed her grandson, but you let him go. Were they not enemies?"

"They were enemies," the old man answered slowly, regarding me with his crinkled, quizzical look. "We were boys and maybe we were thinking of our grandmothers. I could tell you a story about the time when a war party of our people felt sorry for some Crow warriors. They had no horses. They were starving and freezing in the deep snow, and they could not fight any more. So our war party did not kill them. It is a true story. But I will tell you about the time when the Crows were sorry for the Arapahoes. It also happened. The Arapahoes tell it themselves. We know their stories and they know ours, for we are friends. While the people are getting ready for the sun dance, I will tell you.

"It was many snows ago, before I was born. There is a place we call Hide Butte, because the Lakotas once found there many hides staked out to dry by the Crows, and no people anywhere around. It is in the big bend of Duck River, not far from where the Niobrara heads. A whole band of the Arapahoes had a winter camp there, and one morning when they awoke, all their horses were gone. There was not a hoof left. It was very bad. They knew it was the Crows who did it, so they organized a war party and started out *maka mani*, following the trail of their horses. It was very cold, the snow was dry and deep. Afterwhile a wind began to blow, getting stronger. So they stopped to talk about it, and they said, 'We shall freeze looking for horses in this snow. Maybe it is better to wait awhile until it is warmer, and then we can go.' Sharp Nose was the only one who did not say it was better to do that. He said, 'You can go back, and I will go on. If I find where the horses went, I can come back and tell you. I will do my best.' When he said this, he thought some would be brave and say, 'You are not going on alone, for we are going with you'; but nobody said that, and the party turned back towards the village.

"So Sharp Nose went on alone. He came to a ridge, and when he looked back to see the others going yonder, there was one lone man coming. He waited, and it was his woman's younger brother, hardly old enough for war yet. We can call him Little Bear. And Sharp Nose said, 'Brother-in-law, why are you coming?' And Little Bear answered, 'I wanted to come before, but I thought some older men would come and I would go with them; but nobody came, so I am here. I will go wherever you go. I will die wherever you die. That is why I am here.' And Sharp Nose said, 'You are a brave young man.' So they went on in the deep snow, Little Bear behind Sharp Nose, following the trail of the horses. Sometimes it was covered with blowing drifts, but they would find it again. That night they made a shelter of pine bows in a bend of a creek against a high bank that broke the wind, and made a fire; and when they had roasted some *papa* and eaten, they slept.

"When they awoke, the snow was drifted deep about them; and when they had eaten again and started walking, they could not find the trail at all. Then Sharp Nose said, 'The crows have our horses, and we will go on to where the Crows are.' So they went, Little Bear behind Sharp Nose. The wind was strong and cold; the snow was deep; it was hard walking, and it was hard to see for the flying snow.

"When the day was getting old and it was time to make a camp for the night, all at once they could see big dim bodies about them in the blowing snow, and it was a stray band of buffalo just standing there with their heads down. It was like dreaming about buffalo to see them, for the air was like a whirling fog, and night was coming. They did not seem to notice the men, and when Sharp Nose shot a cow back of the shoulder so that she dropped and did not get up, the others drifted away with the wind and were not there any more. It was like dreaming, but the dead cow was there anyway. So they had to skin the cow, and it was hard to do that because the wet hide froze their fingers. But before it was black dark, the skinning was done, and when they had taken some of the hump meat, the liver, and the bladder, they rolled the cow off the hide, and that was very hard for them to do. Then they found a bank that broke the wind, for they were following a creek that ran towards Crow country so that they might not get lost. There they dragged the fresh hide into a clump of brush and made a shelter of it. That helped them to make a fire, and when they had eaten all they wanted of the raw liver they felt good and slept. The wind died in the night, and in the still cold morning they walked again, taking the bladder, some hump meat and some tallow with them. I do not know how many camps they made, but afterwhile they came to the Greasy Grass [Little Big Horn] which is the Crow country. By now a great warm wind was coming from beyond the mountains, roaring all day and all night, and snow was melting on the slopes towards the sun. It was like the time when the tender grasses appear, but it was winter yet. And Sharp Nose said, 'We will go on down the Greasy Grass, and maybe the Crows are camping on the Big Horn yonder; but we must be very careful.' So they made a camp; and when they had eaten, they rested and slept until it was dark. Then they started walking again, Little Bear behind Sharp Nose. And when the day was coming, there was a ridge, and they went up there to look. It was the Big Horn yonder, and in the valley among trees there was a big Crow village, and the tepee tops were beginning to smoke. They were careful to keep from being seen, and when they had found a deep gully full of brush, with the big ridge between them and the village, they made a camp and even had a little fire. Then Sharp Nose said to the boy: 'We have come to get back our horses; but you have seen that there are many people yonder. We have come a long way, and it would not be good to go back with only a story. We cannot steal all the horses we have lost. If we steal any, the Crows will follow us, and we shall die. So it will be just as well to die in there among them, and in the morning when we have gotten ready, we will go in there. And Little Bear said, 'I came to go wherever you go and to die wherever you die.' And Sharp Nose said to the boy, 'You are a brave man. Now we will get ready.'

"So he began making a medicine bundle, and that was the first time the boy knew why Sharp Nose wanted the bladder and the tallow. Maybe he was too bashful to ask, because he was only a boy and Sharp Nose was a great warrior. Of course, Sharp Nose had his pipe with him, also some tobacco mixed with red willow bark. He kept these in a sack made of red flannel that he got from a trader, and he would need that also. So he mixed some sacred tobacco and red willow bark with the buffalo tallow, which was sacred too, because in his vision quest he had seen a spirit buffalo. Then he placed this in the buffalo's bladder, and around the bladder he tied the red flannel; and red, you know, is a sacred color. This is the way he made a medicine bundle, and all tribes know that it is a very sacred thing. But when he had done this, he was not yet ready, for he had to take off his clothes and paint his body with sacred red paint. This he made by mixing tallow with some red paint dust that he always had with him. Last of all he fastened one eagle feather in his hair, so that it would hang down over the back of his neck.

"When he had done all this and was ready, the sun was high; and he said to Little Bear, 'We will go into the village now. You will carry my clothes and gun and the bow and arrows, and you will follow after me.' So they started.

"When they had crossed the top of the ridge, they saw many horses grazing on the slope and in the valley, and some of these they knew for the horses that had been stolen from their people. When they were about halfway down to the village, a Crow, who was out looking for some ponies, came riding out of a gulch all at once, and when he saw the naked man all painted red and the boy following after, he yelled and rode back fast to the village. But Sharp Nose went on walking towards the village with the medicine bundle on his back and his pipe in front of him, and behind him came Little Bear with the clothes and the gun and the bow and arrows in a bundle.

"Then there was shouting down yonder, and they saw that many Crow warriors were charging up the hill. When these came close and saw the naked man all painted red with the sacred bundle on his back and the pipe held out in front, they swung to one side and rode around him in a circle, for he was a mysterious man painted so and carrying the sacred bundle and the pipe; and each feared to strike him first. The boy was not mysterious, so they rode around him, crowding in to coup him many times, and the clothes and gun and bow and arrows they took away from him. They wanted to kill him because he was an enemy, but they were afraid to do that because he was the mysterious man's helper and maybe something very bad might happen. While they were doing this, a chief who was among them got off his horse and went up to Sharp Nose, who just stood there holding the pipe in front of him with both hands. When the warriors saw the chief do this, they swarmed around the mysterious man. They were hungry dogs yelping and snarling because they smelled fresh meat; but somebody was keeping them away from it with a big club. The chief looked hard into the eyes of Sharp Nose for a while. Sharp Nose held the pipe tight and looked back just as hard. Then the chief reached for the pipe and took it; and when he held it up before the warriors, they quit yelling and fell back behind the boy, for there is sacred power in the pipe.

"So now they all started down the hill towards the village. First went the chief with the pipe; then came Sharp Nose, naked and all painted red, with the sacred bundle on his back and the one eagle feather in his hair; then Little Bear with his big bundle; and after him the warriors on their horses. That is the way they came into the Crow village, and all the people crowded in about them, buzzing and wondering about the mysterious man and the boy.

"When they came to the chief's tepee and the chief motioned for the strangers to go in, Sharp Nose took the sacred bundle from his back and held it with both hands in front of him; for I think he was afraid and wanted the sacred power to protect him. So he went into the chief's big tepee with Little Bear close behind him. When they were sitting down inside, the chief sent a crier about the village telling all the sub-chiefs to come into his lodge for a council. So they came; and when they were sitting in a circle about the fire, they began arguing about the two strangers and what should be done with them. Some wanted to kill them right away, for were they not enemies? Maybe it was only a trick they were playing, so that some great harm might come to the people. But there were others who could see only that the man was painted red all over and that he had a sacred bundle. Was it not clear that the man was *wakon* and not to be harmed? Then why not kill the boy and have only one to watch? But was not the boy the sacred man's helper, and therefore at least a little sacred too? Then why not just keep the gun and bow and arrows and drive the strangers out of the village? But might not something very bad happen if the man were really sacred and brought a sacred gift that was refused? But was it a sacred gift that he brought, or was it only something he had put in a dirty red rag?

"So the argument went 'round and 'round the circle, while the man and boy sat there wondering when they were going to die, for they could not understand what the council was saying. While the argument was going 'round and 'round, the day grew old and the sun went down. Then the sub-chiefs went away, still arguing; and it was night; and afterwhile the man and the boy slept with guards watching about them.

"When the sun came back, the sub-chiefs came too, and the argument began all over again, going 'round and 'round the circle; and the man and boy sat there wondering when they were going to die. But after-while the day began to get old, and the voices were not so angry as they had been. Then the head chief stood up tall and looked hard into each face about the circle; and there was stillness waiting for his words to fill it. And after he had looked hard for a while, the chief said, 'I heard many words yesterday, and today I have heard many words. They are all the same. I have closed my ears, for they are tired. Now I will receive this gift the mysterious stranger brings us.' As he said this, he stooped and took the sacred bundle from Sharp Nose, and when he was standing straight and tall again, holding the gift with both hands, he said, 'I have received it and with it I am willing to die. If you want to kill me with this bundle, here I stand.' When the sub-chiefs heard these words, they all cried, 'hiyee! hiyee! as though they had but one mouth. Then one stood up and said, 'I too will die with the stranger's gift; and, one by one, all the others stood and said the same.'

"Of course, only a *wichasha wakon* [holy man] could untie the sacred bundle, and there was one among the sub-chiefs who did this. First he took some red coals from the fire and placed them in front of him. Then upon the coals he put some pieces of dry buffalo dung; and when these gave forth a flame, he lit his pipe therefrom, and presented it to the four quarters and to the sky and to the earth. Then he was ready to un-tie the bundle, and as he took it from the chief, there was no sound in the tepee but what the fire made, and the ring of eyes looked hard upon the bundle. When the holy man had untied the red flannel, a sound went round the circle, 'ah-h-h,' for all could see that this was not just something tied up in a dirty rag. Then the holy man gave the bundle to the head chief, who took it and cried, 'Hiyee-thanks!' The crowd of people outside, hearing the words of the chief, cried out the same, as with one mouth, 'Hiyee-thanks!' Then when the chief had touched his body all over with the sacred gift, he passed it on to the sub-chiefs, and, all around the circle, each in his turn received the sacred gift, crying, 'hiyee-thanks!' But this is not all they did; for when each had cried out thus and touched his body all over with the bundle, he gave a gift to each of the strangers—one horse, two horses, fine buck-skin clothing, three horses or maybe four, so that when the sacred bundle had gone all around the circle, the strangers had all that they could wish for themselves, except food and drink. Then the head chief called for water to be brought, and they drank. After that, they smoked, and all shared the pipe with them. Then food in plenty was brought and they ate like hungry dogs, for they had eaten nothing those two days, nor had they drunk till then.

"Now that gifts had been given and received, it was time to question the strangers. Who were they? Where was their home? What were they doing here? What did they want that had not already been given? Who made the sacred bundle and sent it to the Crows? They had smoked the peace pipe and must tell the truth.

"These things were asked of the strangers in the sign language that all the people knew. When Sharp Nose answered, he had a few Crow words to help him, and this is what he told.

"He and his boy helper were Arapahoes; had come out of pity for their own women and children who were all standing on a hill yonder crying for their horses; for without their horses, they would starve. He and his helper had come to die for their people among the Crows who had taken all their horses, and not a hoof was left. The great Arapahoe chief had made the sacred bundle and sent it as a gift to plead for his crying women and children. The Crows were kind to him and his helper, and he gave them thanks. Would they not be even as kind to all the women and children crying yonder on a hill?

"Sharp Nose was a good man, but, of course, he had lied; for it was not the great Arapahoe chief, but Sharp Nose himself, who made the bundle. It was a bad thing to lie when he had taken the peace pipe that was offered him; but he did it for his people, and he did not care what happened to him.

"When the Crow chief and sub-chiefs understood the story, Sharp Nose told in the sign language with his few Crow words, they just sat still for a while and looked at the ground. Then the head chief said to Sharp Nose, 'How long will you stay here?' And the other answered, 'About four days.' For a while after that, the chiefs all huddled together and talked with low voices; and then the head chief turned to Sharp Nose and said: 'The gift you have brought is sacred and we could not refuse it. Also, we have heard the Arapahoe women and children crying yonder on the hill. When you go back after four days, you shall not go alone, but thirty of our warriors shall go with you, and with these all the horses our warriors have taken from your people. Not even a little colt shall we keep. Also with these shall go one of our chiefs; and his woman and his son shall go with him, to show that our hearts are good.'

"When they understood what was said, the two Arapahoes stood up and raised their hands, thanking the Great Spirit; then they stooped and touched earth, the mother of all!

"So on the fifth day, when the morning star had seen the sun below and was getting dim, the horse-guards had all the Arapahoe ponies bunched near the village, and it was a big herd. Also, the thirty warriors were ready with the chief and his woman and his son. So were Sharp Nose and Little Bear, all dressed in the fine new clothing the Crow chiefs had given them.

"And as they started towards the new sun yonder, people sang.

"The weather was still warm, although it was winter. The snows had melted in the valleys and on the slopes that faced the day, so that there was good grazing for the horses; and every evening there was feasting in the camp, for the hunting was good and the hunters many.

"When they came to the Powder River, they had a last big feast, and then the thirty Crow warriors turned back towards their homes; for beyond that was the hunting country of the Lakota, Arapahoe, and Cheyenne, and it was safe. So Sharp Nose, Little Bear and the Crow chief with his son moved the herd onward a little every day, and every evening the chief's woman fed her family well from a full pot. And afterwhile they were getting near to Hide Butte and the village of the Arapahoe. Then Sharp Nose said to the others, 'You will camp here and watch the horses, for I must go and tell the people to be ready.' So that is what they did.

"All the people were happy when Sharp Nose came back to the Arapahoe village, for his story traveled fast among the lodges. The first thing he did after he had seen his father, was to tell the head chief all that had happened; and then he said, 'I have done a good thing for the people, but to do it I did a very bad thing. I lied, although I had taken the pipe; for I said that you made the sacred bundle and sent us with it as a gift to the Crows, that it might plead for our horses. And now I ask you to do a bad thing also for the good of the people. When the Crow chief comes, tell him that you made the bundle and sent it.'

"When the head chief had smoked and passed the pipe to Sharp Nose, he sat silent for a while and thought. Then at last he spoke. 'This is a hard thing you ask me to do; it is a very hard thing.' Then he sat a long while and looked at the ground. And afterwhile he said, 'If the pipe speak with a forked tongue, who can be trusted?' And after that again he sat a long while without speaking. Then he spoke again. 'It is a great thing you and the boy have done. Alone you went forth into the country of the enemy to die, and it was not for honors that you went, but for the people. If you had died, it would have been a great thing. If you had died, the people would have a great story to tell, but how could they live to tell it without horses? Now they shall live and have both the horses and the story. It is a bad thing, this that you ask me to do; but it is a good thing also, being for the people. Am I greater than the people? I will do it.'

"So while the Arapahoes were getting ready to receive the Crow chief and his family, and to celebrate the strange victory without a scalp, Sharp Nose went back to the little camp where the big herd was waiting, and with him went many Arapahoe warriors to help in bringing the horses back home.

"When the party with the whole herd, and not a colt missing, came near to the Arapahoe village, the Arapahoe chiefs and councilors came forth to meet the visitors, singing welcome as they came. And when these had surrounded the friendly strangers, three softly tanned robes, ringed round with only chiefs and councilors to carry them, were stretched that the visitors might be carried therein. Thus the Crow chief and his woman and his son entered the village of their old enemies that now were friends, all singing welcome with one great voice.

"Four days there was feasting and dancing; but the Crows were too happy to go home yet. Four more days there was feasting and dancing; then they spoke of going home, but the people were too happy to let them go. And when on the twelfth day the Crow chief said he and his family had stayed long enough, they did not go with empty hands nor alone. Twelve pack horses carried the gifts they had received; and not thirty warriors, but sixty, rode with them, not to the Powder, but all the way back.

"And since that time these peoples have not fought."

The Sun Dance

"I think Wakon Tonka knows we are going to remember my first sun dance today," said Eagle Voice with the crinkled look of amusement about his eyes. "You see the sun is shining again this morning; the wind is still and the edge of the air is like a dull knife. There will be a little melting on the day sides of the hills before night."

It was truly a beautiful winter morning, and I had noted a light breath from the southwest. The tepee was cozy, the pipe had been passed, and I waited. After a long silence, the old man began speaking again in a low voice, looking towards me with a long-focused gaze as though I were transparent or not there at all. "She was a pretty girl," he said with seeming irrelevance. "Tashina Wanblee. Her name is like singing when I remember now, far-away singing. When I was riding around the village with the Crow scalp on my coup-stick after we got back with all those horses, I saw her. She was pushing through the tight ring of people to get closer, and she was right under me looking up. I know now that she was very pretty, for she was still both girl and woman. Her face was all shining and she was singing to me. I cannot say what look was in her eyes. I think I did not see the look clearly until I was older and my eyes were getting tired of all I had seen instead. I saw that she was very proud of me because I had become a great warrior, and that made my heart leap. We had played together, and then I was only her horse; but now I was a man at last, high above her, and all the people were praising me. So I made my horse rear and plunge. I did not see her again until I was dancing the sun dance.

"It is the sun dance we are going to remember now.

"When cherry seeds begin to harden, the sun is like a strong man just past his youth and not yet growing old. It is then that the sun is highest in the sky and his power is the greatest. There he stands a little while before he starts back towards the winter again. That is the time for all the people to come together and dance his sacred dance, that his power may be theirs and their hearts may be strengthened for the road of difficulties ahead. Maybe the people have been wandering in small bands, living in little hoops by themselves. Maybe some of them have almost forgotten the power of the great hoop to shield and make them strong. And maybe even in the little hoops some people are so proud they begin to forget that by themselves they are nothing. It is good for them to feel the sacred power of the great hoop again, for it is the power of Wakon Tonka. And at the center of that hoop the Sacred Tree shall grow and spread above them all and fill with leaves and bloom and singing birds. It is a time of happiness for all the people; for it is then that relatives, from far places maybe, see each other again and tell all that has happened. And there is feasting; and the old men and women remember, and the little boys and the youths look and listen, thinking of the great deeds they are going to do. And under many a lover's blanket the girls hear whispered words that make their hearts like birds singing in their breasts.

"It is a happy time; but also it is a time to suffer and endure, for pain is wise to teach and without courage there is nothing good.

"It was the time of hardening cherry seeds when we got back with all those Crow horses and the scalp. Already a wide flat place by a creek was chosen for the sun dance, and the sacred societies were building a big round enclosure for the ceremony. They cut poles and placed them in the ground; and over these, other poles were placed, and on these poles leafy branches were laid to make a circular shade where the people would sit and watch. And around the outside of this big circle of shade, tepee skins would be hung to make an enclosure for the holy place. Inside this circle was the bare flat dancing ground, open to the strong sun; and in the center of this, the sacred tree would stand. They stopped working a little while when we came back, but when the victory dance was over, they went on with the work of getting ready.

"While they were doing this, four old men came to our tepee early in the morning, and one of them was Chagla, Kicking Bear's father-in-law and also a relative to me, but not a very close one. He was *owankara* that year, the one who prepares the dance for the people. It is a great honor, like a victory, to do that. Chagla had a pipe with him, and when he entered our tepee with the three other old men behind him, he held the pipe in front of him with both hands, the mouthpiece forward. I knew what they had come for, and all at once I was afraid and wanted to run away. When we were driving all those horses away from the Crow village in the night, my heart sang and I was not afraid. Now I wanted to run away; but I was ashamed of being afraid, so I waited.

"The four old men sat down, and when my mother had given them something to eat and they had eaten, Chagla began to talk about the sun dance. It was a great thing to be young and brave and to go forth into enemy country to do great deeds or to die. But the heart may be strong to do that because it is proud and hungry for praise.

"In the sacred dance the proud heart dies with pain and thirst, hunger and weariness, that the power of Wakon Tonka may come in and live there for the good of all the people. Many brave men had taken the pipe and would dance.

"When Chagla was through talking, the other old men said, 'hetchetu,' meaning it was so; and then Chagla held the stem of the pipe towards me.

"As I told you before, we boys had made a vow to dance and we had dedicated a pipe to Wakon Tonka. We were back home safe now with many horses and much honor. But I was afraid. This thing I had to do was *wakon* and a fearful thing. I wished I had not made the vow, so that I could refuse the pipe. The four old men and my step-father and mother were all looking hard at me, but for a while I could not reach out and take the pipe. Then when Chagla began to draw it back towards him, all at once my heart leaped within me and I grasped the pipe and held it to my mouth; and the four old men said, 'hi-yay.' Then they went away.

"Now I had to dance, for I had made a vow and I had taken the pipe. I was not afraid any more. When the enemies are many and you are few, and it seems there is nothing to do but to die right there, you raise a death-song, and then you are not afraid of anything, because you are dead already, and what can hurt you? It was something like that with me.

"My step-father and mother were very proud of me when I came back with those Crow horses, and now they were still prouder because I was going to dance. So they made a feast and asked many to come. Many came to eat and they told my mother and step-father what a brave young man their son was, and maybe I would grow up to be a great chief.

"The dancing place was prepared, and the next thing was to find the *chun wakon* [the sacred tree] which would stand in the center of the circle. It must be a tall slender cottonwood and everything had to be done just right. When I was young I heard the old men say why this was so. A long while ago—beyond so many snows and grasses that the oldest man's grandfather and his grandfather before him, and his and his could not remember—there was a beautiful girl who was big with child. The child was a boy and would grow up to be a great *wichasha wakon*. And while he was still inside his mother, at the time when cherry seeds harden and the sun is strongest, he had a great vision about the sun dance, and everything was shown to him just as it should be. So when he became a young man he remembered his vision and taught the people. He was the first *owankara*, the first to prepare a sun dance. This is what the old men told when I was young.

"Four were chosen to go forth and find the *chun wakon*—two men and two women. Both men were great warriors and *wichasha yatapika*, and no bad thing could be said of them. They belonged to the Chante Tinza society [Strong Hearts]. The two women were mothers, neither young nor old, and they were always helping the sick and the needy, and no one among all the people could say anything but good of them. So these four went forth with axes to find the sacred cottonwood, and after them went young warriors wearing their war bonnets and painted as for war. Maybe the tree was a long way off; maybe it was near. But when it was found, standing tall and straight with a fork near the top, the young warriors charged upon it, crying, 'hoka-hey,' as in a battle, and couping the tree with their coup-sticks. When this was done, the two chosen men took their axes and struck the tree; and between strokes they told of brave deeds they had done. Then when the tree was cut more than halfway through, the two chosen women approached with their axes and chopped carefully, so that the tree did not fall all at once, but slowly; and as it fell it cried out as with great pain. When it was lying on the ground, four poles were placed under it and eight men lifted it so, placing the butt towards the quarter whence comes the sun, bringing light and wisdom and the peace that wisdom gives. Then the two women began chopping off all the branches, and only the two forks were left at the top. The young warriors now were riding fast back and forth between the sacred tree and the happy people, who were feasting; and to these they brought the news of the tree, telling all that the four chosen ones were doing. 'They have found the *chun wakon*—they are chopping it—the tree has fallen—the women are cutting the limbs away.' Every little thing the young warriors told the people, riding fast back and forth; and the people heard, crying, 'hi-yay,' and singing as for a victory.

"No one could touch the tree with hands, for it was *wakon*. When it was all ready to be brought home, eight men lifted it on the four poles, four men on each side. And four would change with another four, so that many brought it home. These walked slowly in a sacred manner; and as they walked, the young warriors rode fast back and forth between the holy tree and the happy people yonder, telling where it was now, and where now, and now. And the people heard, cheering and singing as for a great victory. When at last the *chun wakon* had come in sight of home, one of the carriers, who was a great warrior and had counted many coups, raised a long howl the way a dog does when the moon is big, and the other carriers joined with him. Then all the people swarmed forth to meet the tree, singing together as they crowded about it, but not too close. You remember how the warriors at the wagon boxes were like a blooming mountain valley walking; but those were singing the death-song. Now the happy people were singing to the Ever-Living One, and they were all blooming—the girls and women with flowers braided into their hair, and the men with their war bonnets.

So the *chun wakon* came home. The carriers placed the tree in the center of the dancing ring with its butt pointing to where the sun comes up; and there a hole had been dug for the planting. But before it was planted, Blue Spotted Horse, the old holy man—the same who prepared me for my vision quest—came to paint the tree. First he prayed to the Six Powers, as he had taught me, and then he took red paint that he had made by mixing red clay with bison tallow, and painted from the top down to the butt, so that the whole tree was bright with the sacred color. And as he painted the *chun wakon*, all the people sat round about in a great circle and watched, and there was no sound; and the sun watched too.

Next Chagla came with a bundle of chokecherry branches which must be tied in the crotch of the tree. No chokecherries were growing in the country where we were, so a band of young warriors had been sent all the way to Mini Shoshay [the Missouri] to fetch the branches. Below these the bundle of offerings must be tied. It was a pouch made of buffalo skin, and inside were all kinds of little things the people had brought—locks of hair, little pieces of their own flesh, sinew for sewing and bone needles, rings, beads, and many other little things that the people might think of giving so that the sacred power might not forget them; and last of all a flint, an arrow, and a gun were placed in the bundle. Before he tied these bundles in their places with thongs of bison hide, Chagla prayed; holding his pipe towards the sun, stem forward. And when he had prayed, he told the people about a vision that had come to him. It was the vision that had commanded him to prepare the dance for the good of the people, that they might be a nation and live to see their children flourish, and their children's children. Last of all, before the tree was planted, Chagla took a piece of buffalo tallow and dropped it in the hole. It was the gift to Maka [earth], the mother of all living things, the only mother, she who has shown mercy to her children.

"Next, long thongs of buffalo hide were tied to the top of the tree, and when the carriers had raised the tree on forked poles and set the butt upon the hole, young warriors pulled upon the thongs and the tree arose until it dropped into the hole. Then all the people cried out together with one voice, rejoicing.

"So the sacred tree was planted. And the sun went down.

"All the while these things were being done, we who were going to dance had to wait in a big lodge that had been made for us, and when the tree had come home, our attendants told us everything that was being done out there, and we could hear Blue Spotted Horse and Chagla praying. When the people cried out with one voice, we knew the tree was planted. We had all gone through the sweat bath, as I did before my vision quest; and afterwards we were rubbed with the sacred sage and painted red all over with the sacred paint. We could hear the happy people outside and what the young warriors cried to them about the preparing and coming of the tree. High Horse, Kicking Bear, and Charging Cat were in there too, because the four of us had dedicated the pipe and made the vow together the way I told you. But we could not go outside and be seen until it was time to dance. What I have told you is what I have seen many times when I did not dance.

"It was night now. Before we slept they gave us some food and water, and that was the last that we could have until our vows were fulfilled. It was not long before there was snoring all around me, but it was hard for me to go to sleep. Maybe I was a little afraid. Sometimes I would hold my breath because something might happen all at once. When the snoring stopped, now and then, the big night outside held its breath too, waiting for something. Maybe a voice would roar all at once, as when I stole my grandfather's pipe and the thunder beings scolded. Kicking Bear was lying on one side of me and High Horse on the other. Next to High Horse was Charging Cat. I could hear Kicking Bear and Charging Cat breathing deep, as though nothing was going to happen, and I wondered if maybe I was a coward after all. Then I remembered how my heart sang when we were driving the Crow herd away from the village that night. I was not a coward then. Afterwhile I knew that High Horse was not sleeping either. He would turn over and then turn back; and when he was still for a while I could feel he was awake yet. That made me feel better, because I knew he was brave. After we had lain there awake for a long while, he put his mouth close to my ear and whispered: 'Brother, are you awake?' And I answered, whispering: 'Yes, brother, I cannot go to sleep.' He was still for a while, and then he whispered: 'She *was* funny, wasn't she—the fat old woman—the way she bounced?' Then we put our arms around each other and lay close together, snickering like little boys.

"Suddenly someone was shaking me by the shoulder, saying: 'Get up! It is time!' Then I knew that the attendants were waking the dancers, and I had been sleeping deep.

"It was still dark. They told us to put on our skirts of bison fur, and that is all we wore—not even moccasins. Then they led us outside into the still, starry night. Some people were moving like shadows among the tepees and some were coming towards the dancing ring."

The old man ceased speaking and fell into a reverie, blowing softly the while on his eagle-bone whistle, highly polished by years of thumbing.

"I had this in my hand," he said at length. "Chagla gave it to me. I also carried a pipe. The stem was wrapped with colored porcupine quills up to the mouthpiece, and that was covered with the green skin of a mallard. They led us through the opening of the dancing ring, and I was first because I had taken the scalp. Next came High Horse, Kicking Bear, and Charging Cat, because of all those Crow horses and the victory. There were about thirty other dancers.

"As I entered, they gave me a buffalo skull to carry because I was the principal dancer. We went around the ring from left to right, which is walking in a sacred manner, and stopped facing the place where the sun comes up. I put the skull down in front of me with the nose to the coming day. Low down at the rim of earth yonder was a faint streak of light. The morning star was big and bright and still. As I gazed at it, I wanted to cry, but I could feel something like wings lifting me too. It was the same way the star looked down at me that time after I dreamed beneath my father's scaffold and heard him tell me always to be kind to old people and never to be afraid of anything. Then the drummers began singing to the coming sun, and their drumsticks, with bison tails fastened on the ends, made a slapping sound."

The old man ceased. Getting to his feet with some difficulty, he danced feebly, keeping time with drums long silent and blowing on his whistle pointed towards no earthly dawn. "So!" he said at length with a little cackling laugh and panting like a runner. "*Washtay!* It was good. But I cannot dance very well any more. There is no strength in what I eat these days."

Seated again, he waited until normal breathing was restored, and then:

"We danced to the drums and the singing, and I stared at the place where the sky was getting white. Sometimes I could not feel the ground at all, for something seemed to lift me and it was like floating on drumbeats and singing. Then suddenly the great round sun leaped yellow and glaring over the edge of the world, and all the people cried out together with one voice.

The singing and drumming stopped now, and they led us dancers back to the sacred tree, placing us in a circle around it. I had the bison skull in front of me. Chagla told me I must put it in a certain place that was prepared near the tree. There was a heap of white clay, and into this I thrust the skull three times. The fourth time I pushed it deep and left it there. So Maka's sacred gift of the bison to the people was given back to the giver with thanks. Also at that place there were two forked sticks in the ground with another stick lying across. Against this I must set my pipe with the stem pointed up. This was a gift to Wakon Tonka and the life-giving sun.

The drums and the singing began again, and we danced with our faces to the blazing sun, holding our whistles in our mouths and blowing upon them in time with the dancing. Somebody was talking close to my ear, and it was Chagla. 'Do not look directly at the sun,' he said; 'look just a little below.' I tried to do that, but it did not help much at first, it was like white-hot knives in my eyes. After a while I did not feel anything, and it was dark. The drumbeats and the singing seemed far away in empty night, and they lifted me, floating alone. I was lost in the blindness of my eyes, and I kept praying in my mind in time with the whistle and the far-off drums, 'Let me see, let me see!'

"I did not see anything. Then all at once, I could see everything, and far away was near. There was a wide green land; wide, wide, green, green, with hills and valleys and streams glittering bright. And the sky over it was deeper and wider and bluer than I can say. It was the same land I saw when I dreamed under the scaffold and my father came to me on his spirit horse. The drumbeats and singing were dim and far away—more like remembering than hearing. I was looking hard at a hilltop for a horseback to come out of the sky. Then someone shook me by the shoulder, and I knew it was Chagla.

"The drums and singing were still. This world came back slowly out of the dark. I was looking down at my shadow. It was right under me like a puddle. Then I was very thirsty, but I made myself remember the green land and the glittering streams, and when I could do that, I forgot I was thirsty.

All the people were around us in a crowd, watching us while they feasted; but when I thought about eating, it was water that I wanted. Also while the people were watching and eating, the relatives of the dancers were giving away many things—horses and fine clothing, beaded work, and maybe tepees; for giving is a sacred deed and is pleasing to the Mysterious One who gives everything.

"Chagla took my pipe from where I had placed it, and told me I should give it to one of the singers and drummers. So I went to a man, and when he held out his hands I spread his fingers and pretended to give him the pipe. Three times he tried to grasp it, but I pulled it away. The fourth time, I let him seize it. Others were doing the same with other drummers and singers.

"The high sun was burning hot. The attendants came now and rubbed us all over with sacred sage until the red paint was gone and our skins were dry. Then they painted us again. They made my body yellow for the power to grow. Then they took some blue paint made from clay we used to get at Rawhide Buttes. With this my arms were painted from the elbows down, and my legs below the knees. The blue was for the power of the quarter where the sun goes down, the power to make live and to destroy, the power of the Thunder Beings and the rain. With these powers to help me, I would grow to be a great warrior; also a helper of the people, for the hoop of the people and the shielding tree belong to the yellow quarter. When they had done this, they painted something on my back, and it was a half-moon. They did not paint a new moon, because that would have meant going down to the spiritland beyond where the days of man end; and I was to grow in this world and be a great warrior.

"While they were painting us the drummers sang about it like this." The old man lifted a cracked, quavering voice, drumming on one hand with the other:

> "'Father, paint the earth on me.
> A nation I will make over.
> A two-legged nation I will make holy.
> Father, paint the earth on me.'

"Last of all, they fastened strips of bison-hide around my wrists and ankles, that the strength of the bison might be mine.

"I was then told to get my pipe back and place it again where I had placed it in the morning. The man held it in front of him with both hands, and when I reached for it he pulled it away. Three times he did this. Then I placed both of my hands on the top of his head and brought them slowly down along his neck and shoulders and arms. That was the fourth time I reached for the pipe, and he let me take it, saying, *'palamo yelo* [thanks].' Then I placed it against the cross-stick again, with the stem pointing upward. While I was doing this, other dancers were doing the same thing, and so the singers shared in the gift to the Ever-Living One. The power fell on them too, and drew us all closer together.

"Blue Spotted Horse came and pierced the flesh on the breasts of two of the dancers, and through the cut on each he tied the end of one of the rawhide thongs that were fastened to the top of the sacred tree. When he did this, the two dancers only stared at the sun. They did not move; they did not make a sound. I had vowed secretly to do this on the fourth day, and I wondered if I could be as brave as they were.

"Now the drumming and singing began again. I saw the two dancers, with pierced breasts, lean back against the thongs with blood running down their bellies. Then we all began dancing with our eyes to the blazing sun. I did not see them after that, for the hot light stabbed my eyes and the blindness came back quickly. I heard later that one of them fainted when the sun was getting low, and there he hung from the tree until his father had him cut down. But he danced again next day, after the holy men had fixed his wound and he had slept. The other one leaned so hard upon the thong that he soon pulled it through the flesh. After the holy men had washed the wound and put medicine in it, he danced until night.

"I saw nothing. In the darkness of my eyes I floated alone on the drumbeats and the singing, and as I floated I prayed, 'Let me see! Let me see!' I wanted to get back to the wide green land and the sparkling streams; but I saw nothing. Someone came and put a piece of slippery bark into my mouth. I think it was Chagla. I chewed on this, and it made my mouth feel better. I went on dancing and praying in the darkness, 'Let me see again! Let me see!' All at once I did see, and I was not thirsty any more. It was the same wide green land under the wide blue sky. It was beautiful, but it was empty. I looked and looked, but there were no people, and no horseback came out of the sky. When the far-off drums and singing stopped, and this world came back, the sun was down, and the night was coming.

"I dropped down where I was, and I must have gone to sleep right away. Then someone was shaking me by the shoulder, and I thought I heard my father saying, 'Hold fast! There is more!' But when I was awake, it was one of the attendants who were waking the dancers. It was still dark, but there were stars. The sky was fading a little over where the sun comes up. People were moving about in the starlight yonder.

When I stood up and looked at the morning star, a power went through me and I felt good. I was not heavy at all. I felt very strong. Blue Spotted Horse was praying. There was no sound but his voice raised high. He prayed that the nation might live. To the Six Powers he prayed and to the coming sun, and the morning star looked and listened. Then the drumming began and the singing. It was the sun singing while it came up out of the night yonder:

" 'With visible face I am appearing.
In a sacred manner I appear.
For the greening earth a pleasantness I make.
The center of the nation's hoop I have made pleasant.
With visible face behold me!
The four-leggeds and two-leggeds, I have made them to walk.
The wings of the air, I have made them to fly.
The finned of the streams, I have made them to swim.
The rooted ones, I have made them to rise.
With visible face, behold, I appear!
My day, I have made it holy.'

"The morning star went out and the sun blazed over the edge of the earth. The blindness came. I prayed hard, 'Let me see!' I danced hard, like a homesick runner going home. The blindness did not go away. The darkness was burning hot. It pressed down upon me with great power. I did not float on the drumbeats and the singing. I worked hard to keep on dancing. My tongue was a stranger in my mouth. It was hard to blow upon my eagle-bone whistle. I kept on trying to pray and to remember, 'Hold fast, there is more.' I held fast, but I could not see. Someone put the slippery bark into my mouth. It was not easy to chew, but it helped a little. That day, it was like dancing always, but I held fast; and the drums stopped and the singing. I slept there on the ground, and had bad dreams about rivers too far off to reach, or they were not there when I came to where I saw them.

"The third day was harder, and it was very hot. I could not see, and my tongue filled my mouth. Afterwards I heard that five of the dancers fell down that day and could not get up. They had to be carried out. Charging Cat was one of them; but High Horse and Kicking Bear went through. I prayed to see, but it was only words. I kept on dancing because I remembered, 'Hold fast, there is more!'

"That night I dreamed of crawling around in the dark trying to find water. Afterwhile I heard a voice, and I knew it was my father. I could not see him, but his voice was like a wind out in the night, everywhere, nowhere: 'Let your heart be strong—it is nearly finished—you will see —you will see!'

"Then the attendant was shaking me awake.

"It was going to be the last day. When I got up from the ground, my body felt dead and it was hard to lift. But when I looked at the morning star above the pale streak yonder, my father's words seemed to fill the hollow world that listened, and a power ran through me stronger than ever before. While a holy man was praying, the power in me grew; and when the drums began and the singers sang, my heart sang too.

> " 'See where the sacred sun is walking!
> In the blue robe of morning he is walking,
> With his power greenward walking,
> Hey-o-ha, hey-o-ha
> Hey-o-ha, hey-o-ha.'

"I danced, but I did not feel the ground. The star died; the sun blazed up; the drums and singing stopped. It was time to fulfill the vow I made when I saw the Crow village and all those horses from the hill. I had told Chagla about this, and now it was the time. He came to me and said, so that many could hear, and his words spread through the crowd:

" 'Eagle Voice, the people are asking, that you give them a day.' And I answered: 'I will give them a day.' My tongue could not make the words clear, but Chagla said them so that all could understand: 'Eagle Voice has said it. He will give a day to the people. Eagle Voice has said it.' When they heard, the people cheered with one voice, 'hi-ya!'

The attendants began painting the dancers again after they had rubbed our bodies with the sacred sage. My body they painted red all over, except from the elbows and knees down, and that was blue for the power to make live and to destroy, as before. My body was red to make me holy, for through me a sacred gift would come to the people. From each wrist they hung an eagle feather, and one was tied in my hair, standing up. These were for the Great Mysterious One whose gift would come through me, and whose strength must be mine. When this was done, Blue Spotted Horse came and painted something on my back. It was a flying eagle, for the one that spoke to me with my father's voice in my vision on the hill when I was a boy and Blue Spotted Horse prepared me for my quest. That is why I am Eagle Voice. So it was painted on my back.

"While this was being done, another holy man came with some sacred sage to where I had placed the bison skull. He was wearing a bison robe painted half yellow and half red. Into the eye sockets and the ear and nose holes of the skull he thrust the sage. Then he sang a bison song:

> "'A sacred nation, they are appearing.
> They are appearing, may you behold!
> The bison nation, they are appearing!
> May you behold!'

"As he was singing the bison song, all at once the sage was blown out of the holes with great power, and a deep bellowing came forth. I do not know how this was, but I saw and heard; and I could feel the power growing in me, so that I felt strong as a bison and light as an eagle floating.

"When I was painted, they hung the bison skull on my back with a thong across the back of my neck and under my arms. Then they turned me to the blazing sun, and I stared straight at it. The burning blindness turned dark. I heard Blue Spotted Horse praying, and then, far off, I felt the knife in the flesh of my chest and the thong pushed through. If it hurt, I do not remember. I think the power lifted me above my body.

"When the drums and singing began again, I swung backward, leaning from the thong in my breast. It was like waking all at once from a dream. I forgot that I wanted to see. I wanted to cry out, but I did not. It was pulling the raw heart out of my breast. I wanted to stop dancing, but I kept on. This is the first time I ever told anybody; but now I am too old to be ashamed. I forgot to pray. I just kept saying to myself, 'Hold fast, hold fast, hold fast.' All the power had left me alone with my body in the burning dark, and my heart was tearing from its roots.

"This was always; and then it was not. Maybe my body was still dancing on the ground; I do not know. I was swinging in a great hollow night, back and forth, farther and farther, farther and farther. I was doing this always; I could not stop; I could not get loose. There was no one to cry to, there was nothing to grasp, for everywhere it was empty.

"This was always too; and then I swung so far that I broke loose and flew, head first, belly down, with my hands in front of me—like diving —no, like an arrow when a strong man draws the bow—*whang!* I flew so fast that my body sang. Then I saw the morning star straight ahead of me, and day was coming very fast. No, it was not coming; it was yonder and I was going to it. The star went out, and I was there, floating in clear, white light. The sun did not rise, but day was everywhere upon a wide green land—hills and valleys and gleaming streams.

"Then right below me there was a great village, a wide hoop of people, and they were all looking up at me and singing thanks for the good day. The light was so clear that I could see their happy faces, and I knew they were all my people. Many, many of them were glowing, and those were the ever-living ones who had died. I saw many darker ones who were still in this world, but all were united in the clear, happy day. When I looked for my father, he was there all glowing, and beside him was a young man who did not glow. When I looked harder at the young man, I could see it was myself. Then the wide land went out and I was falling, dizzy, in a darkness.

"Blue Spotted Horse was looking down at me and someone was dropping water into my mouth. They told me I had danced until the thong pulled out when the sun was starting down the sky. I had fulfilled my vow, and the water dropping on my tongue felt good; but I was very tired and my breast ached. Then I knew I was lying in a shade, and I could hear the drums and singing out yonder where they were still dancing. Afterwhile when I could talk a little, because the water softened my tongue, I told Blue Spotted Horse what I had seen. He said, 'My grandson, it is good. The power has come to you and you must send forth a voice for all the people to the Six Grandfathers.'

"They rubbed me all over with sage and painted me again—red as before, and blue from the elbows and knees down. While they were doing this they kept dropping water into my mouth a little at a time, and Blue Spotted Horse sang a medicine song. I could feel the power coming back into me while he sang. The water helped too.

"The sun was getting ready to go down, but it was still about the breadth of a hand above the earth. Then Chagla came and led me out into the dancing ring. I was naked now except for a breech clout, for I came naked into the world, and I must go to the Six Powers as I came. When they saw me, the drummers and singers stopped, and all the people cheered with one great voice, for the word had spread among the people. When I heard the voice of my people, it was like my vision and the power came over me stronger than ever. I felt light and happy and my heart·sang again.

"Chagla had made a quirt out of bison-hide fringed into many little thongs at one end, and at the other end was a loop to hang about the neck. This was painted red. He gave it to me, and said, 'Hang this down your back and never let it go. If you do this, no arrow or bullet can ever touch you, for the quirt will brush them away like flies.' I thanked him and hung it down my back, as he said. Then he led me to where a black horse was waiting for me at the entrance to the ring. The horse was painted blue on the nose and blue across the withers. From his tail one eagle feather hung.

"Before I got on the horse, Chagla told me what I must do. I felt light and strong when I put my hand on the horse's mane and sprang onto his back.

"Chagla brought my pipe from where I had placed it and gave it to me. Then I rode to the quarter where the sun comes up and raised my hands, palms out, with the pipe in the right one. There I sent a voice for all the people: 'Grandfather, you have given me this pipe and the morning star. Give me the eyes to see and the strength to understand, so that I may be a nation and live.' And when I had said it, all the people cried out together, giving thanks.

"Then I rode back to the quarter where you are always facing, which was the entrance. It is where the summer brings the power to grow. There I raised my hands and the pipe as before, and sent forth a voice: 'Grandfather, you have given me the hoop and the tree. Make them flourish that I may be a nation and live.' Again the people cried out together, giving thanks.

"When I was riding to the quarter where the sun goes down, all at once there was a face just under my horse's left ear. It was all bright and shining from inside like the people in my vision, and it was Tashina looking up. She was so close that I could see tears on her cheeks. When I was much older I thought about this, and it was like rain when the sun is shining. But it was mixed up with my vision then, and I was full of the great thing I was doing for the people. At the quarter where the sun goes down, I faced the level sun and sent forth a voice: 'Thunder Beings, you who make live and destroy, hear me and give me your power that I may be a nation and flourish.' Again the people raised one voice, giving thanks.

"When I had sent a voice at the quarter where the great white giant lives and asked for cleansing and healing, I rode again to the quarter where the sun comes up. But I did not stop there. I turned and rode straight in to the sacred tree at the center. There I stopped and raised my hands and the pipe to the sky straight above me. Then I sent forth a voice:

" 'Grandfather, Great Mysterious One, you have been always, and before you nothing has been. There is no one to pray to but you. You are older than all need, older than all pain and prayer. The star nations all over the heavens are yours, and yours are the grasses of the earth.

" 'Grandfather, it is finished now, and I have fulfilled the vow I made to you. Send me the good day that you have shown me. I want to be a nation and live.'

"When I had said this, the people cried out again with a great voice, giving thanks, and my horse lifted his head high and neighed and neighed; and the other horses grazing in the valley heard and raised their voices too. People talked about this afterwards. Some said the power was so strong that even the four-leggeds gave thanks. Others said my horse saw his ghost relatives in the world of spirit, and was crying out to them.

"When this was done, Chagla gave me a piece of red cloth, with which I must make an offering to earth, the mother of all. There was a stake pushed into the hole against the bottom of the sacred tree, and he pulled this out. Then I leaned over the horse's neck and held the red cloth above the hole. As I did this, the horse put his nose to the ground. Maybe he wanted to nibble some grass; maybe the power was strong in him and he was giving thanks. I do not know. Then I sent a voice to the earth and said: 'Maka, all creeping things, the wings of the air, those that swim in the waters, the rooted ones, the four-leggeds and the two-leggeds—they all belong to you. You are the mother of all, the only mother, she who has shown mercy to her children. Have mercy on me, for I want to be a nation and live.' Just as I finished saying this, something sucked the red cloth out of my hand and down into the hole. I do not know how this was, but Chagla and I and some others saw it.

"Now I had finished, and as I rode back to where the sun comes up and then to the opening and out of the circle, the voice of the people was loud, giving thanks for the good day. When the voice of the people was still, I could hear Chagla. He was facing the quarter where the sun had just gone down, and he was singing:

> "'A sacred praise I am making.
> A sacred praise I am making.
> My nation, behold it in kindness.
> The day of the sun has been my strength.
> The path of the moon shall be my robe.
> A sacred praise I am making.
> A sacred praise I am making.'

"When I got off my horse at our tepee, the power left me, and my legs would not hold me. My mother and step-father held me up. When I was lying down inside, Blue Spotted Horse and Chagla came. The last I re-member they were washing my body and dropping water and meat juice into my mouth. The people danced and feasted most of the night, but I did not hear them. In the morning, they 'woke me, and when I had drunk some water and eaten a little, I slept. That evening they fed me again and gave me water, and I slept. Next morning I was very hungry and thirsty. So I drank and ate all I wanted. I felt strong again, and my breast did not hurt. Blue Spotted Horse made it heal fast. Look. You can see it yet."

With fumbling fingers the old man unbuttoned his shirt, exposing puckered scars on the skinny chest.

"*Washtay!*" he said, as he rebuttoned his shirt. "It was good. Wakon Tonka sent the people good days when I was young. The hoop was not yet broken, and the people had not forgotten all that is true."

Eagle Voice seemed to have forgotten me suddenly. Gazing at the ground, he began blowing softly on his whistle. "Grandfather," I said at length; "you still have your eagle-bone whistle; but where is the sacred quirt that Chagla gave you?"

The old man regarded me for a while with that crinkled look of amusement about his eyes. "Grandson, you are in a hurry again," he said. "Can you not wait for a story?"

Thanking the Food

"I have been thinking about roads," the old man remarked musingly, with an air of reluctant return from somewhere far off. It was the next morning, and I had waited longer than usual for the story.

"About roads?" I said; "what roads, Grandfather?"

"Good roads, bad roads, Grandson," he replied. "I have been thinking maybe the good road is the one a man does not walk because he does not see it until he is tired and looks back. Also I have been thinking the bad road is bad because he walks it, and maybe does not see it either, until he is very tired and stops to look back. There was a road I did not walk that time, because I did not find it until I had walked across the world."

"And what road was that, Grandfather?" I asked.

"A girl's road," he answered slowly, fixing his long-focused gaze upon something beyond me. "Tashina went away on it."

He was silent awhile, until the focus of his gaze shortened to include me, and then—

"My mother and step-father were proud of me because I had given the people a good day, and they were all praising me. I think I was very proud of myself too. Maybe afterwhile when I was older and had counted many coups and all the old people praised me because I always had a big pot and tender meat for them—maybe then the *wichasha yata-pika* would make me one of them. And maybe when I was still older, I would be a great chief. That is what I was thinking all the time, after the sun dance, and maybe my step-father and my mother were thinking that too. So they said we must make a feast and invite very old men and women to come and eat. Also, we would ask some wise old man to come and thank the food."

"Could not anyone give thanks for food, Grandfather?" I interrupted.

"Anyone could give thanks for food," the old man replied. "A woman could do that. Maybe she has been cooking meat, and before she puts it out, she takes a tender piece and holds it up and says, 'Wahnagi, eat this for me.' She is making a thank offering to the spirits by sharing her meat with them before she eats any herself. War parties would do this too when they sat down to eat. But thanking the food was different. Not everyone could do that.

"They used to say it was not easy to walk the road of difficulties through this world; but of all the hard things, four things were hardest. Getting food was the first, and without food there is nothing else. The second hardest thing was losing your oldest child. The third was losing your woman. The fourth was having to fight a big war party when yours was small. I had an uncle when I was a boy, and his name was Flying By. Once I asked him, 'Uncle, what is the hardest thing you have known?' And he said, 'My nephew, it was not any of the four hardest things people talk about.' Then he told me of a time when he was out hunting alone over by Mini Shoshay [the Missouri], and a party of Rees chased him. He got away, for he had a good start, and hid in the thick willow brush that grew in a swamp. It was getting dark, so the Rees did not find him. He was afraid to leave the brush or make any noise. But he was not alone there. The whole nation of mosquitoes was camped in that swamp, and they were singing and dancing and feasting all night long. My uncle was the meat. 'Nephew,' he said, 'there are not four, but five hardest things, and that is the hardest.' But my uncle was always joking.

"Getting food is the hardest thing, and without it there is nothing. It is great to be brave in battle, but a great warrior must look to the food and remember the old and needy.

"So my mother borrowed some more pots from her friends who came over to help her cook the meat for the feast; and these brought with them some of the tenderest meat they had, for they wanted to help in the giving. And when the meat was all tender and the soup smelled good, I had to go all around the village, inviting the very oldest people. Kicking Bear, High Horse, and Charging Cat went along with me, because we had been brothers in a great deed. When I came to an old man, maybe he was so old that he dozed most of the time, and he would be sitting with his chin on his chest and his nose almost on his chin, and his hair, thin and white like mine, over his eyes. So I would tap him on the shoulder, and he would look up and blink, with his head shaking. 'Heh! heh! heh!' he would say, wondering what was wrong, for he had been far away in a dream, maybe. Then I would say, 'Grandfather, we are going to thank the food over at our lodge, and we want you to come and help us; for we are only young men and you are *gan inhuni* [come to old age] and you are wise.' And when the old man was awake and understood, maybe he was so pleased that he would cackle when he thanked me; and maybe he would show only two teeth, and neither a friend to the other. And maybe he would say, 'You thought I was sleeping when you came; but I was just sitting here thinking about the time when I was a fine, brave young man like you. I was a good dancer, and I was good-looking too! The girls all liked me!' Then maybe he would giggle and poke me in the ribs.

"Or maybe it would be a woman so very old that she could not get fat any more, and she was all skin and bones. And maybe she would be nodding over a moccasin she had been trying to bead for a long while, and her hands were like eagle claws, and her eyes dim, so that the moccasins did not ever get finished. And she would look up and squint hard at me, and say, 'Are you not so-and-so's son?' And it would be somebody whose name I had not heard. I would tell her my father's name, and she would look troubled. Then she would thank me and smile at us just like our own grandmothers, and tell us we were fine boys.

"While we were going around inviting old people, my step-father went over to see Blue Spotted Horse and asked him to thank the food for us. He could do this because he was old and very wise. Also he was a holy man. He had taught me when I went on vision quest, and he had helped me in the sun dance. I was like a younger grandson to him.

"The feast was ready, so we were waiting for the old people. We could see them coming from all over the village, bringing their cups and knives with them. They were all three-legged, the way I am now, for near the end of the black road there is a cane. Some of them would be all bent over and they would be holding their heads up like turtles to see where the pots were steaming. I was a boy, straight and tall, then, and that is the way they looked to me. Some would be holding their hands on their backs where it hurt them to walk. Some of them would be hurrying and some would not be hurrying at all; but one would be coming no faster than the other.

"We could hear them making songs as they came, and when they got near enough, maybe the song would be like this:

"'Hi-a-he! Hi-a-he!
Eagle Voice, you are brave, they say,
And I have heard.'

"Maybe it would start thin and high like singing, and then get tired all at once and be just muttering.

132

" 'To be a man is difficult, they say;
But you are brave and I have heard.
Many horses you have brought;
Many horses, I have heard.
Hi-a-he! Hi-a-he!'

"When we were all sitting in a circle in front of our lodge, with the full pots steaming in the middle and the old people holding their cups and knives, many people were crowding around to see. They were all still when Blue Spotted Horse stood up with his pipe near the pots. He looked very old too, for his hair was white and he stooped, and when he looked at you there were half-moons in his eyes. But when he held his hands and his pipe to the place where the sun goes down, and sent forth a voice, it went with eagle wings. There he prayed to the Power that makes live and destroys. To the place where the Great White Giant lives he turned and prayed to the Power that cleanses and heals. To the place whence come the morning star and the day, he prayed to the Power that gives light and understanding and peace. At the place whence comes the summer, he prayed to the Power of growing. Then he raised his hands and his pipe to the sky, sending a voice to Wakon Tonka, the one who has all these Powers. And last he leaned low, praying to Maka, the mother of all that live.

"When he had done this, he went to his place in the circle and sat down. There was a murmuring all around the hoop and among the crowding people. *Hetchetu aloh!* So it was indeed. Then Blue Spotted Horse looked all around the circle at the old people waiting with their cups and knives, and he smiled at them like a grandfather at his children's children. Then he looked straight at us boys and began talking:

" 'Grandsons, these old people here have been sitting in their tepees with their heads down. They were thinking about where to get some good tender food. They all know you, so they all began looking up to your tepee to see if maybe smoke was coming out. Smoke came out of your tepee, and they were waiting. They were sitting there waiting with their heads down thinking of you. You had done brave deeds, so maybe you would be giving a feast. And while they were sitting there thinking, all at once there you were, inviting them to come and eat! They are not often happy any more, for the black road gets steeper before it ends. But when they heard you, all at once they were happy. You have seen them coming to your tepee, smiling and rejoicing and singing praise of you. So you see them now, all happy and sitting in a sacred manner with you in one hoop. They are holding their empty cups, and their knives they have sharpened. They are hungry, and the food you have cooked smells so good and looks so good. You are young and brave. Who but you will fill their cups with soup and tender meat?

"'What do you want of these old people, that you have cooked all this good food for them? Surely there is something you must want; but you know very well they cannot give you anything now. Still you feed them. What do you want from them? They cannot repay you, for they have nothing.

"'Yes, they do have something. Maybe it is the white war bonnet they wear. Maybe that is what you want them to give you. Maybe it is the wrinkled old buckskin they are wearing [their skins]; but that is almost worn out, and would not keep you from freezing on a winter trail. Maybe you want them to give you their canes; but three legs are slower than two.

"'I think you do not want any of these things now; but maybe this is what you are thinking: I am young and I will look to the old who are worthy. They have seen their days and proven themselves. With the help of Wakon Tonka, they have grown ripe for the world of spirit, and they can see what eyes do not show. What will be, but is not yet, they can tell it; and what comes out of their mouths, it is so, because it is not with their eyes that they see. If I give them of my strength, being young, their power to live will come back to me and my family. So shall we come in our time to where the cane is; so shall we wear the white war bonnet and be ripe for the world of spirit; so we too shall see our children's children.

"'I thought all the while, grandsons, that there must be something you wanted for this food; and now you have told me what it is. It is good, and so shall it be.

"'And now as we sit here together in a sacred manner, smelling all this good meat, we can hear the Food talking. It is talking to you, grandsons, and it says: "I come first, and I am sacred, for without me there is nothing. The Grandfather, Wakon Tonka, has given me to Maka, the mother of all living things, and she has shown mercy to her children that they may live. On her thousand breasts I am grass; in her thousand laps I am meat; and again on her thousand breasts I am grass. The bison's strength is mine. The great warrior, I have made him strong for his deeds. The greedy-for-me, their days shall be easy to count; but those who are liberal with me, upon me shall they uproot their teeth [grow very old]. Unless the great warrior gives me with his deeds, they shall be as a coward's. Let any try without me, I will always win. It is I who am the greatest warrior. If I had weapons, who could count my prisoners by now?"

" 'Grandsons, so it is the Food talks, and you have heard. Surely we must thank this sacred one, and how can we do that? *Plama yelo* is a breath in the mouth; it is easy to say, and no one is the fatter for it. The Food itself has told us how to thank it. We shall give it to the needy and the old.'

"When Blue Spotted Horse was through talking, the old man at his left smiled at us boys and said, 'Ho, Grandsons! *How!*' Then the next and the next spoke to us in the same way, until all the old men and old women had spoken. And when the voices had gone around the hoop from left to right, which is the sacred manner, and come back to Blue Spotted Horse, he said, 'I am sending the food neither down nor up. The people are hungry and ready, so put it out.'

"Then we boys went around the hoop, left to right, beginning with the first old man who had spoken, and filled all the cups of the old people, Blue Spotted Horse's last, with soup and tender meat. And this we kept on doing, until no more cups were emptied. Then we ate, and when we had eaten, the meat that was left we divided among the old people, and they went away with it, making songs about the brave young men who had fed them."

Eagle Voice sat silent for a while, his eyes closed, his hands on his knees. Emerging from his reverie at length, he fixed his crinkled gaze on me and smiled. "You can see," he said, "that the Food was right when it talked, for I have come to where the cane is. Most of my teeth are uprooted, and I am wearing the wrinkled buckskin and the white war bonnet. When I was young and my head was full of brave deeds and horses and coups and scalps, I have heard old men say, 'It is good to be young and die on the prairie for the people. It is not good to grow old.' Maybe they wanted to make us braver. Maybe the black road made them tired where it steepens. When I am all alone, I think and think; and it is about going to visit my relatives in the world of spirit that I think most; but it is good to look back and remember."

"When you look back, Grandfather," I said, "you see a girl's road that you did not walk because you did not see it then. Do you wish you had seen it and walked it?"

"There are many roads, Grandson," he answered. "They all come together, and at that place there stands a three-legged old horse always looking for the grass that used to be." The picture of himself, drawn once before, amused him, and he chuckled over it. *"Dho!"* he continued. "It was the road Tashina Wanblee walked that time, and I did not see it until I had walked across the world.

"When the feasting was over, the bands that had come together for the sun dance were getting ready to scatter and go their own ways. Boys and men would be catching horses. Tepee poles would be clattering. Women would be scolding because the horses would not stand still while the drags were loaded. People would be visiting each other because maybe they would not meet again until next grass, or never. Maybe boys would be sneaking off into the brush to meet their girls, and maybe some boy would run away that night and follow the trail of a girl so that he could talk to her under the blanket once more.

"High Horse was a Miniconjou and Kicking Bear was a Hunkpapa. They were going to Pa Sapa [the Black Hills] with their people. But we had big plans. When the fall hunt was over, they would come back again and find our village somewhere on the Greasy Grass [Little Big Horn] or the Powder or the Tongue. Then the three of us and Charging Cat, and maybe some others, would make war against the Shoshonis or the Crows, or maybe both of them. It was harder to make war in the winter than in the summer, and if we got back with horses and scalps we would be great warriors and everybody would be talking about us again. Maybe we would all be chiefs sometime. We had been together most of the time after the sun dance and thanking the food, and we talked and talked about our plan. We would ride out into the hills alone and talk about how we would do. So we were not thinking about girls. Even High Horse had not been sick, since getting all those horses cured him.

"I was out helping to catch horses, and I was riding back leading three of them. At the creek I stopped to let them drink, and there was some brush there. I was leaning on my horse's neck, and I heard something moving in the brush. When I looked, it was Tashina. Maybe she saw me going after horses, and came down there to see me before she went away. She was just standing there outside the brush with a pretty trader's shawl over her shoulders and up over her head. She was holding it close about her face, and when I looked at her, she pulled it closer and looked down at the ground. I was glad to see her, and I spoke to her the same as to a boy. I joked and said, 'If you are out looking for a horse again, here are three real ones.' I was thinking of when she caught me for a horse and made me pull her drag. She just kept on looking at the ground with the shawl tight about her face. And when I stopped joking, I could hear her saying, '*Shonka 'kan, Shonka 'kan,* you made me proud.' She said it so low that I could just hear her. Maybe I would have jumped off my horse then; but the three horses were full of grass and water and felt good, so when they saw some other horses coming, they neighed and reared. Two of them broke away, dragging their lariats, bucking and kicking and breaking wind. So I said, 'Hold this horse for me while I catch the others.' It was an old horse and it did not feel so good as the others. Then I rode off on the run. The horses were hard to catch again; and when I came back, the other horse was tied by his lariat to the brush, and Tashina was not there."

After a silence, the old man looked up at me and continued: "The bands moved off that day, and I rode awhile with High Horse and Kicking Bear. The people were all strung out, and we would ride up and down, talking to people we knew. I saw Tashina. She was riding an old mare, and when I came up to her, I thought I would joke with her again so I thanked her for holding my horse. She did not say anything and did not look up at me. When the sun was halfway down, I turned back towards our village with others who had come along.

"We had a big bison hunt that fall, the Oglalas and Sans Arcs together, and I was not looking for calves any more. When the advisers chose the young warriors who should kill meat for the old and needy, I was one they chose. It was a big honor for a young man. We went up to Elk River [Yellowstone] first. I was out with a scouting party up there, and we found some stakes driven into the ground. It was where the Wasichus were going to make another iron road. People had talked much about this, but I saw the stakes, and we pulled up all we saw and threw them away. People had talked much about the other iron road too, the one along the Shell [Platte]. It stopped the bison and cut the herd in two. Now the Wasichus would build an iron road on the other side of us also. It was what Wooden Cup told the people long ago. Sometimes when I heard this talk I was afraid.

We found a big herd and followed it slowly, killing only what we wanted. It was a happy time. Before the snow came we were back on Powder River with more *papa* and *wasna* than we could eat. There was feasting and we were happy. I wish I had some of that meat now. It had strength in it. If somebody could thank the food, maybe I would be invited to help."

"I am not worthy to thank the food, Grandfather," I said; "but let us have a feast tomorrow anyway. We can invite two or three of your friends. I will bring the feast and maybe your daughter will cook it for us."

"*Hi-yay!*" the old man exclaimed; "*Washtay!* Let us have a feast. It will be good."

137

XVII

The Woman Four Times Widowed

And so, next day, we feasted—Eagle Voice, No Water, Moves Walking, and I. It was well past noon when we began, for after delivering the makings of the feast to the daughter in the little gray log house, I had gone in search of the guests, taking the son-in-law with me as a guide. Drifted by-roads, that had ceased to be even the desultory trails they were at best, led at last to lonely shacks some miles up the creek valley where the old men lived, or, rather, waited, in apathetic squalor for nothing in particular. Curiosity, chronic loneliness and the immemorial lure of a feast, which is more than eating, assured a ready acceptance of the invitation.

So the four of us were sitting in a close circle with a steaming pot of veal in the center. *Pae zhuta sapa* [black medicine] bubbled in the bat-tered coffee pot on the sheet-iron stove, and there was plenty of *chun humpi* [juice of the tree, sugar] to sweeten it. Bread, cookies, and canned peaches were close at hand. As giver of the feast and the young-est of the party, I had filled the tin cups with meat and broth, passed the bread around, and filled other tin cups with coffee liberally dosed with sugar. I had been greeted by each in turn, *"Ho! Grandson, how!"* To this greeting, Eagle Voice had added: "This is indeed my grandson. See! He has given me these fine warm moccasins. Now my toes do not smart when I get wood in the snow." When the moccasins had been ex-amined and generously approved, No Water, the older of the guests, both of whom were younger than Eagle Voice, had a little speech to make. It was to the effect that I could not help being a Wasichu any more than he could be other than a Lakota. And, indeed, a little brown paint on my face and a blanket—"Could not tell the difference," he said; "could be Ta Shunka Witko [Crazy Horse]." I thanked him for the too generous compliment, and his round, bulbous-nosed counte-nance, that normally bore a vaguely grieved, apprehensive look, glowed with good humor. "Maybe Wakon Tonka gave him a Lakota heart,"

Moves Walking added. "Maybe if all Wasichus were so, things would be better." Wiry and smallish for a Sioux, a cast in his left eye gave to his sharp, shriveled face an air of angry intensity; but now even the recalcitrant off-eye softened a bit with good will.

Having first offered choice morsels of meat to the *wahnagi*, we fell to serious eating with fingers and sharp knives, the latter for cutting off the bite. Eagle Voice broke the silence with a remark to the effect that the meat was tender. "Even I can chew it, and most of my teeth are uprooted. I might be eating the first young calf I killed when I was a boy. I think this will make me stronger."

When it was unanimously agreed that the meat was tender and *washtay*, we resumed the serious business of eating in silence. At last, the peaches and cakes having been sampled and approved, the pipe went round and Eagle Voice spoke: "Our grandson likes to hear stories, and I have told him many already. There is a story about a dog. I have heard No Water tell it."

"*Dho,*" assented No Water; "it is a true story [*woya kapi*]. I can prove it by a Hunkpapa, much older than I am, who told it to me."

He searched our faces with his vaguely grieved apprehensive look. There being no denials, he proceeded: "Sometimes the four-leggeds are wiser than we two-leggeds. A horse will take his man home in the darkest night when the man is lost. If you try to lose a dog, he will find you, even if there is no trail to smell. I do not know how this is, but it is so. I think they are closer relatives to the spirits than we are. Sometimes they can talk too, but not many can understand them. This dog could talk, but only a very little girl could understand, as you will hear.

"This man's name was Sitting Hawk. He was not a noted warrior, but he was a good hunter and took good care of his family, so that they always had plenty to eat. I did not hear his woman's name, and I am telling only what I know. He had two daughters, one of them not quite a woman yet and the other just a little girl—maybe three winters. They had a little dog, and the little dog had four pups.

"The scouts had been out looking everywhere, and there were no enemies; so Sitting Hawk thought he would go hunting and take his family along to have a good time. He liked to do that. There were horses for all the family to ride, and the little dog rode on the pony-drag with her pups when she was not running around smelling things. Afterwhile they came to a place of green grass with plenty of water and wood, and there they made a camp. It was good weather, so they were happy there. Sitting Hawk would go hunting, and his woman and older daughter would stay at home and dry the meat. The very little girl would play with the four pups. That is the way it was, for I do not know how many days.

"One day Sitting Hawk came home early and he was very tired. So he ate and lay down in the tepee to sleep awhile. It was not yet dark, so the others were all up. The woman and her older daughter were scraping a deerskin they had staked out on the ground. They did not notice the little girl much, and the dog was letting the four pups eat. Afterwhile the little girl came and asked for something to eat. So the older daughter gave it to her. Soon the little girl came back and asked again for something to eat. The sister gave her some more meat and said, 'This is all you can have. You will make yourself sick eating so much.'

"So the little girl went away; and this is what she was doing. There were four men hiding out there in the brush, and one of them could speak our tongue. Perhaps they were kind to the little girl. It must have been so, for she was not afraid. When they told her to get them something to eat and not to tell, that is what she did. Maybe it was like a game she liked to play all by herself.

"The four men were so hungry that what the little girl brought only made them hungrier. So they got bolder and came to the tepee where Sitting Hawk was sleeping, and the mother and older daughter were scraping the deerskin, and the dog was feeding her pups. When the woman and daughter saw the four men all at once, they just stared. When the little dog saw them, she made whimpering noises to the little girl that said, 'Why did you feed these men? They are enemies!' And that scared the little girl. When Sitting Hawk sat up and saw them, he knew they were Blackfeet, although one of them spoke our tongue and asked for food. Sitting Hawk could do nothing, so he said to his woman, 'Feed them.' And she did. When they had eaten, the four lay down inside the tepee with their bows and arrows beside them. I think they were only waiting until it got darker. The woman had fed them, and she thought, I will treat them like relatives. So she took off their moccasins and rubbed the bottoms of their feet with warm tallow, the way she would do with her own man when he was tired. This made the men drowsy, and they fell sound asleep around the fire, being full of meat and weary. They were *maka mani* [afoot] and maybe they had walked far.

"Now the little dog began yawning and making strange noises like talking. The little girl listened, and understood. The dog was saying, 'Hurry! Take my little ones and run away from here as fast as you can or you will be killed. These are bad men and enemies.' This scared the little girl more than ever, and she whispered to her mother what the dog said. This scared the woman and she whispered it to Sitting Hawk, so that he was scared too, for he knew these were Blackfeet. And this is what he did. He whispered to his family to follow him with what they could carry. The little girl put the pups inside her dress, and the dog followed her. When the horses were all ready, Sitting Hawk went back to the tepee without making any noise. There were some big pieces of tallow on the ground, and these he put into the red ashes of the fire, with the men sleeping around it. The tallow sputtered. Then a big flame leaped up, and Sitting Hawk ran to his horse where the others were all ready to go. They rode fast, and when they came to the top of a hill they could see the tepee burning and men running here and there. Maybe the Blackfeet got burned with hot grease; I do not know. But Sitting Hawk and his family and the little dog and the pups were safe."

"Ho, ho!" exclaimed Moves Walking and Eagle Voice together by way of applause.

"It is a true story," resumed No Water, "and the very old man who told me—much older than I am—told me more about a dog just to prove it.

"The way I got the story, this man's wife was well known among the Lakota. Her name was Loud Woman. Her man, I cannot give his name, for I have forgotten—but I will call him Good Buffalo. He had two sons and these had wives. Also he had a daughter and a sister. The daughter was just a little girl—maybe four or five winters—and she had a little dog. So it was a family of eight, if you do not count the dog.

"This family was on a hunting party, for the scouts had been looking around and no enemies were seen. So the councilors allowed small parties to go out. They were having a good time, and they were moving back slowly towards the village, which was not far away now and not very close either.

One day Good Buffalo told his wife, Loud Woman, to camp in a certain place with his sister, his little daughter and his two daughters-in-law. It was a grassy place with plenty of good water and wood. So there were four women and a little girl in that camp, if you do not count the little dog. Then Good Buffalo and his two sons went hunting.

"It was getting to be evening, but it was early yet. The little dog had been running around here and there, smelling everything to learn all about the new camping place. This one was a mother dog too, but she did not have any pups yet. You see, they were all women in that camp. Afterwhile the little dog was sitting on top of a hill near the camp, and she was barking. Soon she raised her nose to the sky and began howling in a queer way. The little girl listened, and all at once she knew her dog was talking, and this is what the dog was saying: *Wahoo—oo-oo!* It is going to be terrible! We should run away! It is going to be terrible! We should run away! *Wahoo-oo-oo!'*

"The little girl ran to her mother and told what she heard the dog say; but her mother was very busy doing something—and she kept on doing it—so that she did not hear the little girl very well. Then the little dog came running down the hill with her tongue hanging and all out of breath. She leaped up on each one in the camp, wagging her tail, and yawning with queer noises in her throat. Then she would whine and yelp. And the mother said, 'What is the matter with that dog? She acts crazy!' And the little girl said, 'Mother, she is talking. I told you she was talking. She says it is going to be terrible and we must run away.'

"While the mother was looking hard at her little daughter and wondering if she might be making it up, the little dog ran back to the hilltop as though she might be chasing a rabbit.

"They were all looking up at the little dog, and she was howling that queer way again, with her nose to the sky. The little girl understood again, and she began to cry, because she was scared and nobody could understand. Then the mother said, 'Why are you crying like this?' And the little girl answered, 'The dog is telling us it is going to be terrible. My father and brothers are coming and enemies are coming too. It is going to be terrible. We must run away now, for it is going to be terrible. My dog is saying it!' Then she cried harder than ever. And the mother said, 'You must stop crying. We must wait until your father and brothers come back and they will know what to do.' So they waited. And the little girl cried, and the little dog mourned on the hill.

"It was just before dark, and the three men came back. Loud Woman told Good Buffalo about the little girl and what the dog said. But Good Buffalo was tired from hunting all day, also he was hungry, and he said: 'Of course we will go away from here when we are ready. We are camping here now.'

"Just then the little girl heard the dog talking up there again, and the dog said, 'They are here! *Wahoo-oo-oo!* They are here! You have no ears, so I am running away! *Wahoo-oo-oo!*' Then the dog was gone from the hill, and her howling was getting dimmer.

"Now the little girl was crying so hard she could hardly talk, and she said, 'They are here! Enemies are here! My dog said it and she has run away!'

"So Good Buffalo said to his sons, 'Let us go and see what all this is about. We can eat when we get back.' But they did not go, for just then there were shots from out in the dark. The camp was surrounded. The women raised the tremolo. Good Buffalo began a death-song, and the sons sang with him as they ran out to meet the enemies. They did not sing long, for they were killed. Then Loud Woman beat her breast and grasped a butcher knife and went out yelling after the men. And after her the sons' wives ran with butcher knives to help their men. Soon there was only a galloping of horses, and then it was still out in the night.

"Good Buffalo's sister and her little niece hid under a buffalo robe inside the tepee. They thought soon they would be killed and scalped. But nothing more happened. All the enemies wanted was the horses, and maybe they thought a big camp was near.

"When it was morning, Good Buffalo's sister and her little niece went to find the others. It was terrible—the way the dog said it was going to be. The three men and the three women were scattered around, all dead. The sister was shot in the leg—but it was not in the bone, so she was strong enough to drag the six dead people into the tepee and to place them side by side. She thought, the enemies may come back and it will be just as well to lie dead here with the others. And there she mourned, waiting for death, and the little girl cried and cried.

"When the little dog quit trying to make the people understand, and ran away, she went straight for the village. When she got there, the people were sleeping, but she ran around and around among the lodges yelping and howling, and that set all the other dogs barking. So the people awoke and ran out of their lodges to see what was happening. The little dog ran up to some relatives she knew and leaped up on them, whining and yawning, and making queer noises in her throat. And the relatives said, 'This dog belongs to Good Buffalo's little daughter, and he is gone hunting with his family. Something bad must have happened to them. We must go and find them.'

"It was past the middle of the night, but they did not wait until morning. They formed a war party and started in the direction Good Buffalo had gone hunting. One of them was carrying the little dog, and when they had been riding awhile, they put her on the ground. She whined and whimpered and ran ahead, and the war party followed.

"When it was getting day, they could see that the little dog was limping and could hardly carry her tail. So one of them picked her up and let her ride in front of him. Afterwhile, they came to the bottom of a hill. The little dog leaped down and limped off up the hill, howling all the way. The party followed her; and when they were at the top, they saw three tepees in the valley and no smoke coming out. It was where Good Buffalo's sister and little daughter were waiting for death with the six who were dead."

Ho, ho! Ho, ho! But surely there was more!

There was; but No Water was not in a hurry to divulge it. Adding the emphasis of silence to the impact of his tale, he searched our faces for a while with narrowed, penetrating eyes.

"It was not a small war party that followed the little dog," he continued. "The way I heard about it, there were forty-two. When they saw what they saw in that tepee and heard what they heard from Good Buffalo's sister, and the little daughter crying and crying, their hearts were bad, and every warrior of them was like three. So eight of them started back afoot towards the village with six led horses and the dead across them, and the sister mourning with her hair cut off, and the daughter holding her little dog and crying. There was mourning in the village; but after six days the victory songs were louder. That was when the war party came back from following the enemies. The way I heard, they were Assiniboins, and they are like cousins of the Lakota! Caught them camping and feeling safe. Fifteen scalps that time! Fifteen, the way I heard! And all the horses, too! It is a true story. The old man who told it is living yet."

When all approving comments had been made, I ventured a question. "Grandfather, I wonder why the little girl could understand and the others could not."

"I have thought and thought about that, Grandson," No Water replied. "The two-leggeds and four-leggeds are relatives. Maybe a long time ago they had one tongue. When people are still little, they are four-leggeds yet, just like their relatives. Maybe they have the same tongue too when they are little and four-legged. Then when they begin to be two-leggeds they begin to forget, and they forget more and more. Maybe the little girl could remember yet. This is only what I have thought. I do not know."

Ah-a-a! It was clear that we all felt the cogency of the idea. "And maybe," Eagle Voice suggested with his crinkled, quizzical look, "maybe then when we get three-legged, we are beginning to remember again! Next time I hear a dog, maybe I can learn something!"

Laughter dwindled to chuckling, and in the following silence the pipe went round again.

Finally, Moves Walking, regarding us with his self-contradicting gaze —fierce from the glaring off-eye and friendly from the other—ended the meditative silence.

"I want to tell a story, but it is not about a dog. It is about a woman who was four times widowed, because nobody would believe her—just the way they would not believe the little girl. This also is a true story. A Sisseton who was *gan inhuni* [come to old age] told it. I was over there and this old man told me. His father told him. They are both dead, and I cannot prove it, but it is true. All of the Sisseton Lakota know it, so I must be very careful to tell it right.

"This woman, I could say that I know her name, but I have forgotten it so I will give her the name of Sees-White-Cow. I could say that maybe she had a dream about seeing a white bison cow and it gave her a power to see more than other people, because a white cow is *wakon*. But I do not tell this because I do not know it. I must be careful.

"Sometimes the tribe is all gathered together and sometimes it is scattered. This happened when the tribe was scattered, and it happened at a place they call Minnesota. There was a man by the name of Turning Hawk, and he did not belong to Sees-White-Cow's band. He had been wanting her for his woman when the bands were all together, and he had talked to her under the blanket. When the bands parted and went different ways, he felt very sad; so he thought he would not stay with his people. He would follow his girl. At that time there were few horses, but Turning Hawk had a good one, so he followed where his girl went.

"Sees-White-Cow was the only girl in the family, but she had two brothers, both brave warriors. When Turning Hawk came to where she was, he had a talk with her family, and offered his horse for the girl. She was the only daughter they had, but they did not have any horse at all; so Turning Hawk got the girl for his woman. Of course he wanted to go back to his people with her, and she was willing. So Sees-White-Cow got everything ready, and because he had traded his horse off, they had to go *maka mani*.

"They started early in the morning, and on the second day they were coming down to a lake with trees and brush growing around it. They thought it was a good place to camp and rest awhile, for the grass was soft and green under the trees.

"Just then Sees-White-Cow saw something, and she said, 'Look! There is a man peeking out from yonder brush!' Turning Hawk looked and answered, 'That is not a man; it is an otter.' And Sees-White-Cow said, 'Look there and there! They are men looking out of the brush!' Still Turning Hawk could not see, and he said, 'They are only otter.' But the woman was frightened at what she had seen. 'They are enemies, and I am going.' So she dropped her pack and began running back the way they had come."

Moves Walking had risen spryly to his feet, hand at brow, the better to see otter yonder in the brush. Apparently he was less certain about the otter now, for he glanced nervously back over his shoulder at the fleeing woman. Suddenly it happened. He clapped his hands, simulating the sound of bows released and arrows in flight. "*Whang—whoosh—whang—whoosh—whang—whoosh!*" Tugging at imaginary shafts in his breast and belly, he slumped slowly, and sat down. After pausing long enough to emphasize the fatal nature of the incident, he resumed.

"Turning Hawk was dead, full of arrows; but Sees-White-Cow got away. I think she was a fast runner. When she came to the band of her people and told the story, a war party set forth and her two brothers were in it. They found Turning Hawk butchered like a deer and hung up in a tree. Afterwhile they caught the Chippewas who did this. There was a big fight. Many enemies were killed and scalped, and the two brothers were so brave and got so many scalps that everybody was talking about them; and there was a big victory dance.

"So the husband was dead, and maybe if he had listened to his woman he would have lived. Sees-White-Cow cut off her hair and mourned for a while. But she was a young woman and good to see; so when a brave young man by the name of Chasing Otter asked for her, she became his woman. He was a Sisseton.

"Afterwhile the band was camped by a lake, and on the other side of it there was a high bank with trees and plum brush. Someone said there were big ripe plums there, so Chasing Otter said to Sees-White-Cow, 'Why don't we paddle over there and get us some good ripe plums?' And she said that would be good. So they got in their canoe and paddled to where the ripe plums were. They were having a good time picking the plums, and then Sees-White-Cow thought she would climb up the bank to where the plums were even bigger and riper. When she got up there and looked over, there was a man peeking at her out of the brush. So she dropped back down the bank and whispered to Chasing Otter, 'An enemy peeked at me! Let us get away from here quick!' Chasing Otter was eating ripe plums and they tasted very good. So he said, 'It is only some other people who are picking some plums for themselves. I will go and see.' He started climbing up the bank. But the woman was frightened and she said, 'They are enemies! I am going!' So she leaped into the canoe and began to paddle away."

Moves Walking fell to paddling violently, peering anxiously ahead. Suddenly, he looked back over his shoulder. "The enemies are charging!" he announced excitedly—"*Wham! Whock!*" He lashed viciously at the air with an imaginary tomahawk. "Chasing Otter is dead, scalped. *Whang—whang—whang!*" With left hand extended and right hand at ear, Moves Walking released arrow after arrow in the direction of the galloping canoe.

"They shot at Sees-White-Cow, but did not hit her. When she got

146

back to the village and told the story, a war party set out after the enemies and her two brothers were in it. When they found the enemies they were Chippewas again, and there was a big fight. Only a few of the enemies got away. The brothers were so brave and got so many scalps that people talked and talked about them, and there was a big victory dance.

"So the second husband was dead and Sees-White-Cow was a widow again. She cut her hair and mourned awhile. But she was young and good to see; and when her hair was beginning to get long, a brave young man, called Tall Horse, asked for her, and she became his woman. Tall Horse was from another band and he had been visiting some relatives. He wanted to go back home with his woman, and Sees-White-Cow was willing, so they got ready and started out afoot, because there were few horses in those days.

"They traveled all day, and when it was getting dark they came to a rough country, hilly and wooded. Sees-White-Cow did not want to lose another man. She was thinking hard about this, so she chose a place to camp where they would be hidden and safe. There they made a tepee of brush and grass. Tall Horse was tired and he went to sleep right after they had eaten; but Sees-White-Cow could not sleep at all for thinking and thinking. It was getting near morning when she heard an otter calling. When she had listened awhile, she knew it was not an otter at all, but a man making like an otter. Then she heard another—and another— and another—"

Moves Walking, with his hands cupped behind his ears, listened breathlessly for some time.

"They were not otter! They were enemies! She could hear the difference. So she shook her man and whispered, 'Tall Horse, get up! There are enemies and I think we are surrounded! We can crawl down the ravine and escape.' Tall Horse listened, and when there were more calls, he yawned and said, 'They are otter. They are mating and calling to each other. I am tired, so let me sleep.' But the woman was frightened and she was thinking of the other husbands too. 'Man, I know! They are *not* otter! You'd better come if you want to live, for I am going.' But he yawned and said, 'They *are* otter, and I am sleepy.' Then he lay down again.

"Sees-White-Cow started crawling down a wash and thought her man would still believe and follow her when he knew she meant what she said. She was not far down the wash yet, and some men were coming up it. So she made herself flat in the grass and they nearly stepped on her. When they were gone awhile, she listened, and heard Tall Horse yell just once. After that, men were talking all excited. Then she got up and started running, for she knew her man was dead up there. After-while, she could hear men running after her. There was an old moon coming up, not very bright, but it helped her to see. She came to where there was a flat place with a big tree standing alone in its shadow. So she ran into the shadow and made herself flat against the tree. Soon the men came running by in the dim moonlight. She could hear them puffing. When they were gone, she ran back down the wash and into a ravine. There she hid again just as the day was coming. After two more nights she was back home.

"When the people heard her story, a war party started out after the enemies, and the two brothers went along. The enemies were Chippewas again, and there was a big fight. Not one got away. The two brothers of Sees-White-Cow were braver than ever. They brought back so many scalps and counted so many coups that people talked and talked about them even more than before; and there was a big victory dance. Seemed like every time their sister lost a man, they got more famous.

"So the third husband was dead, and Sees-White-Cow was a widow once more. She cut her hair again and mourned and mourned, and she did not want to get married to anybody at all. She always had such bad luck that she thought she would just live alone and maybe save a few men. But she was still a young woman, and she was good to see, after her hair began to get long again.

"There was a brave young man called Red Horse, and he was very handsome. After a while he wanted Sees-White-Cow for his woman. She already had three dead husbands and maybe he would be the fourth. So she would not listen to him for a long time. But her brothers liked Red Horse, whose father was a chief, and when he offered four good horses to her father, she forgot about her dead husbands for a while, and took him.

"Red Horse was from another band and he was visiting relatives. Of course he wanted to go back home and take his woman along, but she would not go. She would not even let him go on war parties, and she was always watching him, for she was afraid something might happen.

"They got along well together that winter, and afterwhile the grass appeared again and got tall in the valleys. One day Red Horse came back from taking care of his horses, for he still had some after he traded off the four; and horses were few in those days. So he said to his woman, 'I saw many turnips, and they look good. Why do we not go out and get ourselves some?' And Sees-White-Cow said, 'I think it would be good to do that.' So that is what they did. It was not far, so they went afoot.

Many people were out there with their sticks digging turnips, laughing and having a good time. The scouts had been all around, and there were no signs of enemies, so the people were not afraid.

"Sees-White-Cow and her man had some food with them, and when it was getting evening Red Horse said, 'Why do we not make a little camp in the ravine yonder and stay all night? We can peel and braid the turnips we have, and in the morning we can dig some more.' The woman was afraid, for she was thinking about her other husbands. She said, 'There may be enemies.' But Red Horse laughed and said, 'The scouts have been looking all around, and there are no enemies here. I think it will be good to camp and braid the turnips.' Sees-White-Cow did not want to do this, but afterwhile she gave in. So they made a little shelter with their turnip sticks and a blanket thrown over these. When they were through eating and braiding turnips by their little fire, they lay down to sleep under the blanket. But Sees-White-Cow could not sleep at all for thinking and thinking. Afterwhile an otter whistled— then another one whistled—then another."

Moves Walking paused, listening tensely, mouth open, hands cupped behind his ears.

"Of course," he continued, "otter are mostly in a lake, but she heard this whistling and she was frightened. These were enemies! She could tell the difference. So she shook Red Horse and whispered, 'Enemies! Listen!' Red Horse was only half awake, and when there was another whistle, he said, 'Foolish woman! That is an otter! Do not bother me!' But Sees-White-Cow was more frightened than ever. She had heard two dead husbands talk the same way. So she said, 'They are enemies! I am going!' And she started crawling away. All at once two men were coming, bent over and looking all around. She flattened herself in the grass, and they went by. Soon she heard just one big yell. Then she got up and ran towards camp as fast as she could."

At this point, No Water grunted and Moves Walking paused to scan his friend's face, one eye glaring fiercely, the other questioning. "Four dead husbands," said No Water with his grieved, apprehensive look. He held up four fingers. "One, two, three, four. How many more husbands has that woman got?"

Eagle Voice chuckled, and Moves Walking, ignoring the question, continued. "When the people heard about this, a war party started out to catch the enemies and the two brothers went along. There was a big fight and nearly all the Chippewas got killed and scalped. The brothers were braver than ever before, and I can not say how many scalps they got, because I do not know that, and I must be careful when I tell this true story. All the people talked and talked about them again, and by now I think they must have been *wichasha yatapika,* maybe *akichitas,* or even councilors. I think if Sees-White-Cow got a few more husbands those brothers would be head chiefs!

"Sees-White-Cow cut off her hair another time, and mourned and mourned. Seemed like every time she got a husband it was the same as murdering him herself. So she was never going to do that again as long as she lived. She was going to live alone after that.

"Afterwhile her hair was getting long again—"

"Ah-a-a-ah!" commented No Water.

"—and she was still not old," continued Moves Walking. "Also she was good to see. About that time a very handsome young warrior came visiting his relatives, and I do not know how many horses he had, but they were many. This handsome young man's name was Flies Back, and he wanted Sees-White-Cow for his woman. I think he had not heard this story. So when he offered six horses, her father thought maybe it would be better for her this time; also there were few horses in those days. Her two brothers liked Flies Back and they coaxed her to take him, so that she would not be living alone. Maybe they wanted to get more famous, but I do not know this, and I do not tell it.

"So afterwhile Sees-White-Cow gave in, and they got along well together all that winter. Then it was spring and the ducks were coming back.

"One day Flies Back said to his woman, 'There are many ducks on the lake. Why do we not go out and get some for ourselves? We can go out this evening and make a camp near the water. Then when it is early morning we can get some for ourselves. I am hungry for ducks.' When he said that, Sees-White-Cow began to remember, and she did not want to go. But she was hungry for ducks too, and she thought it might be all right this time. So they went and made a good warm camp close to this lake, and Flies Back went hunting, crawling through the grass and reeds. While he was gone, Sees-White-Cow kept looking all around, for she was afraid." Moves Walking, with hand at brow, peered anxiously about him for a while and No Water soberly joined him in the silent search. "All at once," resumed Moves Walking with a start, "she saw a man run from behind a tree and disappear behind some brush."

"Ho—ho!" exclaimed Eagle Voice.

"—saw a man running and hiding behind some brush," Moves Walking continued, "and she was more frightened than she had ever been. About that time Flies Back came with two ducks, and Sees-White-Cow told him about the man. 'It is only somebody out getting some ducks for himself,' Flies Back said. 'There are no enemies here. The scouts have been out looking all around.'

"Sees-White-Cow thought maybe her husband was right this time, and she was hungry for ducks. So they cooked the ducks and ate them, and then it was dark, so they lay down to sleep.

"But Sees-White-Cow got to remembering, and she could not sleep at all. I did not tell that they had a little dog with them, but I tell it now. And when the night was old, the little dog began growling and barking. Sees-White-Cow knew all at once that it *was* an enemy she had seen and no duck hunter. So she shook her man and whispered 'Enemies! We are surrounded! We must run away from here!' She got up and started running. He got up and started running too, but he ran the other way. When he came to the village, Sees-White-Cow was not there. He 'woke the people, and when they heard, a war party got together and started after the enemies. The two brothers went along. In the early morning they found Sees-White-Cow, and she was not going to have any more husbands. The little dog was curled up beside her whining, and she was scalped. Maybe she was hiding, and the little dog ran to where she was and barked, so that the enemies came and found her. I do not know this, and that is why I do not tell it.

"It was Chippewas again, and there was a big fight. The two brothers couped and killed and scalped I do not know how many. Big victory dance! People talk and talk about it. Maybe the two brothers were made chiefs that time. I do not know, and I must be careful when I tell this true story. The Sisseton who told me was *gan inhuni,* and he heard it from his father who was *gan inhuni* also."

"*Ho-ho! Ho-ho! Ho-ho!*" No Water and Eagle Voice applauded in unison. "*Washtay!*" remarked No Water. "One husband got away that time! *Washtay!*"

"It was not so," said Moves Walking. "Brothers were very sad. Had bad hearts. Killed Flies Back for running away from their sister. All dead! Five!" Holding up his spread right hand, he slowly counted with a careful forefinger.

Eagle Voice chuckled, and No Water, his grieved look intensified, shook his head sadly in silence.

XVIII

Falling Star, the Savior

Having filled the coffee cups and set the meat pot within easy reach of
the guests, I went outside to get a chunk of cottonwood, for a chill had
crept into the tepee. Under a dull sky the afternoon was waning fast,
and already the edge of the still air was sharpening with the approach of
night. While chopping, it occurred to me that we would soon be sitting in the dark, so I went to the little log house and borrowed an oil
lamp—the only one, but freely given. The family would go to bed soon,
the daughter explained, and it would not be needed. Also, if the old
men did not want to go home, they could sleep on the floor by the stove,
and go home in the morning.

When I re-entered the tepee, Eagle Voice was lying down, his knees
drawn up, an arm across his face. Apparently he was asleep. No Water
and Moves Walking were having a friendly argument between mouth-
fuls. No Water was convinced that it happened in the winter when the
four Crows were killed, while Moves Walking held out for the winter
when the tree fell on the old woman. When I had put the cottonwood
chunk on the embers and placed the lighted lamp on the ground near
the stove, it soon became clear to me that both contenders had the best
of reasons, with a glaring eye to reinforce them on the one hand, and
a deeply grieved look on the other.

What it was that had happened, whenever it had, was not revealed.
Eagle Voice sat up, brushed the straggling gray hair from his eyes,
grinned pleasantly, and said: "*Kola,* it was not the winter when the four
Crows were killed; it was not the winter when the tree fell on the old
woman. It was the winter when the Shoshonis were chased over the
bank; and that is a story I could tell."

"*Ah-a-a-a!*" agreed the erstwhile contenders in unison. Was not Eagle
Voice much older than they?

When we had eaten in silence for a while, Eagle Voice fumbled in
his long tobacco sack, charged his pipe and lighted it. "*Dho,*" he said,

152

starting the pipe on its rounds; "I could tell the story about the time when the Shoshonis were chased over the bank, for I was there. Maybe I will tell it to my grandson here, but I will not tell it now." He searched our faces with the amused, crinkled look about his eyes. "I do not want to kill any more people today. Too many dead husbands around here already." No Water slapped his knee and bellowed with laughter. Moves Walking fixed us in turn with the glaring eye. "It is a true story!" he protested; the good eye belying its fellow with a gleam of amusement. "Woya kapi! I can prove it!"

"Dho! It is a true story, kola," resumed Eagle Voice soberly, "and it is a good story; but there were thirty Shoshonis, and I am full of good tender meat. I do not feel like killing so many more people today. It is getting dark, so I can tell an ohunka kapi [fairy tale the old people make up]. If I tell it in the daytime, maybe I get long hair all over my backside. That is what I heard my grandfather say. But it is getting dark now, so I am not afraid of that." Having shared in the chuckling of his hearers over the hoary joke, he continued. "Maybe the story was true so long ago that we cannot believe it any more. I do not know. It is about Falling Star."

"Ho, ho!" exclaimed No Water and Moves Walking together. "Washtay!" said the latter. "My grandmother told it to me when I was very little. There were two girls and they married stars." "Dho," No Water agreed, "they did that. I think it was my grandfather told me first. And the girls fell through the sky."

"One girl," corrected Moves Walking.

"You are in a hurry to tell my story for me, kola," said Eagle Voice; "but I am going to tell it myself, and now I will tell it."

"This happened so long ago that I think the oldest person who ever told it had heard it from his grandfather. So I cannot prove it. In that time there was a big village, and I think the people were not even Lakotas yet."

No Water and Moves Walking sat with their hands on their knees, leaning towards the story-teller with eager expectancy, something childlike in their age-scarred faces.

"—and in this village there were two girls who were just beginning to be women; and these girls were sisters."

"Ah–a–a!" agreed No Water and Moves Walking, sharing the pleasure of recognition.

"They were pretty girls and they were sisters. So one summer night when the wind was still, and most of the people were sleeping, and no dog barked, and the sky was full of stars, these two girls were not sleeping. They were outside in the warm, still night, lying back against the side of their tepee and looking up at the sky. They were looking at the star nations, and they were saying to each other they wondered how far it was up yonder, how many sleeps it would take to get there, and how pleasant it would be to live in that country among those bright, happy people.

"Then they just lay back against the tepee for a while, and I think by now they were looking at the star nation we call Carrier [Big Dipper]. Then the older sister yawned and said to the younger sister, 'Do you see that big star up there—the biggest one?' And her sister yawned and said, 'Yes, I see it.' And the older sister said, 'That is the very star I like best of all.' And the younger sister said, 'Can you see that small star not far away from the big star?' And her sister said, 'Yes, I can see it.' And the younger sister said, 'That is the very one I like best of all the stars.'

"So they yawned and were still for a while, just looking at the two stars they liked best of all. Then the older sister said, 'I think I will marry my star if you will marry your star.' And the younger sister said, 'Yes, let us do that; but I am so sleepy now, I think I will not get married tonight.' And the older sister said, 'I too am sleepy; I can hardly keep my eyes open. We can dream about our stars tonight, and then we can marry them when we are not so sleepy.' And the younger sister said, 'Yes, we can do that.'

"So the two sleepy sisters started walking around the side of the tepee to the opening, for they wanted to go to bed."

"Ho, ho!" exclaimed No Water and Moves Walking, keenly aware of what was about to happen.

"Sh-h-h!" Eagle Voice raised an admonishing forefinger and continued slowly, speaking scarcely above a whisper. "They were in front of the flap and the older sister was reaching to lift it. But she did not lift it."

At this point the teller ceased abruptly, with a surprised stare into vacancy. It was clear by the faces of the three old men that the tale was still unfolding in the tense silence.

"Two men were standing there," Eagle Voice continued, speaking low and with an air of mystery. "They were men, but they were not like other men, for they made the light they lived in, and there was no shadow where they stood. This light was soft and kind, and when the two men smiled, it spread about the sisters so that they were not afraid at all. Then they saw that one man was young and one was very old. The younger one was taller than any man the girls had ever seen; but the older one was even taller. I think he stood above the other like a tree, and the light he made was that much brighter. He was old, old; but he was young too. I think he was much older than the other because he had been young so much longer. I think there are no canes where these men came from, no wrinkled skins, and no uprooted teeth, and no white hairs.

"Then the older man said to the older sister, 'We heard you talking, and I heard you say that you would marry me; so I am here.' Then the younger man spoke to the younger sister, and said, 'We heard you talking, and I heard you say that you would marry me; so I am here.' The girls could not say anything at all, but their hearts were singing in their breasts, and the two men heard. So the older man said to the older sister, 'Put your arms about my neck, and we will go.' And the younger man said to the younger sister, 'Put your arms about my neck and we will go.'

"That is what the sisters did, and so they went.

"It was like eagles flying, only faster, higher than eagles fly. And all at once there was no village down below and no earth. There was only air—blue air, blue air; and nothing anywhere but two men made of light and two girls with their arms about the necks of those, flying fast and higher, very fast and very high. Then all at once there were shining villages of star people on a wide blue prairie, and from all the villages came singing as the fliers passed, for all the people there were happy. And afterwhile there was a village bigger than all the others in that wide blue country, and there the flying men of light came swooping down like eagles to their nests.

"Then the older star-man said to the older sister, 'You are my wife now, and I have brought you home.' And the younger star-man spoke to the younger sister, saying, 'You are now my wife and I have brought you home.'

"The sisters did not say anything at all, but their hearts were singing. And all at once the whole hoop of the village about them was one great song, and all the bright star people came from every side, singing together as they came to welcome their great head chief and his son with their new wives. And the singing was like many happy colors in the brightness of that place.

"So there was dancing as for a great victory, and there was feasting. Four days and nights the people danced and feasted and were glad."

The teller ceased, gazing out and upward as into wide blue air. The two silent collaborators, with their hands upon their knees, gazed also in the same direction, like children lost in wonder. Were they really only feigning for the sly fun of it, or had they for the moment lost the burden of their years?

When, at length, it seemed the tale was waiting for the dancing and the feasting to be ended yonder, No Water turned suddenly upon Eagle Voice with his grieved and anxious look. *"Turnips!"* he prompted in an explosive whisper. Moves Walking fixed a glaring eye upon him, and with a raised forefinger Eagle Voice deplored the interruption. *"Sh-h-h-h!"*

But the spell was broken, and the tale continued. "So the two sisters lived with their husbands among the bright star people, and they were happy. Then one day it was the time when the turnips are getting to be good, and there were many growing on the wide blue prairie. So the older sister said to the younger sister, 'I think my husband would like to eat turnips, so I will go out and dig some.' And the younger sister said, 'I think my husband likes them too, so I will go along with you, and we will dig some.' Then they made themselves two sharp sticks and went out to dig the turnips that were growing big and juicy on the wide blue prairie.

"Many other women were out there getting turnips for their husbands, and they were all happy and joking together as they dug. One of these was a wise and good old woman, and the great head chief was her son. So she came over to the older sister and said, 'Daughter, you are already big in the belly, and I see it will not be long until I shall have a grandchild. So I wish you would be very careful, and do not press the stick against your belly when you are digging, for that might hurt the baby.' And the older sister said, 'I will be careful, Mother.' And she was.

"But it was much harder to dig the turnips if she did not lean against the stick, for then she had to do it all with her arms. She had to chop with the stick, and it was not easy to make the sharp end go deep enough. So she was chopping harder and harder, harder and harder, harder and—"

The tale stopped with a shock of surprise. *Ah-h-h-h!* Open-mouthed, wide-eyed, No Water and Moves Walking stared appalled upon an approaching catastrophe.

"Chop—chop—chop," the teller resumed slowly, wielding an imaginary turnip stick. "Chop—chop—chop—*chop!* It was too hard that time, and all at once the blue ground broke wide open right under the older sister, and she fell head-first through the hole. The younger sister screamed and came running, and all the other women screamed and came running; but they could not do anything at all. So they all crowded around the hole in the sky prairie and looked and looked. They saw the older sister tumbling over and over, over and over, getting smaller and smaller, smaller and smaller as she fell. And then they saw nothing at all.

"It was a long way down to the earth, and I cannot say how many sleeps the older sister fell. But afterwhile she got here, and when she struck the ground she broke wide open, pop!—just like a seed-pod—and a baby boy rolled out on some thick, soft bunch grass that was growing there. I think some buffalo manure made the grass soft and thick in that place, so the baby boy did not get hurt at all."

"That will be *me!*" exclaimed No Water, with an air of gloating triumph. "No, it will be *me!*" challenged Moves Walking, the off-eye glaring, although the rivals were grinning at each other. Clearly, the explosive interruption at this point in the story was a traditional obligation of the co-operative hearer.

Eagle Voice raised a conciliating forefinger and smiled benignly upon the two, like a kindly grandfather silencing over-eager children. "It was a good day," he continued; "and so the baby was just lying there in the bunch of thick soft grass with his thumb in his mouth. And afterwhile there was a magpie who saw something and came to look. This was an old-woman magpie, and she walked around and around the baby, with her head on one side and then on the other, for I think she had never seen anything like this before."

[With cocked heads, the three collaborators curiously examined the baby in the grass for a few moments of silence.] "But a magpie knows everything, and when this one had looked for a while, she said to herself, 'This is a baby of the two-legged people without wings. It has four legs, but it is not a four-legged because it has no fur, and all four-leggeds have fur.' Then she said to the baby, 'You *are* a fine big baby, and you *are* a boy too, aren't you?' And the baby said, '*Goo-oo,*' like that. And the magpie said, 'But how are you going to live, for I see your mother lying dead over there?' Then the baby took his thumb out of his mouth and began to cry.

"This made the old-woman magpie feel very sad, and she said, 'Somebody must come and take care of this baby that has no mother. I cannot, because I have to fly around and talk so much that I could never take care of him. And if I did not fly around, telling people everything, how would they ever know anything?'

"So she flew away; and as she flew around all over the prairie, she kept crying out to the four-leggeds and the wings of the air and those that crawl on their bellies in the grass, and she said, 'Come quick! Come quick! There is a two-legged baby without a mother! Come

157

quick and help! Come quick and help! There is a baby without a mother!'

"So in a little while all the four-leggeds and all the wings of the air and all of those that crawl on their bellies in the grass were going to see the baby without a mother. They were coming from all sides, galloping and crawling and flying; and when they came to where the baby was lying in the soft, thick grass, they made a big hoop all around it. Everybody was there except the finned people. They had to stay in the streams and lakes, and that is why they did not come to see.

"Then the old-woman magpie stood beside the baby in the center of the hoop of peoples, and she made her voice big and sent it forth like this: 'Wings of the air, four-leggeds, and belly-crawlers, you have come to see the baby without a mother. Here you see him lying all alone with no one to care for him. Will you let him die here on the prairie?'

"Then she pointed her long nose at the bison bull, and said, 'You are the biggest and strongest of all the four-leggeds. Will you not take care of this baby?' And the bison bull said in his voice like thunder, 'My wives and I would like to take this baby, but we have no tepee at all to live in, and the baby would die.'

"Then the magpie-woman pointed her sharp nose at the bull elk, and said, 'Elk, you are almost as strong as the bison, and you could carry the baby in your antlers. Will you take care of him?' And the elk said, 'Even though I am stronger than the bison, I cannot take care of this baby, for I have no tepee but the sky.'

"So the magpie-woman spoke to the grizzly bear, and said, 'Bear, you are very big and very strong, and you have a warm den to sleep in. *You* could look after this baby that has no mother.' And the bear said, 'I wish I could take this baby, for he is much like a cub, except that he has no fur. Maybe he would get some fur afterwhile. But I cannot take this baby. You all know I am a very hard sleeper, and when I go to sleep I do not 'waken for a long while. Who would feed this baby while I was sleeping? He would starve before I could 'waken; or maybe I would roll over on him in my sleep.'

"Then the old-woman magpie spoke to each of the other four-leggeds in turn, the bigger ones before the smaller ones. They all felt sorry for the baby without a mother, but not one of them could take him. The wolf and his wife had too many children already. The jack rabbit and his wife also had all the children they could feed. The gopher's home was too small, and the mouse's was even smaller.

"Just then the magpie saw the snake standing up on his tail, so that he could look upon the baby without a mother. She could see that there were tears in the snake's eyes, and he was moving his head back and forth in sorrow. So the magpie thought, 'Here at last is one who will take the baby,' and she said, 'Snake, can you not take this baby into a cave somewhere and look after him?' And the snake said, 'My wife and I would like to have the baby, for often we are lonely. We could bring him frogs and mice to eat, and we could scare all the bad people away so that he would be safe. But we must not take this baby. Nobody likes us, and it would be bad for him to grow up with us.' Then all at once he was afraid again, and he slid into the grass and flowed away like fast water, making a sound like *sho—sho—sho sho—sho sho*.

"So the old-woman magpie pointed her sharp nose towards the wings-of-the-air who were sitting together on their side of the hoop of peoples. And when she saw the eagle, she said, 'Eagle, you are the great head chief of all the wings of the air, and you always make a kill. You are so strong that the baby could ride on your back between your wide wings. I am sure *you* can raise this baby that has no mother. And the eagle said, 'Yes, I am chief of all the winged ones because I am the strongest of them all, and I always make a kill; but I cannot take this baby, for I live in such high places that it is always cold up there, and the baby would get sick and die.'

"While the eagle was talking, everybody was very still, and when he was through, nobody said anything for a while. You could hear the baby whimpering in the grass. Then all at once the wren sent forth a small thin voice, and she said, 'If I were as big as some of the winged ones around here, I myself would take this baby to raise, for it makes me sad to hear him crying for his mother. Small as I am, I would take him anyway, but my tepee is so little I could never get him into it. I think Hawk could take him. *He* is big and strong, and *he* does not live high up where it is cold.'

"When the tiny oriole heard the wren putting it out so boldly, it made her brave too, and she sent forth *her* thin little voice. 'I am small too, and little as *I* am, I would take this baby; but my tepee is so narrow that even I can hardly get into it. I too think Hawk should raise the baby. He can always get something good to eat.'

"'Who! Who! Who!' cried the owl, which is the same as when we say 'how! how!' And the bluejay screamed, 'hiyay! hiyay!' It pleased them to hear the smallest of the winged ones making so brave.

"Eagle turned his head slowly and looked hard at Wren and Oriole. Hawk turned his head slowly and looked hard at Wren and Oriole. All the people were looking too, and they saw Wren and Oriole fluffing up their feathers and pulling their heads in, the way they do when they are cold; for all at once they did not feel brave at all."

The story-teller paused, turned his head slowly, and cast a penetrating hawk-stare upon No Water and Moves Walking; whereat they hunched their shoulders, drew in their heads, and were frightened little birds, but they were grinning. With an approving grandfatherly smile, Eagle Voice continued:

"When Hawk had looked hard for awhile, he said, 'You know I have no relatives. You know I do not belong with anyone. You know that everybody is my enemy. How could I raise this helpless being with no wings?'

"Nobody said anything at all for a while, and it was so still you could hear the baby whimpering in the soft bunch grass. Then the old-woman magpie said, 'Will nobody take this baby to raise? Will he die here on the prairie all alone?'

"When the baby heard this, he began crying very hard. So the prairie hen felt very sorry for the baby, and she said, 'I think Mudswallow ought to take this baby. She has a good home and she daubs it up so that it is safe and warm. I think she could raise this baby.'

"And Mudswallow answered, 'It is true that I have a good snug home, for I am very careful how I build it. But it is high up on the bank, and even if I should build it big enough, the baby would fall out and be killed.'

"'Heh—heh—heh! Heh—heh—heh!' said the kingfisher. He was feeling very sad, for it seemed that nobody at all was going to help the baby live. And when it was so still that there was nothing to hear but the baby crying in the soft grass, the kingbird sent forth a voice: 'I know who can raise this baby! Meadowlark can do it! He can build a big nest around where the baby is now lying! It will be no trouble at all! Meadowlark is just the one to raise this baby!'

"When the people heard this, they all made the happy noises they knew how to make, and for a while the hoop of peoples was one big sound. Then when they were still again, Meadowlark hopped out to the center of the hoop and sent forth a very kind voice that was like little waters falling into a quiet pool, and he said, 'Kingbird is right. My wife and I can take care of the baby, and we will. I did not say so before, because so many here are greater than I am. We can build a big soft nest all around the baby where he is lying, and we can bring him plenty of seeds and worms to eat. It will be no trouble at all. Our children can play with him, and he will make our home happier.'

"When Meadowlark had said this, his wife sang a song of joy she knew, and it was like sweet water gurgling when everything is thirsty. Then the wings of the air and the four-leggeds and the crawlers in the grass sent forth one great voice—squawking and squealing, chirping and screaming, barking and howling and whistling; and the bison cows lowed and the bulls thundered. That is how glad they were to know the baby would not die all alone on the prairie. They were so glad, I do not know how far away they could be heard; but all the finned peoples heard, and leaped and glittered in all the lakes and streams. I think the star nations also heard and began singing together all over the heavens; but this I do not know, because they are so far away.

"So that is how it was; and soon the hoop was broken up and all the peoples scattered to their homes, galloping and flying and crawling. And the baby went to sleep with his thumb in his mouth.

"Of course, old-woman magpie could not go away with the others. She had to stay there awhile and help. So she sat on top of some brush near by and told Meadowlark and his wife what they must do and how they must do it. Sometimes she would scream at them and say, 'No, not *that* grass! It is not soft enough for the baby! And you are not making the nest big enough! Don't you know this baby is going to grow? *Bigger! Softer!*' All the while Meadowlark and his wife went on building the nest around the baby the way they learned from their grandparents. But they were very kind people, and sometimes they would say, 'Yes, Grandmother—you know best, Grandmother. —we thank you for helping us, Grandmother.' And so afterwhile the nest was finished, and the baby sleeping in it with his thumb in his mouth.

"Then old-woman Magpie hopped down and walked around the nest, turning her head this way and that way to see what she thought of it. And afterwhile she said, 'It is not built as I would build it, but it will do. Now you must take care of the mother's body lying over there. You are not strong enough to build a scaffold for it, so you must cover it up with grasses and little stones; for if you do not, her spirit will make trouble for you. And when you have done this, one of you must mourn all night by the body while the other watches the nest. I cannot stay longer to help you, for I have so much talking to do in so many places that I shall never get it all done if I do not hurry.'

"So old-woman magpie flew away as fast as she could flap her wings.

"The sun was nearly down. It was very still in that place. For a while Meadowlark and his wife stood beside the soft, warm nest, just looking at their big new baby sleeping. And afterwhile Meadowlark said, 'He must have a name. What do you think would be a good name?' And his wife said, 'Let us call him Falling Star.' And her husband said, 'That is a very good name. I like it. So let us call him Falling Star.' And they were so happy that they forgot about the work they had to do, and they began to sing together like little waters falling into a quiet pool. You can hear them do that yet if you listen in the evening.

"Then all at once they remembered what they must do next. So they began working as fast as they could, carrying grasses and little stones to cover the mother's body. When the work was done, it was night.

"Then Meadowlark and his wife took some bison tallow that they had for their children, and this they mixed with red clay to make sacred paint. With this paint they greased the baby all over, and when this was done, they fed him some fine big earth worms that lived down by the creek, also some seeds that they had chewed to make them soft. The baby felt so good he went to sleep again right away. And all the star nations came forth to look upon the baby sleeping in his soft, warm nest, and the mother meadowlark watching there, while her husband sat beside the mound of grass and little stones and mourned in his throat.

"Meadowlark and his wife had been working very hard, and I think they could not stay awake long. The morning star came to see, and they were sleeping. He stood higher and higher, but they did not 'waken. The star nations were very tired from watching all night, so they all began going to sleep—the little ones first and then the big ones. The morning star got sleepy too and went back to his tepee.

"Then all at once the mother meadowlark awoke, and the young day was everywhere. She looked first at the nest. Then she screamed. It was empty. She screamed and screamed until her husband awoke and came hopping and flopping his wings. 'What is the matter? What is the matter?'

" 'Our baby is gone! Our big new baby is gone! Somebody has taken Falling Star! What shall we do? Eagle has stolen him, or maybe Hawk! What shall we do?' The mother meadowlark was crying very hard.

"Meadowlark was so frightened that he could hardly talk, but he had to make brave, so he said, 'No, no! Eagle did not want him. Hawk did not want him. Nobody stole him, because we are the only ones who want him. Stop crying, and let us look around.'

"So they began looking around, and all at once they were very happy again. For over yonder, not very far away, Falling Star was sitting up among some flowers that were growing there, and he was playing with the flowers and saying '*Goo-oo*' to them."

"*Hiyay! hiyay!*" applauded No Water and Moves Walking, mindful of their privilege and duty as sympathetic hearers. The tale continued:

"When Meadowlark and his wife hopped over there in a hurry, they could hardly believe it. 'See how our Falling Star has grown!' the wife cried, flapping her wings. 'He is nearly twice as big as he was!' cried the husband, flapping his wings. Then they were so happy that they raised their heads and sang—like two little waters falling together into a quiet pool. And the young day was still to listen. You can hear them yet, if you listen in the still morning.

"Then Meadowlark said to his wife, 'Woman, this baby is getting too big to live on worms and seeds. Already he can crawl, and tomorrow maybe he will walk. I heard Grandmother Magpie say once that two-leggeds without wings like to eat bison and are always hunting them. So I think I will go hunting today.' And that is what he did.

"The day was young when he started. He hunted and hunted, and the sun was above him. He hunted and hunted, and he saw many bison, many, many; but they were very big and he had no bow and arrows, so he went on hunting. The sun was halfway down, and still he was hunting. Then all at once he saw a dead bison calf, and wolves and crows feasting there. So he thought, 'I am small. If I can sneak in there where they are feasting, maybe nobody will notice me and I can get some bison meat for the baby.'

"So he sneaked through the grass, making himself even smaller than before, until he was right in among the feasters with their bloody beaks and muzzles. He was afraid, but he had to feed the baby. The wolves were snarling and snapping at each other while they ate, and the crows were quarreling because they all wanted the pieces of meat the others had. While they were doing this, Meadowlark sneaked between the legs of the wolves until he was inside the dead calf that the wolves had torn open. And right in front of him was a big fat liver!"

"*Washtay!*" exclaimed No Water and Moves Walking. "*Washtay!*"

"Meadowlark had to hurry, because the crows might notice him in there and kill him. So he pecked and pecked as hard and fast as he could; and in a little while he had cut off a big chunk of fat liver. But how was he going to get out of there with the liver? He was thinking about this, and then all at once he could hear the wolves fighting harder than ever outside, and the crows flying about with whistling wings and loud battle cries. He peaked outside, and all the wolves were snarling and yelping and snapping and rolling over each other. Some of them were trying to run away with the calf's entrails, and the others wanted them too. So there was a big fight, and I think the crows were cheering the four-leggeds. Maybe if they all killed each other, the crows would have more meat for themselves, and that is why they were cheering.

"Meadowlark thought it was a good time to sneak out of there. So he began pulling the piece of fat liver a little at a time. Nobody noticed him. He pulled it a little more. Everybody out there was fighting and yelling so hard that nobody knew Meadowlark was around. So he got a good hold on the piece of fat liver, jumped outside with it, and began flying. The liver was so heavy that he could hardly keep above the ground; but he thought about the baby and how glad his wife would be, and that made him stronger. Maybe it was good that he had to fly so low. Maybe if he had been stronger, the crows would have seen him."

"Maybe the star people helped him with their power," No Water remarked. "*Dho*," agreed Moves Walking, with a solemn air of finality, "the star people helped."

"I think that is how it was," Eagle Voice continued with a grand-fatherly smile; "the star people gave him power. But he was so small that he had to stop often and pant. Then he would fly some more; then he would stop and pant awhile.

"Then when the sun had just gone under, Meadowlark got back home with the fat liver—"

"*Hiyay! hiyay! hiyay!*" Slapping their knees, the collaborators applauded, like delighted children, grinning at each other the while.

—"And his wife was so happy that she made a new song for her happiness. From the top of the brush near by she sang her new song, and it was like this." Eagle Voice fitted the Sioux words, meaning "calf liver rich," to the familiar notes of the meadowlark's song.

"*Pin-hin-chla pinapin!*
Pin-hin-chla pinapin!

"That is the song she made for her happiness, and the prairie was still to hear it. If you listen in the quiet evening you can hear it yet.

"*Pin-hin-chla pinapin!*
Pin-hin-chla pinapin!

"So they had a big feast, and the baby ate most of the liver. After this, they greased the baby all over again with the sacred paint, and pushed the soft nest close about him, and he slept.

"Next morning Mother Meadowlark awoke early, just when the morning star had come to see. She looked first at the nest, and again it was empty. But she did not scream that time! Instead, she looked around; and what do you think she saw?"

"Walking already," said No Water eagerly.

"Dho," continued Eagle Voice. "That is what he was doing down by the creek; and where he walked it was like day, for a light came out of him all over.

"So Mother Meadowlark whispered to her husband, 'Wake up and see! Wake up and see!' And when he awoke and saw, they both just stood there looking hard, with their beaks wide open. For they did not see any baby at all. They saw a fine big boy walking there, and he was making a little day about him where he walked.

"When the morning star went back to his tepee and all the star nations slept and the sun came, they ate what was left of the liver. Then Falling Star spoke for the first time, and he said, 'I think I will make me a bow and some arrows today.' And he walked away down the creek.

"Meadowlark and his wife waited and waited for their boy to come back home. And when the sun was halfway down the heavens, Mother Meadowlark began to cry, and she said, 'I am afraid something has happened to our boy, and he will never come home.' But her husband said, 'Nothing will hurt him. Did you not see the little day he made where he walked? He is *wakon* and nothing can hurt him.'

"And Meadowlark was right; for all at once they saw Falling Star coming up the creek. And what do you think he was bringing?"

"Muskrat or maybe rabbit!" exclaimed Moves Walking.

Eagle Voice shook his head.

"A big fat beaver?" queried No Water.

"Dho," continued Eagle Voice. "In his right hand he had a fine bow and arrows. In his left hand he had a big fat beaver. And when he came closer, Meadowlark and his wife could see that he had been growing all day. Mother Meadowlark was so happy that she jumped up and down, flapped her wings and cried, 'O see what our grandson has brought us! O see what he has brought us and how big he has grown!' And when Meadowlark tried the bow, it was so strong that even he could not pull it at all.

"So they feasted on fat beaver, and while they feasted, Falling Star told the story of his hunting. Then they slept.

"So it was early morning again, and the nest was empty as before. But Meadow Lark and his wife were not afraid, for they knew Falling Star had gone hunting. They just sat and waited and waited, and wondered what he would bring this time. 'It will be a big jack rabbit, or maybe two,' Meadowlark guessed. But his wife did not think so. 'It will be a fawn,' she said. 'I am sure it will be a fawn, or maybe a bison calf.' And her husband said, 'How could he carry a bison calf or even a fawn? I am sure it will be a jack rabbit or maybe two.'

"While they were arguing, the morning star went back to his tepee and the day was coming over the edge of the world. And when it had come, Falling Star came also, but he was not a boy any more. He was a tall young man, and what do you think he was bringing home?"

"Jack rabbits!" exclaimed Moves Walking. "Two, maybe—big fat ones!"

"It was not so," Eagle Voice went on. "In his right hand he had his bow and arrows, and in his left hand he was holding the legs of a fawn which he carried on his back. Meadowlark and his wife just stood and looked with their beaks wide open. He was so big and handsome that he was a stranger, until he smiled. When he did that, starlight came out of him all over, and it was so kind that he was not a stranger any more. So they had a big feast, and sang much.

"Next morning, Falling Star went hunting again before Meadowlark and his wife awoke. And what do you think he brought home?"

"Big buffalo bull!" blurted Moves Walking.

Eagle Voice shook his head.

"Buffalo cow, maybe?" queried No Water; "—Big fat one?"

"No—o—o!" said Eagle Voice, raising a forefinger by way of emphasizing an important correction. "Two fat calves! That is what he brought. Two fat buffalo calves!"

"Ah—a—a!" breathed the two in unison, dutifully acknowledging error.

"That day, Falling Star made some drying racks, so that Mother Meadowlark could make *papa* of the calf meat, for they could not eat it all.

"Next morning Falling Star went hunting again—"

"Buffalo bull!" exclaimed Moves Walking, his off-eye glaring triumph.

"Fat cow?" queried No Water with his mildly grieved, anxious look.

"*Dho!*" said Eagle Voice. "A fat cow that time. Big fat bull next time. And by now Falling Star was bigger and stronger than any man ever was; and when he smiled, there was starlight all around him. So he made some more drying racks, and they all worked hard cutting the meat into strips and hanging it up to dry.

"Every morning Falling Star went hunting, and he was still getting bigger and stronger. Sometimes he would bring an elk. Then he would bring a fat cow and a deer. Then maybe he would bring an elk and three or four antelope. And afterwhile enough *papa* was drying around the camp to feed Meadowlark and his wife for many snows."

Eagle Voice began fumbling in his long tobacco sack. No Water and

Moves Walking, with hands on knees, leaned towards him expectantly. When the pipe was filled and lighted, Eagle Voice, his merry face emerging from the cloud he blew, said, "I think I will be a little boy now. I have raised Falling Star and made much *papa*. That is the hardest part. Now Moves Walking, my grandson here, and I will listen. No Water will be the grandfather and he will tell us all that happened next."

X I X

The Labors of the Holy One

Hands on knees, we leaned and waited for the tale to continue. Having taken the pipe, No Water drew a deep draught with hollowing cheeks.

"I am very old and wise," he began, speaking out of a slowly thinning fog, "and what I tell, my grandmother told it to me when I was very little like you. She heard it from her grandmother, and she from hers, and she from hers. I must be very careful to tell it right, so that you can tell it when you too are old and wise.

"Meadowlark and his wife had enough *papa* for many snows. When their hungry relatives came to visit, I think there was more than they could eat too.

"Falling Star was bigger and stronger by now than any man ever was, and he was very handsome. I think he looked like the star-chief who was his father, and there was a light that came out of him all over.

"So one day he said to Meadowlark and his wife, 'Grandfather, Grandmother, you have plenty to eat now, and I must go far away, for there is much that I came to do.' When Meadowlark and his wife heard Falling Star say that, it was like waking in the night, and it is still and many stars are looking.

"And Meadowlark said, '*Dho,* Grandson, you are going on a long journey. On that journey you will meet certain people who are sad. Have pity on those people.' Mother Meadowlark did not say anthing; she just sang the song she knew, the one like little waters falling; for she was very proud of the baby, and he so big and strong now.

"Then Falling Star began walking, and all at once he was far away already. Afterwhile, as he walked, he was coming to the top of a hill. There he saw somebody peeking at him." No Water paused to peek, dutifully assisted by the others. "Somebody was peeking yonder, so Falling Star thought he would go and see who was peeking. It was an old man, and he said, '*Hun-hi,* Grandson! Where are you going?' And Falling Star said, 'I am going on a journey, Grandfather.' And the old man

168

said, 'On this journey, there will be difficulties, and you must remember me, always remember me when you meet difficulties. So I give you this.' It was an eagle feather, and that meant the Great Mysterious One. Also it meant that our thoughts should rise high as eagles. Falling Star thanked the old man, and said 'How.' Then he started walking with the feather; and when he looked back, the old man was an eagle and flew away.

"While Falling Star was walking, he came to a little tepee made of grass. In this tepee lived an old, old woman, and when she saw Falling Star coming, she said, 'Hun-hi! My grandson is coming! Falling Star is coming. Grandson, you are on a long journey, and there will be many difficulties, so I give you this.' It was a cap with a hawk's feather in it. 'And I give you this.' It was a long knife. So Falling Star thanked the old woman and started walking again. When he looked back he could see it was a hawk standing back there in front of the little grass tepee.

"We must remember these gifts that Falling Star had, for we shall need them." No Water raised his left hand, counting the gifts on his fingers. "An eagle plume, a cap with a hawk's feather, a big knife. Three! We must be careful not to forget these gifts.

"Falling Star had been walking very far by now, and he was going towards where there is always snow. So it was getting very cold. And when he came to a high ridge he could see a big village in a white valley without grass, and winds were mourning there, and from the tepee tops no smoke came out. Only one tepee gave smoke in all that village. It was much bigger than the others, and it stood to one side all alone. Then Falling Star saw a little tepee made of old hides all pieced together, and from the top there came no smoke; and it was not to the big tepee that he went. When he came to the little patched tepee, the wind was mourning around it and the snow was trying to get in through the patches.

"So he opened the flap, and there inside he saw an old, old man and an old, old woman, and they were huddled together under a patched skin. Then the old man looked up and light came on his face from what he saw. And he said, 'Hun-hi! Our grandson has come at last! Falling Star has come to see us!' Then the old woman looked, and on her face also there came a light from what she saw. And the old man said, 'Grandson, we are having a hard winter. You see this village here. The people are starving, and we are starving too. You saw a big tepee over yonder, and in that tepee lives a man of evil power. All good things are in that tepee, *wasna* and *papa* in plenty, and a warm fire; but this man has the people in his hands and will not let them eat. We are all afraid of him and no one is strong enough to face him, for he is a giant and his name is Wazya [source of snow]. When the people go out to hunt, this man follows them and howls and roars and drives the game away.'"

"*Sheetsha! Sheetsha!*" muttered Eagle Voice and Moves Walking, hunched against the bitter cold of the tale.

"*Dho,*" No Water agreed. "It was bad. And when Falling Star had heard, there came a little boy into the tepee, and he was thin and shivering. And the old man said to Falling Star, 'This is our little grandson, and he too is starving.' And Falling Star said, 'How! I think your grandson and I will go visiting where there is plenty of *wasna* and *papa* and a warm fire.'

"So all at once he changed himself into a little boy just like the old man's grandson, and he was thin and shivering too. And he said 'Now we will visit Wazya.' So the two little boys went out into the white valley with no grass, and the wind mourning there. And the other little boy was not afraid, because Falling Star was with him. Then they came to the big tepee smoking all alone outside the village where no smoke at all arose. And all over the outside of the big tepee more *papa* was hanging than a village could eat in a hard winter. Also *wasna* was stacked all around the tepee. And when Falling Star lifted the flap and looked in, there was a big giant, with long white hair hanging down around his face. You have seen a rocky hillside that looks away from the sun in the Moon of Popping Trees [December]. That is how his face looked. He was sitting by a warm fire, and on the other side there was a giant woman with long white hair hanging around her face, and that was like the same hillside. And back of these, all around the tepee, were sitting many children, and all of them had long white hair, and they were fat.

"When the two thin little boys peeked in there, the giant Wazya looked hard at them, and said '*Hin!*', which meant they were not welcome. 'Why do you come peeking here?' His voice was so big that it made the tepee shake, and the smoke flap quivered. Falling Star made his voice small and said, '*How, kola;* we have come to visit.' And Wazya did not say '*how*'; he said '*hin,*' just like that. And the fat children with white hair stuck their tongues out at the two thin little boys, and they made a sound like snow hissing through dead grass.

"By now Falling Star and the other thin little boy were looking around the big tepee at all the good things to eat. Also, they were looking at the soft warm skins for the giants and their children to sleep in. Then Falling Star saw a big bow and big arrows in a quiver, hanging on a pole. And he said to Wazya, '*Kola,* do you use these when you go hunting?' And Wazya grunted, 'hin.' Then Falling Star said, 'It is the biggest bow I ever saw. You must be very strong to pull it. I wish I could try it.' When Falling Star said this, and he so thin and little, you could hear laughter rumbling deep down in Wazya's belly. When ice is getting ready to break in a river it sounds the same way.

"So Falling Star took the bow down from the pole. It was so big that his two hands could not reach halfway around it. But he remembered his eagle feather, and all at once he lifted the bow with his left hand, and with his right hand he pulled the string back behind his ear. Then the smallest of the giants' little boys pointed to Falling Star and said, 'I know him. He looks just like Falling Star, and he is Falling Star.' Then he just sat and stared like the others. Then there was a big noise like the ice breaking up in a river and the flood smashing through. And there on the ground was Wazya's bow, all in pieces."

"*Washtay! Hiyay!*" Eagle Voice and Moves Walking applauded.

"Wazya did not say anything," No Water continued. "His woman did not say anything. The fat children with white hair did not say anything. They all just sat and stared at the bow all in pieces. It is like that when the winter is old and the sun is warm, and there is no cloud, and no wind blows; but if you listen hard, you can hear little waters." No Water, with his left hand extended and his right hand back of his ear, drew the giant bow.

"So while the giants and their children were staring, Falling Star and the other thin little boy went outside and took all the *papa* they could carry. And the other thin little boy said, 'That boy who spoke to us, he is the one who sometimes sneaks over to our tepee and gives us *papa* to eat. He is not a bad boy.' And Falling Star said, 'We will remember him.'

"So the two thin little boys went back to the little patched tepee with the *papa*; and while the grandfather and grandmother were eating, they heard about Wazya's bow, and were happy again. And while they were eating and hearing, there was a crier going around the village outside, and it was good news that he had for the people. He was shouting, 'Moon Necklace,' for that was the head chief of this village, 'Moon Necklace, the valleys where you used to hunt, they are full of bison! Many bison they have seen in the valleys where you used to hunt! Men, get ready! Women, look to your children's moccasins and sharpen your knives!'

"So the grandfather and grandmother and their grandson and Falling Star went outside. All the people were coming out of their tepees, singing as they came. Even the wind had stopped mourning, and the valley was no longer white. It was all in brown patches, and the tender grass was peeking through.

"So there was a big hunt. Falling Star had only one arrow, but that was all he needed; for he tied his hawk feather on the end of it, and the feather had the sacred power of the hawk, to see and swoop and kill. He would shoot a bison with this arrow, and it would go on through to another bison, and on through to another and another. I cannot say how many, because my grandmother was too old to remember that; but it went through many. Then Falling Star would find his arrow and shoot again, and again, and again. I think the women were very busy by now, cutting up the meat.

"All at once Wazya and his woman and all his children were coming running, and Wazya was roaring, 'Leave my bison alone! Those are my bison, and you cannot have any!' He began putting all the dead bison into a big sack he carried. Then Falling Star grew very tall, taller than any man ever was, and he was burning all over, for he was very angry. When Wazya and his woman and his children saw this, they began to run away. But Falling Star ran faster, and with one swing of his knife he cut off Wazya's head!"

"*Hoka hey!*" cried Moves Walking and Eagle Voice. "*Hoka hey!*"

"And water came rushing out of the giant's neck," No Water went on. "Then with another stroke, the giant woman's head rolled off, and gushing water came out of her neck also."

"*Hoka hey!*" the two cried in unison.

"And when this was done," No Water continued, "Falling Star chased the children and cut off their heads also, the biggest ones first and then the smaller ones. And out of all their necks came running water. So Wazya and his woman and his children were dead, all but one little boy, the smallest of them all. And when Falling Star saw this one, he said to himself, 'This is the boy who sometimes sneaked away from home and fed the old people. I will chase him, but I will let him live.' So he chased the smallest boy into a big crack in the ground, and you could see frost coming out of the crack where the smallest boy hid. If Falling Star had not let that one get away, maybe there would be no winter at all. That is what my grandmother thought. I do not know. But old, old men always say the winters used to be much harder than they are now. Deeper snow! Colder, much colder! Maybe that was before Wazya and his woman and children got their heads cut off. I do not know this, and I must be careful what I tell.

"So the people of this village feasted and danced and sang, every tepee-top gave smoke, and all the valley was green.

"Then the chiefs and the councilors and the *akichita* and the *wichasha yatapika* got together, and in the center of the happy village they made a big tepee of many tepees. And into this place they brought Falling Star that each might thank him in turn for saving the people. And when they had thanked him, the oldest of the *wichasha yatapika* stood up on three legs, and said, 'Falling Star, the people want you to live with them and be their great head chief forever.' And when the people heard this, they all cried, '*Hiyay! Hiyay!*'

"Then Falling Star stood so tall that the people had to look straight up and far to see his face; and it was so bright that it blinded them. But in the darkness of their eyes there was the voice of Falling Star, and the voice said, 'I cannot live with you always, my people, for I have much to do and a long journey to go. But in the moon when cherries blacken, look for me and I will always come again.'

"And when the voice was still and the people looked about them, Falling Star was gone and the high sun was shining on the happy village in the wide green valley."

No Water ceased, and sat in silence, gazing as upon something far away, while Moves Walking and Eagle Voice leaned forward waiting. At length Moves Walking broke the silence with a forceful whisper. "*White crow!*" he prompted.

With that mildly grieved, questioning look of his, No Water turned upon Moves Walking. "Falling Star has gone on a long journey," he said. "I was waiting to see where he went. You know this story so well, Grandfather, you tell it yourself."

"*Dho,*" said Moves Walking explosively, the off-eye glaring, the other revealing a suppressed amusement. "I know this story from my grandfather. Don't bother me, and I will tell it right."

Evidently No Water had become an eager little boy, hands on knees, leaning to hear.

"So Falling Star had to go on another long journey," Moves Walking began, "and he was far away already. He was walking, walking—walking; and my grandfather said you could see where he walked by the flowers. And while he was walking he came to the top of a hill. An old man was standing there, and this old man said, '*Hun-hi*, Grandson, where are you going? And Falling Star said, 'I am on a journey, Grandfather.' And the old man said, 'Grandson, you are going to meet some difficulties. There is a big village yonder. In that village there is no meat, and the children are crying for it. What you must do will be hard, so you must remember me and I give you this.' It was a grasshopper. Falling Star thanked the old man and started walking again. When he looked back, a meadowlark was standing on the hilltop yonder, and that made him feel very kind.

"So Falling Star walked far, and afterwhile he came to another hilltop, and in the valley yonder was this big village the meadowlark man told about. It looked as though nobody was young down there—people sitting by their tepees with their chins on their breasts, boys walking around like old men without canes. And when you listen, you hear little children whimpering and crying, like being very hungry and no meat.

"While Falling Star was looking, he saw a little tepee made of old skins patched together; so that is where he went. And when he lifted the flap an old, old man and an old, old woman were sitting inside with their chins on their breasts. When the old man lifted his head to look, it was shaking, and he said, '*Hun-hun-hi*, here is my grandson! Sit down.' When the old woman lifted her head to look, it was shaking too, and she said, 'It is good that you came, my grandson, for the people are all starving. I can see that you are Falling Star.' And the old man said, 'It is true. We are all starving. When the hunters go out, there are bison; but there is a white crow that talks, and he tells all the bison to run away for the hunters are coming. So no bison are there when the hunters come, and we are starving.' "

"*Sheetsha! Sheetsha!*" commented No Water and Eagle Voice, their heads shaking with feebleness.

"*Dho*," Moves Walking agreed. "It was bad, very bad. So Falling Star said, 'Grandfather, I think you should call the head men of the village here, for I want to say something to them.' The old man felt much stronger now, so he went and told the head men. And when the head men were there, they all said, '*Hun-hun-hi!* It is good! Our grandson, Falling Star, has come to visit us!' And the head chief said, 'We have no meat to give you, for we are all starving. There is a white crow that talks. He always flies ahead of the hunters and tells the bison to go away; and when the hunters come, no bison are there at all, and we are starving.'

"Then Falling Star said to the head men, 'You must do what I say. Set up a tepee in the center of the hoop and make it tight without even a smoke flap; for nobody is going to live in this tepee. Make a little fire in there before you shut it tight. There are bison not far away. I will go there and change myself into a bison. When you come to hunt, there will be only one bison left, for the white crow will tell the others to run away. This one bison will be I, but do not fear to kill and butcher me, for you cannot hurt me. Do not take any meat for yourselves—only enough for the little children who are crying. Then you will see.'

"So Falling Star asked for a bison robe, and this he tied about him. Then he began rolling on the ground and bellowing. All at once he was a big bison bull, and he galloped away to where the other bison were feeding, and the white crow was hopping around among them.

"Soon the hunters were coming, and the white crow began flying around over the bison and screaming, 'Run! Run! The hunters are coming!' All of them ran away from there except one big bull, and he just went on feeding. So the white crow flew down onto the bull's back and began pecking and screaming, 'Did you not hear me, bad one? I told you to run away! The hunters are coming!' But this big bull just made thunder in his belly and went on feeding.

"The hunters were close now, and the white crow had to fly away. But he was watching while the hunters killed and butchered the big bull. When they had butchered they took some tender meat and good warm liver for the little children who were crying, and went back to the village.

"Then the white crow came flying around and around the bull that was butchered, and he was thinking, 'I must be careful. Maybe this is a trick.' But the fresh meat smelled so good that he could not stay away from it. So he hopped around the butchered bison, with his head on this side, then on that side, then on this side, then on that side. [Three heads wagged, illustrating the point.] All the while he was hopping a little closer. When he could not wait any longer he pecked at one of the eyes. But the way the other eye looked at him, he was frightened, and he said, 'This looks like Falling Star's eye.' So he flew away and sat on top of a plum thicket to watch.

"While he was watching, the black crows and the magpies and two hawks smelled the fresh meat and came swooping down on it to feast. This made the white crow hungrier than before, and very angry too. So he came flapping and screaming, 'Get away from my meat! This is my meat, and I will eat it myself!' But nobody listened. So he hopped right inside the butchered bison and began poking around for some good warm liver. *Peck-peck. Peck-peck-peck. Peck-peck-peck-peck.* The meat was good and he was greedy, so he forgot to be afraid.

"That is just what Falling Star was waiting for, and all at once he was not a butchered four-legged any more; for he changed himself into a two-legged and caught white crow by the legs!"

Having silenced the exclamations of triumph with a lifted forefinger, Moves Walking continued: "Don't bother me. I must tell this right.

'Squawk! Squ-awk! Squ-awk-k-k!' the white crow screamed; 'Let me go! Let me go! I will give you my power if you will let me go!' But Falling Star said, 'You have been bad to the people long enough. I will not let you go.' So he went back to the village; and when the people saw him coming with the white crow that was flapping and screaming, they all cried, 'Hiyay! Hiyay,' with one big voice.

"Then Falling Star went to the tepee that the head men had made tight with a little fire inside, and he pushed the white crow in under the bottom of it. All at once it is like Thunder Beings fighting inside that tepee! People all watch and listen! Hardly breathe! Squawk! Squawk! Flap! Flap! Big noise in there! Looks like that tepee is going to fall down! People come running to hold it up. Everybody holding that tepee up. Then all at once, the tepee-top breaks open, and out flies the white crow with the smoke!"

Moves Walking clapped his hands violently, then paused, open-mouthed, to follow the escaping culprit with one astonished, and one angrily glaring eye.

"Sheetsha! sheetsha!" muttered the others, deploring the unfortunate situation. His excitement having subsided, Moves Walking continued.

"No, Grandsons," he said with a reassuring smile, "it was not bad. It was good, very good. The white crow got away, but he was black, black from the smoke, black all over just like all the other crow people. No power any more. Tries to say something to the bison. Squawk, squawk—that is all he can say. Bison let him squawk, go right on feeding. Hunters come. Plenty bison. Children stop crying. Nobody hungry any more."

"Washtay! Washtay!" Eagle Voice and No Water applauded the happy outcome.

"So there was a big feast in that village," Moves Walking continued. "Then Falling Star said to the old, old man and the old, old woman in their fine new tepee, 'Grandfather, Grandmother, there is another village, and they need me over there. I must go on a long journey.' So he went."

After a waiting silence, Moves Walking turned to Eagle Voice. "Grandfather," he said, "you started this. You finish it."

"Chief's arm!" urged No Water.

"Dho," Eagle Voice began. "The chief's right arm. It is stolen and somebody must get it back. So Falling Star was walking again. When he had walked far, he came to the top of a hill, and there was an old man. And this old man said, 'Hun-hi, Grandson, where are you going?'

And Falling Star said, 'I am on a journey.' And the old man said, 'You will come to a big village, and there will be great difficulties. I do not give you anything; but you must remember the gifts you have received already, for you shall need them. This is going to be very difficult.' Then Falling Star said, 'I will remember all my gifts, Grandfather,' and he went on walking.

"Afterwhile there was a high ridge, and in the valley below was this big village. While he was looking, there was a little patched tepee on one side, and he thought, 'That is where I will go.' So he turned himself into a little boy like you, Grandsons—six, seven winters maybe—and went to the little patched tepee. When he lifted the flap and said, 'How,' there was an old, old woman sitting in there all alone, with thin white hair and the point of her chin close to the point of her nose. And she said, 'Grandson, my Grandson, I am so glad you have come! Your grandfather did not come back from the war-path. I am always waiting, but he does not come, and I am all alone here.' And Falling Star said, 'I will stay with you and bring you tender meat, Grandmother.'

"So that is what he did. He would go hunting, and when he was out there he would turn into a very tall young man. Every time he would come back with plenty of tender meat for his grandmother. But when he came back, he would be a little boy again. People did not know who he was, so they called him Lives-with-his-Grandma; and that was his name.

"Then one day his grandmother said, 'Something very bad has happened, Grandson. The Thunder Beings have stolen the head-chief's right arm, and with only his left arm he has no power and cannot protect the people. He has one daughter, and all the young warriors want her for their woman. They have brought many horses, but he waves them away and says, 'Bring me my right arm and I will give her to you.'

"Then Falling Star laughed and said, 'Grandmother, I think I will go and peek at the head-chief's daughter.' So that is what he did. And when he had peeked, he said to himself, 'I will go and find that arm and I will bring it back, for I am Falling Star, and even the Thunder Beings shall not stop me!'

"There was a long line of young warriors waiting their turn to talk to the daughter, and she sitting in front of her tepee. One by one, she waved them away and said, 'The arm! Go find the arm!' So the long line shortened, and Falling Star was the last one. He was a tall young man now. When he looked at the daughter, his eyes were stars in a still night. She looked back at him, and her eyes were stars too, shining in a still clear night. And while they were looking, there was a soft starlight that grew, and it covered them like a lover's blanket, and they were alone together in there.

"Then the daughter said, 'You are Falling Star, and I have been waiting so long. Go quickly and bring the arm, for it is so long that I have waited.' And when Falling Star heard this, all at once he was like the sun when it is rising.

"Then he was gone from there. So Falling Star was walking again. And afterwhile there was an old woman living by a creek. Maybe it was Rapid Creek in Pa Sapa [the Black Hills]. My grandfather thought this, but I do not know. And the old woman said, 'Grandson, I know what you are looking for. I saw the Thunder Beings with the chief's right arm. They came roaring through here. This is going to be the most difficult thing, and you will need help. So I give you this piece of sinew. When you need to go away fast from somewhere, just put a live coal on one end of this sinew, and all at once you will not be there at all. When you come near to Where-the-Bears-Live [Bear Butte], you will see your grandfather, and he will help.'

"Falling Star thanked the old woman and went on walking. Soon he saw an old man standing by his tepee with a blanket around him. '*Hun-hun-hi*, Grandson, you are doing a very difficult thing, I have heard! Come in and eat.' So they went inside the tepee, and it was full of eagles lying down with their wings stretched out—like a robe of eagles on the ground. And while they were eating the old man said, 'As you go, there is a place called He-Ska [White Buttes, north of the Black Hills]. Your grandfather lives there. Be sure to see him before you get to where you are going. And take this feather with you.'

"Falling Star thanked the old man with the eagles and went on. Then he was coming to He-Ska, and on top was a tepee. And from the tepee an old man called down to him. 'Grandson, I am your grandfather. Come up and I will help you.' So Falling Star climbed up, and the old man said, 'It is very difficult, what you are doing, I have heard. I am small but I can help you. Take this.' Then Falling Star saw that the old man was a split-tail swallow, and it was one of his wing feathers that he gave. 'Go on with this,' the old man said. 'You are very near now.'

"So Falling Star thanked the old man and went on into a wide flatland deep in grass. And in that flatland was a big village. I think maybe the people were dancing in that village, because Falling Star could hear drums—like thunder when it sleeps and snores under the edge of the world.

"When Falling Star was going into the village where the thunder slept, there was a thin little voice coming from a bull-berry bush. He looked, and it was a wren. And the wren said, 'I am not much of a man myself, but I can help. Take this feather from my wing, but I want it back. The chief's right arm is in that big tepee you see yonder. Put the feather in your hair and fly over to that woodpile by the big tepee. Then you must say, "Zuya wahi! Zuya wahi! [On the war-path I come]." They will hear and let you in. And be sure to give me back my feather.'

"Then Falling Star said, 'You make me thankful, Holds-back-the-Buffalo [for that was his name]. I will not forget, little Grandfather.' So he put the feather in his hair. All at once he was a wren, and he flew over to the woodpile by the big tepee.

"There was a little boy Thunder Being who came out of the big tepee and heard what the wren was saying on the woodpile. So he went back inside and said, 'There is a wren sitting on the woodpile out there, and he says he has come on the war-path.' Falling Star could hear Thunders laughing inside, and a big voice said, 'A wren on the war-path! Ho ho! Bring him in! A wren on the war-path! Ho! ho!'

"So the little boy caught the wren and took him inside the big tepee that was made of cloud. There were giants sitting around a pot, and the pot was boiling. Falling Star knew they were Thunder Beings the way their bellies rumbled when they laughed, and there were blue jagged stripes all over their bodies. He could see something wrapped in hide hanging from a pole, and what do you think *that* was?"

"*Chief's right arm!*" exclaimed Moves Walking and No Water in unison.

"*Dho*, the chief's right arm! The wren knew it too, and he began saying, '*Zuya wahi! Zuya wahi!*' as loud as he could. Then one of the Thunder Beings roared with laughing, seized the wren and threw him into the boiling pot.

"But the wren was Falling Star, and when he flapped his wings, the boiling soup whirled like a great storm and fell on all the Thunder Beings. They howled with pain; and the way they were feeling around for the wren while they howled, you could see they were nearly blind with the scalding soup in their eyes.

"Then Falling Star seized the arm and flew out of the tepee built of cloud and all on fire with sharp lightning. First, he flew to He Ska where his grandfather Wren lived, and he said, 'Little Grandfather, here is your feather. You have made me thankful. I must hurry.' Then he put the feather of the split-tail swallow in his hair. And as he turned into a swallow, all the Thunder Beings came roaring and howling and flashing with sharp fires. If you have seen how split-tail swallows fly in front of a storm, that is how Falling Star flew. Up and down, back and forth, rise and swoop, he flew and dodged so fast that the arrows of the lightning could not hit him.

"The Thunder Beings were howling and roaring close behind when he came to where his Grandfather Swallow lived; and he said, 'Quick, Grandfather! Take your feather! You have made me thankful! I must hurry!'

"Then he put his eagle plume in his hair. You may think he changed into an eagle, but that is not what he did. He changed into an eagle feather that floated and flew on the back of the great wind ahead of the Thunder Beings. When he came to his grandfather of the eagles, he said, 'Quick, Grandfather! Take back your plume! You have made me thankful. I must hurry!'

"Then he put a live coal on the end of the sinew. And when it sizzled and began to shrink and curl, all at once he was not there at all. He was right in front of his old grandmother's tepee in the big village he had started from. When he looked back, he saw a big, boiling, black cloud full of Thunder Beings that were howling and roaring and shooting blue fire arrows as they came. They were coming fast, and Falling Star thought, 'I have used the powers of the wren, the swallow, the eagle, and the sinew. What can I do now?' He still had his grasshopper and hawk feather, but the hawk would be too slow. When he touched the ground in front of the old grandmother's tepee, he had changed into a little boy again, the one they called Lives-with-his-Grandma.

"He was going to change into the grasshopper so that he could hide in the grass until the Thunder Beings had gone by. But he did not do this, for just then his old grandmother came running out of her tepee with a hatchet. She was very angry, and she was yelling at the Thunder Beings. 'What are you doing to my grandson?' *Whack!* 'This is my little grandson, and don't you dare hurt him!' *Whack! Whack!* 'You go away from here, you bad Thunder Beings!' *Whack! Whack!* The last stroke of her hatchet cut right through the boiling black cloud, and the sun blazed out. That made the Thunder Beings turn and fly away as fast as they could fly, and you could hear them rumbling and howling, rumbling and howling until they were back under the edge of the world."

"*Washtay! Washtay! Washtay!*"

Eagle Voice waited for the applause to cease. After it had ceased, he still sat in silence, as though enjoying the golden peace of a world delivered.

"Maybe he can have the girl now—?" No Water ventured timidly.

"Chief's daughter!" Moves Walking exclaimed.

"*Dho*," said Eagle Voice, smiling benignly upon the two. "The chief has his right arm again and Falling Star has the chief's daughter. Also, he still has his first eagle plume and the hawk's feather and the grasshopper. He did not need these powers; but he is going to have a son when the young grass comes again, and his son must have these, for there are more villages that need help, and his son will help them.

"You come back with the young grass and I will tell you all about it then."

The Battle in the Blizzard

"There was strength in that meat," remarked Eagle Voice, when next we sat alone together in his tepee and the pipe was passed. "Almost as strong as fat bison cow, and even I could chew it. Good meat and stories told with friends make young awhile. When I was getting wood this morning I could smell melting in the wind. It is far to the young grass yet, but I think there will be a little water running before the wind changes. It was like that to eat good meat with No Water and Moves Walking and you, and to remember together."

When we had talked awhile about our two guests at the late feast, the old man said: "They are younger than I am, but Moves Walking is not much younger. No Water was only a boy when we fought the soldiers of the Gray Fox [General Crook] on the Rosebud, and when we rubbed out Long Hair [Custer] on the Greasy Grass. But Moves Walking was almost a young man already, the winter when the thirty Lakota were killed. That was the winter after my first sun dance that I have told you about.

"Yes, Moves Walking was with us when the thirty were killed, and I will tell you how that was. After our fall hunt when we made our winter camp on Powder River with plenty of *papa* and *wasna*, High Horse and Kicking Bear came back from Pa Sapa [the Black Hills] and the hunting with their people yonder. We had talked, the way I told you, about great deeds that we would do that winter; and so they came. It was when the Moon of Falling Leaves was young that they came, and there was not yet any snow.

"Charging Cat was going along with us again, for he had helped us when we drove off all those Crow horses. Nobody ever noticed him much, and he did not talk until he had to do it, like saying, 'Yes,' or, 'No,' maybe, or 'We can do that.' He had a long jaw, and he looked sad, like an old horse. But whatever we would say, he wanted to do that. The four of us were going alone, *maka mani* like the last time. It would be braver that way, and if we found deep snow, there would be no horses to starve—until we got some from the enemy.

"When we were getting ready, people noticed us because we had made names for ourselves. Young men came to us, and said, 'We are men too, and we are going with you.' So when we started, there were many of us. Some were hardly more than boys and some had sons, and some had scars from many fights.

"So when we were all ready, we started southwest, for we were going against the Shoshonis over where the mountains are. We called them snake men, because that was their sign-language name. When we had slept twice, there was a creek with plenty of wood and good water and signs of game, and there we camped to hunt and rest and eat fresh meat.

"We were camping there one sleep, and the sun was just going down again. There was no wind in the brush. Our fires were warm. Meat was boiling in the paunches of deer. They were set up, each with four sticks, and hot rocks made the water boil in them. The soup was smelling good already, along with ribs and entrails roasting over coals. It was not enemy country yet, and we felt safe there.

"All at once somebody was yelling; and when we looked, it was Last Dog running fast towards us down a little hill. He was saying, 'They are coming! Get ready to die here! Enemies are coming!' He was all out of breath when he came to us. 'I was creeping up to the top of a ridge,' he said, and he was panting hard; 'A deer went that way, and I was creeping up, but there was no deer. There were men in the brush! I do not know how many, but there were many. Many! They were peeking out at me, and I came here to tell you. That is why I did not fight and die there. I am a man, and I will die here protecting my brothers.' Then he began singing a death-song.

"Nobody liked Last Dog very much, because he was always talking about how brave he was. Sometimes we called him Big Mouth. But some Crows might be roving around there, so we got ready to fight right where we were. Anyway, the meat smelled good and we were hungry. There were more than fifty of us, and was not one Lakota better than two Crows? We could eat while we were waiting to fight, and that is what we did.

"It was beginning to get dark along the creek when Last Dog jumped up and said, 'Look! They are crawling over the hilltop yonder!' We looked and it was so. They were crawling out of the sky there, and all at once many were charging down upon us, yelling. But they were saying, 'Hoka hey, Kola! Hoka hey, Kola!'

"They were Lakotas from our village, all *maka mani* like us. When we were gone two sleeps, some others thought they would follow, and others followed after them; and they had camped where we had camped. Moves Walking was with them. I think they saw Last Dog coming and wanted to watch him run. Also they were having fun with us.

"So there were about a hundred mouths around the boiling paunches and the fires, eating and laughing that night. Some of the youngsters joked Last Dog about his enemies, and one of them asked when he was going to begin dying. That made Last Dog angry, and he shouted, 'You shall see who is a man around here!' Then his brother-in-law He Crow, who was a good warrior and a quiet man, said, 'Look around you, brother, and count us. We are all men around here.' And Last Dog looked down his nose.

"Next morning we started out again for Shoshoni country. When we had slept once, we walked until the sun was high and we camped in a good place to hunt and rest, for those who had followed were more tired than we who went first. So we were eating there when the sun was just down, and a big moon was coming up. The air was sharp and it was blowing a little from the way we were going. There was a low bank along the creek on that side, and it broke the wind. Our little fires felt good, and we were not looking for enemies yet.

"But all at once—men were there on the bank looking down at us, and they were not some more Lakotas! They were Crows! The country was rough on that side and the wind was at their backs. They were going to camp where we were, and they ran right into us. My mouth was full of meat, but I forgot to chew—I think all of us forgot to chew. They were looking at us and we were looking at them. It seemed long, but I think it would have been only a breath or two, if any of us, Crow or Lakota, were breathing."

Eagle Voice paused to stare open-mouthed. Then he clapped his hands. "*Whang!* One yonder yelled and sent an arrow among us. Then everybody was yelling; and there was nobody on the bank. They were runinng away.

"When we were up the bank, they were strung out and running fast towards a high butte yonder. There were about thirty of them, all *maka mani*. One was leading a horse with a pack and another was running behind, beating the horse with a bow. There was a dog, and he was running and leaping among them and yelping. Maybe he was saying, '*Hoka hey!* It's a good day to die, brothers!' But nobody was stopping to die. We were shooting at them by now, and one of them tumbled. Most of us just couped the man as we ran past, and some boys got the scalp.

There were plenty of scalps running away yonder, and we wanted to stop them before they got to the butte.

"But they had the start and got there first. There was a way up into the butte through some big rocks, and it was narrow at the bottom where the rocks were. Most of them ran in there with the horse, while the others stopped to shoot at us. Then those ran after the others.

"It was beginning to get dark and the big moon was back of the butte yet. They had some guns too, and we shot at each other for a while; but there were many rocks around there and we were scattered out among them. It was getting dark fast, and maybe the Crows were too scared to hit anything. Between shooting we could hear them rolling rocks into the narrow way, and we knew we could not charge up in the dark. So we sent some scouts around the butte to see where the Crows could get down and run away. It was high and steep all around, and they could never get down alive, even if they left the horse.

"There was a rocky draw with brush in it not far from the narrow way up the butte, and we camped in there. The enemy could see the light of our fires, but they could not shoot at us. In the morning we would see what we could do. So we sent men back to bring the paunches and the meat from the other camping place, also the blankets and robes that we had left there. Some took turns watching the opening, and we feasted by many little fires.

"While we were eating, the big moon looked over the butte. The air was sharp without wind. When we listened, there was nothing to hear but a stick popping in a fire, maybe. When new guards went out and the others came back, they had heard nothing up there, and we wondered about this.

"Many were asleep. Charging Cat was snoring in his blanket, but Kicking Bear and High Horse and I were sitting in our blankets by a little fire. The big moon stood tall above the butte. I dozed and awoke. The moon was overhead. There was a voice up yonder in the butte, and it was mourning. Many of those who had slept, sat up and listened. Sometimes the voice was like a falling wind in a tree. Then it rose high and thin, high and sharp and thin, as high as the moon, and fell again like a wind moaning. The dog began to mourn too with a long low howl. Then he would yelp and his voice would rise high and thin, higher than the man's, farther than the moon. Then it would be a low long howl again. Some wolves heard and sang back.

"The voice stopped mourning and the dog was still. High Horse said, 'I think we hit somebody up there.' And Kicking Bear said, 'Maybe they are mourning for tomorrow while they can.' Then the man's voice began again, and it was singing a death-song, and the dog sang too. A guard came running, and said, 'One is singing a death-song! Maybe they are coming down to die here!' So we all got ready to fight. We waited and listened. The man and dog stopped singing. The moon stared and started down the sky. The air was sharp and bright and still. Afterwhile a guard came and said, 'There is no sound up yonder. We have seen nothing move in the moonlight.' New wood cracked on the low fires, and it was loud. Charging Cat began to snore in his blanket. Many slept. I sat and dozed.

"The moon was staring low over the edge of the world. I was shivering in my blanket by the embers. Day was coming and the butte was dark against it.

"When we had eaten what was left of the meat, it was time to go up into the butte. Many wanted to go first, but Kicking Bear, High Horse, and I had started the party, so they let us go. Charging Cat did not say anything. He just came along the way a dog does.

"The others were waiting to see what would happen. And we crawled up over the rocks that the Crows had piled in the opening. There was nobody. So we climbed on up a crooked way among rocks. Sometimes we crawled, then we would lie flat and listen. There was nothing. When we were nearly up the butte, we could see the others waiting, so we waved to them and they started up. The top of the butte was broader than we thought, and almost flat. Some brush grew here and there, and at the far end there were some crooked little trees half dead. We stood and stared around. There was nobody. There was a hawk floating high in the morning. We came to the little trees that were half dead at the far end of the butte top, and looked over. There was a wall of rock straight down to a slope at the bottom. A many-knotted rawhide rope was hanging there, and we saw that it was tied around the thickest little tree.

"The others were running about the butte top, looking down over the steep sides and staring around. When they saw the knotted rawhide rope hanging, some were angry and wanted to follow; but there were more who laughed. Some could not believe all of the story the rope told. How could a horse get down there? Somebody said he just made himself some wings and flew. So it ended in laughing.

"I was almost an old man when I heard all about that night on the butte top. It was long after we had all settled down on reservations, and some of us went over to visit the Crows. There were two old men there who had the ends of their right forefingers cut off, and they were in that party. It was a holy man who told the other Crows how to get away. First he prayed to Wakon Tonka for help, and if help came and they all got home, each man would cut off his forefinger as an offering. Then he told them to cut up their robes in broad strips and tie these together. When this was done, they let two men down over the cliff. If these saw anybody, they would jerk twice on the rope and the others would pull them up again. If there was nobody down there, they would jerk once. After a long while, the two men jerked once, for they had been crawling around and they had seen what we were doing on the other side of the butte. Then the Crows on the butte tied the horse's legs together and let him down over the side with the rope sliding through a crotch of the thickest half-dead tree. There were thirty-two in the party, so there were thirty holding the rope. That was when the holy man with his dog began to mourn so loud. He mourned until most of the men were down too, and then he began the death-song to keep us watching over there while the main party was getting away with the horse. When he stopped singing, two who were left let him down with his dog; then they climbed down with their hands on the rope and their feet against the cliff. It was a good joke on us, and we laughed as friends with the old Crows who told the story.

"But that was many snows afterwards. We had lost our Crows, and, anyway, we were going against the Shoshonis over by the mountains. We traveled two more sleeps, but now we were careful, for it was enemy country. Scouts went before us and behind us, also on our right and left. It was a good country for game and our scouts killed plenty of meat with their bows.

"When we were camping the third time after the Crows fooled us, I awoke in the night. There was no moon. The still dark was soft and full of whispers. Snow was falling thick and the embers of our fire made spitting sounds. I put more wood on, and that wakened Kicking Bear and High Horse. Charging Cat was snoring. If there was no fighting or eating to do, he could sleep. We talked about the snow. It was going to be hard for us, but we were men, and the Shoshonis would not be looking for us in deep snow. Kicking Bear said, 'Dho, it will be hard for us, and the Shoshonis will not expect us. But we are only men and we shall need help if this snow falls deep. Last time we made an offering and came back safe with seventy-five horses; but there was no snow. We must make an offering.'

"Our camp was in the brush by a creek, and there was a hill not far away. We could not see it, but we knew it was there and that is where the three of us went. Charging Cat was snoring, so we did not bother him. What came to us would come to him also. On top of the hill we raised our hands and our faces to where the sun goes down, for from thence comes the power to make live and to destroy. We wanted to live and to destroy our enemies. Kicking Bear had his pipe and he prayed, offering it to the power we needed. If we came home safe with many horses, we would give them all away. Only a few we would keep maybe, for hunting and war. Also, if we should win a great victory, we would dance again, piercing our flesh. When Kicking Bear had prayed, we said, 'hetchetu aloh,' and waited awhile with our hands and our faces to the dark sky, so that the power would go into us. All around us we could hear the still night whispering, and the snow was wet on my face. Then we left the pipe on the hill with the mouthpiece towards the sunset, and went back to where the lights of the low fires looked fuzzy in the snowfall.

"When we had eaten in the morning and were walking again, the snow was three hand-breadths deep, and still it fell and whispered. The air was getting colder and the snow fell finer and finer until it was like white dust. It stopped before we made a camp, and the sun looked out when it was setting. We thought our prayer was heard on the dark hill and our offering accepted.

"We had not seen any Shoshonis, but we knew we were in their country. They would be staying in their winter camps and the snow would help, for they would not be wandering about. Next day was dark with clouds and the wind was changing. We walked slowly, waiting for what our scouts might see. There would be a puff of wind and the snow would whirl about our feet and slide along the ground like snakes —shosho—shosho. Then it would be still; then it would blow again and stop.

"The sun was overhead, but we could not see it. It was halfway down, maybe, and still we could not see it. The wind was getting stronger. Four scouts were out ahead of us and one of them was Last Dog, the big-mouthed one. We came to a ridge and stopped to look over. There was a white valley with low snow hurrying down it, for it lay with the wind that was getting stronger. Beyond the valley was another ridge, and as we looked yonder—" Eagle Voice paused to listen for a moment, then clapped his hands. "Boom!—boom! There was shooting yonder under the far ridge. We crouched there and waited. Maybe we would have to fight right where we were. We waited, with the snow whirling about our knees. We waited; then the four came puffing and running. Last Dog had killed, and he was bragging. He showed a wet scalp and bragged; but the three others looked down their noses. They had seen two horsebacks yonder, a man and a little boy, and the boy was tied to his horse. 'My three friends here,' Last Dog said, 'wanted to hide and let them go, but I am a man and I am not afraid. I could not catch the other, for his horse ran away with him and I am afoot.'

"Many were angry. 'We cannot surprise them now,' they said. 'They will come with horses, and we must fight them where they find us.' Then He Crow said to Last Dog, 'Brother-in-law, we may have to give many scalps for one you have taken too soon.' And Last Dog, being angry, yelled back at He Crow, 'Go and see where your husband butchered! You are afraid to go and see where your husband butchered!'

"That was a bad saying for a brave man to hear, and for a while He Crow looked down and said nothing. He was thinking how it would be if he did not go and they both got back home. Last Dog could say, 'Wife, how did you like the way your husband butchered?' Anyone could laugh. Maybe little boys would hear and point at him and laugh. Then He Crow looked hard at Last Dog, and said, 'Brother-in-law, you know I am no man's woman. I am a man and I can die.'

"He Crow had five brothers and all were with us. When he started alone for the far ridge yonder, we all stood and watched him walking fast. He did not look back. When he was nearly to the valley, the oldest of the brothers said to the youngest, and his name was Running Wolf, 'Stay here. We are going.' Maybe he was thinking of their father and mother and wanted the boy to live and get back home. Then the four older brothers started running after He Crow. When they were halfway down the hill, the youngest brother cried out to the others and started running after them. Then I saw that Charging Cat was going too. He did not say anything; he just started running.

"The wind had been getting stronger, and the light snow was lifting and flying. There were many rocks along the ridge, and we were getting ready to fight there on that high place with the rocks to help us if many Shoshonis came with horses. They would be coming. We knew by the little boy tied on his horse that a winter village was near. They would be coming soon, and it would be better to fight among the rocks.

"When we saw Charging Cat starting down the hill, we looked at each other, Kicking Bear and High Horse and I. Then we started too, running after Charging Cat. The wind was howling down the valley when we crossed it. We were nearly up the hill when I looked back. Some others were coming too. I do not know how many. They were dim in the flying snow. Those ahead were dim in the flying snow; and then they were over the ridge.

"We were coming to the top and there was shooting ahead of us. The sounds were dull and mixed with the wind and snow. I looked back again, and many, like shadows, were coming towards us yonder. Our people heard the shots, and they were not waiting to fight among the rocks on the ridge. They were coming to help us. Then we looked over the top of the ridge ahead. Some horsebacks were coming and shooting. They were floating and blowing with the snow; sometimes only horses' heads and riders blowing in the wind with no legs under them and no sound of hoofs. Our warriors who had gone ahead were in a bunch down there shooting at the horsebacks. We yelled, 'Hoka-hey,' and charged down towards where they stood."

Eagle Voice closed his eyes, and for some time sat in silence. At length he looked at me with half-raised lids and continued in a low, steady voice that expressed no emotion. "Some horsebacks cut us off. We three were together. Kicking Bear pulled us close to him and yelled in our faces, 'Do not get separated! Stay with me and we will die together!' So we clung to him. It was a killing, but not a battle. It was like dreaming. Soon the wind was full of horsebacks floating and flying with the snow, and the cries of men were part of the roaring of the wind around us. We knew the others had come to help us, for some of them stumbled into us as we fought. A horse's head and neck blew out of the flying snow in front of me. We were fighting with our knives. I slashed at the neck. The horse screamed and was gone. We did not look for enemies. We clung close together and struck at horsebacks appearing and blowing in the wind. I had my quirt hanging down my back under my shirt, the way Chagla told me to wear it always in battle. I remembered it and was strong, for it would protect me. But once there was a crowding of horsebacks around us, and I thought we were going to die. Then I remembered the eagle's voice in my vision, 'Hold fast, there is more. Hold fast, there is more.' A horse reared, and Kicking Bear was holding it by the thong on its lower jaw. He was slashing at the throat. I leaped at the man. He struck but could not touch me. High Horse and I pulled him off, and he would not fight again. We did not stop to scalp him.

"It was like dreaming, and then it was like waking in the half-dark. We three were alone together and there were no horses in the wind. The day was going blind, and the snow howled and whirled. We had not seen Charging Cat.

"Kicking Bear pulled us close together and yelled in our faces, 'Keep the left shoulder to the wind and cling to me.' We knew that would set our faces towards home. So we clung together and walked with our left shoulders to the wind. Then it was black, and the darkness howled and was full of whips. We stumbled often. Once we fell over a creek bank into drifted snow. It was warmer there and the drift was soft. Kicking Bear would not let us stay. We could not start a fire, and if we did not walk we would die. We stumbled into some big rocks, and when we tried to climb over, there was a wall. So we went to the right. The wall broke the wind, but the drift was deep, and we wallowed in it until the wind struck us again, and we could keep it on the left shoulder. Afterwhile the dark was going. The day came howling, and it was blind with flying snow. We could not stop, and so we walked and walked with the wind upon our left.

"There was a creek hollow with brush in it, and some stray bison were standing there behind the brush with their heads down. We ran right into them and they did not move. They seemed asleep, and we killed three with arrows. It was easy to drive the arrows back of the forelegs, and we were hungry. While we butchered, the others moved away and disappeared in the flying snow. The hot blood froze on our fingers, but we got them skinned, and in the brush we made a shelter of the fresh hides before they were too stiff with the cold. We could light a fire in there, and when we had feasted on raw liver, Kicking Bear told us to sleep awhile and he would watch the fire. I was dreaming about Charging Cat when Kicking Bear 'wakened me. Then he slept, and afterwhile I 'wakened High Horse and slept again.

"When night was coming, we were all awake and very hungry. So we feasted. It was hard to cut the ribs apart before we broke them off. The frozen meat was like wood. While we roasted the ribs and ate, we talked about the others back yonder and how many would get home. Would Big Mouth get away? We wished him dead. But most we talked about Charging Cat. Was our prayer heard on the dark hill and our offering accepted? Were we not feasting, safe and warm? Would the power protect him too? Or would it pass him by because we did not take him with us to the dark hill? We wondered about this.

"Next day the wind was dead. The sun came pale between two cold fires. The air was like a knife.

"The next day after that we started home with all the meat we could carry through the snow. We blackened our faces against snow blindness with charred sticks from the fire.

"It was a long road, and the cold did not soften. When we came to our village on the Powder, Big Mouth and another were there. They were telling brave stories of the fight and were mourning for so many comrades dead. They told of horses taken in battle from the Shoshonis, and when the fight was over, they had ridden until the horses died. We did not speak to them, and people wondered. Maybe they did not fight at all. Maybe they caught loose horses straying yonder in the snow, while we were killing riders, and started home. They could have found our second camp back before the night. I do not know. It was a good place to camp.

"People waited for their sons and brothers, and some for their fathers. Two would come, and three, and four, with frozen feet and hands, and some snow-blind. There were no songs of victory and no feasts with brave stories. We were beaten and ashamed. People waited and waited, and when a moon had passed, there was mourning in some tepees. And when another moon had died, there was more mourning. He Crow did not come back, nor his four brothers. Only the youngest brother, Running Wolf, came back. The young grass appeared, and there were thirty who never came. We did not see Charging Cat again."

The Cleansing of a Kills-Home

"I have been thinking of Last Dog, the big-mouthed one," Eagle Voice began. Having attended to the fire, I had waited over long, while the old man sat with closed eyes and drooping head, blowing softly now and then upon his thumb-polished eagle-bone whistle. "Also I have been thinking of He Crow and his brothers—of Running Wolf, the youngest, most of all.

"Running Wolf was sick that winter and people said that he would die. There was mourning for his brothers in his old father's tepee where he lay. He was hot all over with a fire that burned inside, and he would cry out to his brothers in the battle. He would cry out, 'Wait for me! I am coming! Look back, for I am coming!' and try to get up. No *wichasha wakon* could help him. The bad spirit would not go away, and people said that soon he would go to his brothers.

"But he did not die. When the young grasses were appearing [April], he got up and walked again. His face was sharp, and he was thin and feeble, like an old man who has come at last to where the cane is. Also he was like a ghost that comes and goes and will not talk to anybody. People said he was *witko*, and tried not to notice him.

"I think the moon when ponies shed [May] was young when he disappeared. His father's best horse was gone too, and people talked and talked. Maybe he was going forth to find an enemy and die. Maybe it was like dreaming, the way he was, and some *witkokaga* [crazy-making spirit] told him he could find his brothers. The moon grew big, and withered, and was dead in the dark. Then Running Wolf came riding back. He was coming over the ridge, and the sun was going down behind him. His horse was walking slow, and he was singing. All around the village people watched him from their tepees to see what he would do, for when a man is *witko* he is *wakon* [mysterious, sacred], and whatever he will do they let him do it. When he came to the opening in the village hoop, he stopped his horse, and we could see that his face was blackened and his hair was cut off. He sat upon his horse and sang a song that he had made, and the people, looking from their tepees, listened. The song was like this, but I cannot remember to sing it right.

"In a far country I have seen.
Their bones I have seen.
The wings of the air have feasted
And the wolves are fed.
On a lonely hill I have seen,
In the country of the stranger;
And my heart is cut into strings.

"Four times he sang it, sitting there on his horse; and while he sang, he wept. Then he started his horse and began riding at a walk about the hoop to the left, in the sacred manner. When he had ridden a little way, he began singing again, and it was a death-song. He looked straight ahead and sang, and the people watched him.

"When he came to Last Dog's tepee, he stopped his horse and cried, 'Last Dog, come out and look at me! You are a brave man, Last Dog! Come out and make my heart glad!'

"Then Last Dog came out, and after him his woman, who was He Crow's sister, and Running Wolf's, and she was holding her man back by his arm. When Last Dog straightened up from stooping through the flap and looked at Running Wolf, they say he tried to smile, but only looked sick all at once. He was saying, 'Kola, kola [friend],' and was holding out his hand. And Running Wolf looked hard at Last Dog for a while, and said, 'I have seen where Last Dog butchered.' Then he leaped from his horse upon Last Dog and bore the man to the ground. His knife was out, and the people near by saw it slash the throat, and stab and stab into Last Dog's breast, and with each stab, he grunted, 'hawnh!' It was still around the village where the people were looking; still between one breathing and the next. Then the woman screamed and seized her brother. But he threw her off and leaped upon his horse, and cried, 'Let my brothers come and see where Running Wolf has butchered!' And then he put his horse into a run and fled, not through the opening into the village but through the hoop of tepees; and the people watched him over the ridge.

"That night the sister mourned in Last Dog's tepee; and there was mourning in the tepee of the dead man's father, Standing Hawk. Some of us who had fought Shoshoni horsebacks in the snow listened that night and talked. A young woman could find another man, and maybe a better one, when her hair grew long again. But Standing Hawk was old, and Last Dog was the only son he had left. We did not say evil things of Last Dog, for his spirit would be hearing; and we did not call him Big Mouth; but we did not like him, and Running Wolf we liked, for we knew how it was in his heart. We talked of Standing Hawk and of his sorrow. He was a good old man. Everybody liked him, and he was one of the *wichasha yatapika*, men of whom no evil could be said. For he was a great warrior when he was younger, and he had always given to the needy; and often when men spoke of *wachin tanka* [magnanimity], they remembered stories about him.

"We talked of Running Wolf too, hardly more than a boy, and of what he had done. Hardly more than a boy, and a *te-wichakte* [kills-home, murderer], and all the people against him. We spoke low when we spoke of him, for he had done the worst thing a man can do; and we liked him. Maybe we would have done it, too, with five brothers feeding the crows and wolves yonder. But we spoke low when we said it, for it was the worst thing that he had done. Kill a stranger, many strangers, and the people cried, *'hiyay,'* and sang the victory song, and danced the victory dance. Kill a Lakota and you killed a home, you broke the sacred hoop of the people a little. Maka [the Mother Earth] herself you struck when you killed. It was the worst thing a man could do.

"When the day came, the council got together; and when they had talked, they sent for two *akichitas,* and to them the head chief said, 'Find Running Wolf and bring him here. If he will not come, then leave him for the crows to eat where you find him.' And the two *akichitas* rode away.

"They did not have very far to go, for the day was still young when we saw three horsebacks coming over the ridge; and Running Wolf rode in the middle with his chin upon his breast. Afterwards I heard how they found him sitting on a hill and weeping, with his horse grazing near. I think he had been crying there all night, and his anger was washed out of his heart. When the two rode up and stopped their horses, he stood, and looked at them; and if he had been *witko*, he was not so any more. He just said, 'I am ready.'

"While the three came riding, the people were out in front of their tepees, watching all around the hoop. Old Standing Hawk was sitting in front of his tepee, with his dead son, Last Dog, lying beside him, washed and dressed, ready for the world of spirit. They had not wrapped the dead man yet, so that the kills-home might look upon his face again. In the center of the hoop the council and the chiefs and the *wichasha yatapika* were sitting, watching too. And there was nothing to hear but the voices of the mourning ones.

"The three rode in through the opening and around the hoop, to the left, with their horses walking slow, until they came to where the old man sat beside his dead son. There they stopped and waited, facing the mourner, and in the middle Running Wolf sat upon his horse with his head hung low. When they had waited so for a while, old Standing Hawk lifted his face to Running Wolf and said, 'Come here and sit with me, young man.' Running Wolf got down and came. Then the old man pointed to the body on the ground and said, 'Sit there upon him while I speak to you.' And Running Wolf sat down upon the man he killed, with his face in his hands. Then Standing Hawk raised a mourning voice, like singing, and said, 'I had a son, and he was all I had. One son I had, and now my son is dead, and I am old, and there is none to look to in my need. One son I had and Running Wolf has killed him. My days are made empty now, and I am old.'

"People near by saw Running Wolf's shoulders shaking and tears running through his fingers.

"Then Standing Hawk took his pipe and filled and lit it, and to the four quarters of the earth he offered it and to Wakon Tonka and to Maka, the mother of all. And when this was done, he held the mouthpiece of the pipe towards Running Wolf, and said, 'Look up and do not fear.' And Running Wolf looked up with tears upon his face, and took the pipe and touched it with his mouth. And when the people saw this done, they knew that he was sorry and would do whatever he was told; and with one voice they cried, '*Hiyee!* Thanks! *Hiyee!*'

"When the voice of the people was still, Standing Hawk spoke to Running Wolf again, 'My son, you have done the worst thing a man can do, but I have seen your tears and looked into your heart. Do not be afraid of anything, my son, for when you come again to me and are cleansed with lamenting, you shall be my son until I die.' Then he asked that a cup of water be brought to him; and when it was brought, he gave Running Wolf to drink, and tears fell into the cup. Then Standing Hawk said, 'Bring food that my son may eat.' And when meat was brought to him, he cut it up himself and gave it to the killer of his son, and Running Wolf ate a little of the meat with his tears upon it.

"Then the oldest man among the *wichasha yatapika* stood up among his brothers where they sat. He leaned upon his cane and looked around the hoop where the people waited for his words, and his head shook. They listened hard, for he was feeble and his voice came thin. 'My people, this day we have seen something that was given to the *wichasha yatapika* when they were chosen. It is a hard thing to do that we have seen, but a man whom all praise must hold fast to his pipe and do what he was taught when he was asked to sit among us. He was told that a wounded dog with an arrow in his body would be brought to him, but he would not be angry. He would hold fast to his pipe. This is what was meant. This is what we have seen; and Standing Hawk has not forgotten. His son has been murdered and brought back to him. You have seen him hold fast to his pipe and remember what he was taught. It is *wachin tanka* [magnanimity] you have seen, and it is good to see.' Then the old, old man looked at Running Wolf sitting there upon the dead man, with his tears upon his face, and said, 'Young warrior, my grandson, you have taken the place of him you killed. But first you must be cleansed by praying and lamenting. To the four quarters you shall go forth, and there shall be only strangers everywhere. The faces of your own you shall not look upon. Three moons you shall wander and lament and pray, thinking of this worst thing that you have done. For you have killed a home. Maka, the mother of all, you have wounded, and the sacred hoop of the people you have broken a little. Have a strong heart, and come back cleansed, my grandson.'

"When the old, old man had spoken, the people did not cry out; they only murmured all around the hoop, for they had seen and heard a great thing.

"The two *akichitas* had prepared a sweat-lodge, using only four sticks to hold the hide. It was made to cleanse a *te-wichakte,* and he must wander to the four quarters; so that is why they used four sticks. And when the rocks were heated in a fire and placed inside the lodge with forked poles, the unclean one went in there naked, and water was thrown upon the stones. Then the two *akichitas* dug a shallow hole in front of the sweat-lodge, as deep as the thickness of a man and shaped like him. And when the lodge was opened and Running Wolf came out, they placed him in the hole, face down, and left him there a little while. Thus they gave him back to the mother of all, who has shown mercy to her children; and even this they could not do until his body was cleansed in the sweat-lodge. But his heart was not yet clean, and he was dead to his people. Those near could hear him weeping there and see his shoulders shaking. And in a little while, they lifted him and led him to where Standing Hawk was sitting. There he stood, naked and weeping. And the old man said to those about him, 'Bring clothing for my son who is going on a long journey and may never come back. Also bring to him my best horse and my bow and arrows and all that he shall need, for I think his journey will be long and hard where there are only strangers.'

"And when this was done, and Running Wolf was clothed, Standing Hawk stood up and, for a little, held the young man's head upon his shoulder, then pushed him off and turned away. Then the *akichitas* lifted the kills-home to the saddle, and with whips they struck him and the horse, and drove him forth alone into the world of strangers. And the people watched him going towards where you are always facing [the south], until they could not see him any more."

Eagle Voice ceased, and when he had sat motionless for some time with closed eyes, I prompted, "And did Running Wolf come back?" Ignoring the question that had brought him out of his reverie, he continued: "It was good to die on the prairie for the people and to make a story for men to hear. But if the kills-home died out there, no story would be told and no song sung about him. A dead dog makes no story. The crows and wolves are glad, and the voice of mourning is not heard. His very name is evil in the mouth.

"Kicking Bear and High Horse had gone back home, and Charging Cat was in the world of spirit; but some of us who fought Shoshoni horsebacks in the snow would get together where we knew that no one heard, and talk about him; but we could not take his name into our mouths. He would be lamenting and praying at night on a lonely hill in the country of the strangers until he slept. And when the day came, even Maka would be staring at him with all her hills—like a stranger. When he sought for food, there would be enemies watching him and lying in wait to kill him. And if maybe a wandering band of Lakotas came in sight, he must flee from them that they might not see his face. We liked him, and when we talked of him our hearts were sad. We might have done it too if we had seen the bones of our brothers scattered yonder.

"They did not put Last Dog upon a scaffold. Because he did not die as men should die, they buried him face down upon a hill. His relatives could not follow him to that place, to mourn beside him through the night. But some people said they saw his woman, the sister of the kills-home, sneaking back to her tepee when the day was just beginning.

"When this was done, the village had to move, for there was an evil spirit in that place. The game all went away to where Maka, the mother of all, had not been wounded. And so the village moved over to the valley of the Rosebud, where grass was good and there was wood in plenty, and the game was not afraid.

"My heart was sick, and I wanted to see High Horse and Kicking Bear. Also I thought much about my father lying yonder on his scaffold. Sometimes I thought I would go and see him again. Then I would think how still it was on that hill. Yonder I would listen, and maybe there would be only the wind blowing. Then I would remember the voice of the eagle on my hill of vision, 'Hold fast; there is more.'

"When the first moon was getting old, I rode alone towards where the sun comes up. The Hunkpapas and Miniconjous would be camping near Pa Sapa [the Black Hills], and I would see High Horse and Kicking Bear. We would make plans for some great deed as we had done before; and if we came back with scalps and horses, people would praise us again. If we did not make a kill-come-back, we could die on the prairie. Then Charging Cat would ride with us again, and I would see my father.

"While I was riding alone, I would be thinking these things. I would be thinking more and more about High Horse, because we were brother-friends. But when I would be thinking about him, I would be seeing Tashina, maybe because she was a Miniconjou too and she would be in the village. As I rode, I would be thinking of her standing by the brush with her blanket about her face and looking at the ground. I would hear her saying she was proud of me. Then I would hear the horses squeal and break wind as they ran away. I was going to see High Horse, but it would be good to see Tashina too. Maybe I would talk to her, and we could laugh about when I used to be her horse.

"I came to Pa Sapa and saw the ashes of camping places. There were some roving hunters of the Brûlés, and they said the villages had moved beyond Pa Sapa, maybe beyond the Mini Shoshay. So I thought I would ride yonder and look for High Horse and Kicking Bear. Maybe while I was seeing my brother-friend, I would talk to Tashina alone, and we would remember and laugh. It made me want to sing when I thought that. But while I thought, I began to feel ashamed because she would not be proud of me any more. The story of our fight with the Shoshonis would have the wings of an eagle, and she would know. So I turned at last and rode back towards the sunset and the Rosebud, for my power had left me and my heart was sick.

"When I got back, the people were getting ready for the sun dance. No one spoke of the kills-home or of Last Dog. They were gone where the smoke goes when the fire is dead and there is only air. Their names were gone where a cry goes when the echoes stop.

"My heart was sick, but I remembered how the power came to me in the sun dance. So I danced again, and the hurt of the thong in my chest was good. I saw again. I did not faint, for the power came strong upon me, and the voice of the eagle was greater than the pain, 'Hold fast; there is more.' "

The old man ceased and sat meditating with closed eyes. After a decent interval I urged, 'And Running Wolf?' He regarded me with an absent gaze that slowly focused upon my face.

"The Moon of Blackened Cherries [July] was gone," he said, "and a new moon had grown big. The day was young. There were some loose horses coming over the ridge towards where the sun goes down. Some people saw and pointed, and many were looking. We had no horses yonder, for ours were all grazing in the valley. Then there was one horseback coming behind the three loose horses. They were coming at a trot. It was Running Wolf come back from being dead, and when the people knew, a cry went up around the village, and the chiefs and councilors went forth to welcome him. I think the people liked him and were happy, for he was hardly more than a boy.

"When he drove his horses through the opening of the hoop, and rode around the village, left to right, the song of welcome was so loud that no one heard the song that he was singing; and he was holding up a coup-stick with a scalp upon it. He had made a kill-come-back with horses. There were tears upon his face—and it was thin, but it was shining while he rode and sang.

"In front of Standing Hawk's tepee he stopped his horses, and they stood, with hanging heads, for they were very tired; and Standing Hawk was waiting there. The song of the people was still, and everybody listened. Then Running Wolf said, 'My father, I have come back with a clean heart to be your son until I die, and I have brought you horses. They are few, but they are Shoshoni horses, and it is far to that country. I was all alone and could not hold the others.' Then Standing Hawk raised his arms for his son to come to him, and Running Wolf got down and put his head upon his new father's shoulder. And all the people cried, 'Hiyee! Thanks! Hiyee!'

"There was a victory dance for Running Wolf. When he made his kill-talk, he was bashful and the words came broken. And when the people praised him and the drums beat and the women's tremolo was loud, he stood like one ashamed, looking at the ground. And when the voices and the drums were still, he said, 'I prayed and prayed and Wakon Tonka heard me.'

"Standing Hawk made a feast for the people and gave away all that he had, because his son who was dead had come back home to him. But when his hands were empty, the people began giving to him and his son, until they had even more than before.

"And after that there was no Running Wolf. They called him Many Horses."

Why the Island Hill Was Sacred

"I did not know it then, for I was young," the old man began after a prolonged meditative silence. "All that time the sacred hoop was breaking, but I did not know. Red Cloud's people were calling us the wild Lakota, because we would not eat Wasichu food and went on living in the sacred manner. The hoop was smaller, but our country looked the same. Only what we heard was different, but the words had traveled far; and when we looked around us, the prairie and the hills were there and the round sky above them. The morning star did not forget to come. The sun measured the days and the moon the seasons. The creeks and rivers ran, the wind blew, the snow came, the rain brought forth the young grass for the bison and the elk and the deer. And Wakon Tonka heard on any hill.

"But we were living on a big island, and the Wasichus were like great waters washing all around it, nibbling off the edges, and it was getting smaller, smaller, smaller. It is very small now. The people have lost the sacred hoop, the good red road, the flowering tree. We young men heard the others talk about Wasichus killing bison along Shell River where the iron road had cut the herd in two; and beyond that, farther towards where you are always facing [south], the land stank with bison rotting. I heard them say Wasichus killed the bison for their tongues, so many that no man could ever count them. Our old men remembered Wooden Cup and what he saw and said before our grandfathers were born. But I was young. Sometime we would get together and kill all the Wasichus. We were young and we would do great deeds and make a story for our grandchildren, and for theirs, and theirs.

"I think I was maybe seventeen winters old when I heard about horseback soldiers with their wagons in Pa Sapa [the Black Hills], and Long Hair [Custer] was their chief. That was the first time I heard his name. Maybe I helped to kill him two grasses after that, for I was fighting on the hill where he died; but I never saw him. I think if our people had been living in one hoop, he and all his soldiers would have died in Pa Sapa that time. Maybe that would have been better. I do not know.

"It was our land and it was *wakon*; for it was promised to us in a vision so long ago that the fire and the bow were new to our fathers then, and the sacred pipe had not yet been given to us.

"I will tell you what I heard the old men tell about Pa Sapa, and they heard it from old men, and they from others; and no one knows how long ago it was. The people were living then in a land that is many, many sleeps yonder [pointing southeast]. Towards where you are always facing [south], there was a great water [Gulf of Mexico]. Towards where the sun comes up, there was a great water [the Atlantic]. The people had become many, and I think they were not a nation yet. All were relatives, but sons did not know their fathers, nor fathers their sons, nor brothers their sisters. These people ate small animals and birds that they could kill with rocks or maybe slingshots, and also roots and berries that they could find. Their knives were only sharp pieces of rock or shells; and all they ate was raw, because they had no fire.

"But there was a man among the people, and his name, they say, was Moves Walking, the same as with our friend who ate with us. I think he must have been the first *wichasha wakon,* for one day he had a vision of the sun, and what the vision taught him, he showed to all the people. He could bring fire down from the sun, and this he did with the soap-weed as he had seen it in the vision. The root of this plant was like hair, and when it was rotten and dry it was very soft. So he put some of this on some hard dry wood. Then he took a dry stem of this weed and made it square. The end he made pointed and round, and this he pressed down through the soft stuff against the wood. When he had made it whirl between his hands awhile, the sun gave him fire, as he had seen it in his vision. This was a wonderful thing, and after that the people could begin to be a nation.

"But they were not ready yet, for they were weaker and slower than the big animals. So another man came up among the people, and they say his name was Wakina Luta [Red Thunder]. I think he must have been the second *wichasha wakon,* for one day when he was out hunting in the woods all alone, he got lost. And when he had walked and walked and could not find the way back, and was so tired he could hardly walk any more, there came a great storm of wind and thunder. So he crawled in under a rock. There was no rain—just wind and big thunders. And there under the rock he went to sleep. All at once as he slept, there were great voices calling, and they say it was the Thunder Beings that he heard. Theirs is the power to make live and to destroy, for theirs are the bow and the cup of water; and they live in the quarter where the sun goes down. And the great voices said, 'Arise, Wakina Luta, and come with us. We are taking you to where there will be a great decision, and by it the people shall live or they shall die. So in his dream Red Thunder arose and followed the voices flying very fast, until he came to a far place that was called The Island Hill; for it was a great hill of many hills, standing high in the center of the hoop of the world. Therein all animals lived with the birds, and the grass was green in the valleys, and the trees on the slopes were many beyond counting, and tall. Clear, cold streams were running and leaping and singing. All flowers were living there of many colors, and among them happy deer made fat and were not afraid. It was more beautiful than any land Red Thunder ever saw before; and while he looked at it from above where he was floating, the voices of the Thunder Beings came again, and they said, 'Here shall be the great decision; look about you.' And when Red Thunder looked, he saw the hoop of the world all about him, and at the center was the Island Hill. And he saw that all the four-leggeds of the earth were gathered on one side, and on the other all the wings of the air, who are two-leggeds like us. They were all waiting for something. Then the thunder voices spoke again and said, 'These that you see shall race around the hoop of the world. If the four-leggeds win, they will eat you and the wings of the air. If the two-leggeds win, your people shall live; the children of your children's children's children shall possess this land; and the four-leggeds shall feed you.'

"Then the race began. The magpie, who knows everything, had a plan; so he flew down and sat on the ear of a bison bull and there he rode and waited. It was a long race, for the hoop of the world is great. Sometimes a big wind came, so that the wings of the air could hardly fly, and the four-leggeds were far ahead. Sometimes there would be a very hot day, and the four-leggeds could hardly run, so that the wings would be winning. A great rainstorm came roaring and many wings of the air were killed. But still the race went on, and all the while the magpie sat on the running bison's ear and waited for something. Nobody knows how long they raced, but it was long. Then one day they were getting near the end. The four-leggeds were ahead, and they began to cheer. All the kinds of four-leggeds were making the noises that they knew, howling and roaring and screaming and barking, and growling and neighing, so that the whole sky was filled with the fearful sound, and the wide earth was afraid.

"But just before the end, the magpie, who was not tired at all, 'rose high' into the air and came swooping down upon the goal ahead of all the others. Then the voices of the four-leggeds died away, and the wide air was full of happy wings that soared and darted, swooped and floated; and the geese cried high, and the crane; the eagles screamed, and every bird that knows a song was singing.

"Then Wakina Luta heard the voice of thunder speaking once again, and it said to him, 'Your two-legged relatives, the wings of the air, have won the race for your people. Your people shall live and possess this land and the Island Hill after many snows and grasses, and the four-leggeds shall keep and feed them.' Then to the magpie the voice of thunder spoke, 'By thinking, you have won the race for all your relatives, the two-leggeds. Hereafter you shall wear the rainbow in your tail, and it shall be a sign of victory.' And what was said is true, for you can see it yet on every magpie. Also, it was true, as the voice said, that the people should be like the birds, their relatives; for it is like birds of prey that we fought, circling and swooping, and in the beauty of the birds we dressed ourselves for battle and for death.

"For a while the world was still, until the voice of thunder filled it once again, and to Wakina Luta in his vision it was speaking: 'Your people still are weaker and slower than the big four-leggeds, so I give you this that you may be stronger than they, and their fleetness shall be slow.' And when Wakina Luta looked, it was the great bow of the Thunder Beings with a pointed arrow that was tailed for guiding as the birds are tailed for guiding to a mark. And as he looked hard to see how it was made, the bow twanged, and the arrow rose high with the whisper of wings, and swooped like a hawk or an eagle; and yonder far away a great bison bull went down with feathers sprouting from his chest.

"The thunder voice rose again, 'Behold!' And Wakina Luta in his vision saw a strange four-legged that might have been a dog, but was not, for no dog could grow so tall. It was a *shonka wakon* [sacred dog, horse], and as he looked and wondered, it raised its head and sent forth a high shrill voice that ran far and was like a victor singing. And the voice said, 'You shall know him after many grasses in this land, and he shall be your friend and give you fleetness.'

"Then Red Thunder awoke under his rock and the world was still. So, with the vision living in him, he found his way back to the people; and all that he had seen, he told. Also he made a bow like that he saw and a feathered arrow; and he showed the young men how to make and use it.

"After that, the old men say, another man came up among the people, and Slow Buffalo is what they called him. I think he was the third *wichasha wakon*, for what he did a vision must have taught him. One day he called all the people together, and from among them he chose the oldest and wisest to sit with him. To these he gave a name, calling them a council. And to these he told what I think a vision must have shown him, while all the people listened. He said the people had grown to be too many for that place, and now with fire and the bow they could wander and go anywhere. For the first time he gave a name to each of the quarters of the world: Where the Sun Goes Down [west], Where the White Giant Lives [north], Where the Sun Comes Up [east], and Where You Are Always Facing [south]. Towards the last place the people could not go, for there the great water was near, and from thence a race of strangers would come. The people should be divided into three, and each should become a nation. One would go towards Where the Sun Comes Up, one to Where the Sun Goes Down, and the last towards Where the White Giant Lives. Each as it went must name all things, and these names would be a tongue.

"Then Slow Buffalo told them about fathers and mothers, sisters and brothers, grandfathers and grandmothers. These he named for the first time. They should live together with one fire, and the fire would be holy. The old would guide the young; the young would give their strength to the old; and all together would give one strength to the nation, that it might be strong and live. The nation, he said, was itself a being with a grandfather, a grandmother, a father, and a mother. The Great Mysterious One is the grandfather, the Earth is the grandmother, the Sky is the father, and the mother is where the growing things come out of the ground and nurse with all that live. When Slow Buffalo had done this, he got together with the council and they chose leaders for the nations and called them chiefs. Each nation he divided into seven bands. Then the people started, each band with its central fire, which was holy, and its chiefs and council.

"I think the Lakotas came from those who wandered towards the Great White Giant; and it was while they were going that a vision was sent to them. I will tell you how the old men told it. Two young men were out hunting together when they saw something coming; and when it was nearer they knew it was a young woman, very good to see, dressed in fine white buckskin, and all about her was a shining white mist. And when one of the young men saw her, he had bad thoughts of her, and this she knew. So she said to the first young hunter, 'Come, then, and do as you wish with me.' But when he came near to her, the shining mist enclosed him and became a dark cloud with lightning in it. And when the cloud was gone and the shining white mist came back, the young man's bones were scattered on the prairie. Then the young woman said to the second young hunter, 'Your thoughts are good, and to you I give this sacred thing for all the people. Behold!' It was a pipe; and while she held it out, she told the meanings that it had. The eagle feather, hanging from the bowl, meant the grandfather of all, the father of fathers, Wakon Tonka. Also it meant that the thoughts of those who smoked should rise high as the eagles do. The bison-hide upon the mouthpiece was for the grandmother of all, the mother of mothers; and he who touched it with his lips would know that he nursed with all living things. The four thongs hanging from the stem were colored like the quarters of the world—blue, white, red, yellow. The pipe and the morning star would stand for the power of the quarter where the sun comes up. Yonder the morning star brings light and wisdom and understanding. The pipe gives peace that comes from understanding. With the morning star and the pipe we should love each other and live together as brothers.

"I think the people forgot these things. Maybe they multiplied so fast that they got to quarreling and split up into many new bands that grew to be strangers with different names for things, different tongues. And maybe one of these bands grew big and became our people, the Lakotas. Even then, the old men say, there was not yet any war. But once the Lakotas found one of their hunters killed and scalped by a band of these strangers. So our people were angry; and when they came upon the band that had done this thing, they cut off all the strangers' heads, so that there could be no war again. Maybe that is why the strangers used to call us cut-throats. But I think all the heads must have grown back on, for we have been fighting ever since. And after that, whatever people did not speak our tongue, we knew them for our enemies. But within the sacred hoop of our own people the ancient teaching lived and the power of the pipe was mighty.

"After these things had happened, there were many snows and grasses; I do not know how many. Then we came at last to the Island Hill that was promised long ago, and it was a sacred place. Because the pines upon it made it black a long way off, we called it Pa Sapa [black heads, the Black Hills]; and all the land around it was ours.

"Farther on towards where the sun goes down, there was a people that we called the Shyela [Cheyenne]. It was they who found the *shonka wakon* [horse] first. They were hunting from where they lived towards where you are always facing, and in a valley by a spring there stood this strange four-legged with long hair upon its neck and tail. It was living wild, but it was tame. At first the hunters were afraid, but after there was a council to talk about it some hunters were sent to catch it, and this they did with lariats of hide. And after some moons, this *shonka wakon* had a young one. Then one day when it was making a high shrill noise, another *shonka wakon* came, and this one was a stallion. So after that the Shyela had horses, and the Lakota traded for them, giving bows and arrows and beaded moccasins and clothing. The Arapahoes also found many horses and with them too the Lakota traded; and these peoples and the Lakota were friends after that, although their tongues were not the same. The old men said it was from the Wasichus who were towards where you are always facing [Spaniards] that the first horses ran away, and that is why they were so tame at first.

"So we had come at last to the Island Hill as the vision had foretold, and the land around it was ours and it was holy. There we lived in the sacred hoop with the sacred fire and the pipe; and the bow and the *shonka wakon* made us mighty.

"But when I was about seventeen winters old, a long dust of horse-back soldiers with their wagons came down upon Pa Sapa, and I heard their chief was Long Hair. They came to look and went away; but they had seen the yellow metal [gold] that makes Wasichus crazy; and I think the whole Wasichu nation heard about it. So when the young grass came again and died, big trouble started."

Fighting the Gray Fox

As the old man had foreseen, a melting wind had risen with the waning of the softened day, and the night came roaring with no cloud. Next morning, when again we sat together, the puffing wood-fire grumbled to the gusts of false April, and the tepee canvas bellied, whipping the poles.

"It was a wind like this," said Eagle Voice; "a big wind, strong and roaring, but it was full of snow and cold. I think I was eighteen winters old that time, and it was in the Moon of Snowblinds [March]. We of the Oglala band had our winter village in the valley of the Powder, not far from where the Little Powder comes in. I think there were fifty or sixty lodges of us; and when our Cheyenne friends came from Red Cloud's agency to visit and trade with us, I think there were a hundred smokes in our village. We had plenty of *papa* and *wasna* and buffalo robes, and the Cheyennes came with powder and guns and canvas tepees they had got from the Wasichus. Also, they came with more word of the big trouble about Pa Sapa. They were saying down yonder that the Wasichus would drive us into those little islands that Wooden Cup had seen long ago; and there we would have to turn ourselves into Wasichus, so that our country could be taken from us. We knew that Gray Fox [General Crook] was in the country and that he had many walking soldiers and horsebacks waiting for the young grass. I was out on a hunting party just before this happened that I am going to tell you, and we saw some of the soldiers. But it was long before the grass, and not yet the time for war, so we were not afraid.

"When our Cheyenne friends came to visit us, there was feasting, for we had plenty, and I heard much talk around the fire at night about the trouble, and about a big village the crazy Wasichus had built in Pa Sapa. But there was talk about the old times, too, when everything was better; and old men told stories that were good to hear, so that those who told and we who heard did not sleep soon.

"It happened when the day had just come and the people were sleeping yet. I thought I was dreaming of many horses galloping and guns shooting and men yelling; but I was not dreaming. We all ran out of our tepee, but I thought of my quirt and hung it around my neck, down my back, as I ran with my gun. Out there all the people were running towards the bluff—men and women and children mixed up and running, screaming and shouting; horseback soldiers galloping and shooting all over the village; women running with babies, old people hobbling, horses rearing and knocking tepees over! It was day, but there was no sun. The wind was strong and full of snow and horses' heads—something like the fight with the Shoshonis. It was very cold, and we had little clothing, but I did not feel the wind's teeth. I ran against a man, and when I saw his face, it made me strong, for it was Crazy Horse. He was carrying some little boy on his back, and he was yelling for the men to gather about him behind the women and the old ones. Some near by heard and others saw, and many gathered about him, and more and more. We fought back of the running women and children, but we could not do much. When we were crowded up along the side of the bluff, the canvas tepees were burning down yonder, and the powder the Cheyennes had brought was going off—*boom, boom, boom!* Tepees and poles flying in the snow wind.

"On the bluff I was not far from Crazy Horse and I heard him crying, 'We are going back! Let us die today, brothers!' Then we all began singing the death-song and started back, charging down the hill— Lakotas and Cheyennes, all mixed up and singing. The cowards and baby-killers yonder did not wait long to fight us. I think they did not want to die that day. They galloped away up the valley of the Powder; and there was only the sharp wind blowing full of snow. A few tepees were standing, and some were smoking yet. I saw dead children trampled by the iron hoofs of the horses, and women with babies dead or wounded in the snow.

"When the soldiers ran away, the women and children and old people came swarming down from the bluff; and the mourning was louder than the wind among the scattered homes.

"There were two bands of horseback soldiers, and only one attacked the village. The others were driving our horses away—five or six hundred, maybe more. So we made a war party to go after our herd. When we had put on what clothes we could find we started after the soldiers, *maka mani*; and Crazy Horse led us, Lakotas and Cheyennes. The soldiers were in a hurry, and some of the horses got away from them. We had to catch strays, and the horseback soldiers had a big start. They did not stop all day. *Lela oosni!* It was cold, very cold; and the wind was strong. Sometimes we would have to run and lead the horses to keep from freezing.

"When it was dark we were near where another creek we called Lodge Pole comes in, and we began to be careful. The soldiers could not run away all night, and we knew that was a good place to camp. So four scouts went out on foot, and I was one. We ran into the herd. They were huddled together with their heads down and rumps to the wind.

"They were like the bison we found in the snowstorm that time, and they did not notice us. I think there were no guards. We did not find any. At the mouth of the creek there were little fires that did not make much light; and when we crept up through the brush to look, it was good to see what we saw there. The Wasichu horses were standing with their heads down and rumps to the wind, and some that I could see had their saddles on. Maybe all of them had. The soldiers were humped up over little brush fires that could not warm them. It looked as though the baby-killers were going to freeze to death. That was good to see.

"When we told the others, Crazy Horse said it was not the time to fight. There would be plenty of fighting when the grass was new. We came for our horses, and we would not stop to kill soldiers. Let the cold do it. So we began driving the herd. It was hard to start them back into the wind, but we got them moving and pushed them hard down the valley. The soldiers must have heard us, but they did not follow. It was good to think maybe they were freezing to death back there.

"When the night was old, we drove the herd against a bluff that broke the wind, and made good fires with some logs we found there. Crazy Horse said we could sleep and he would watch. It was the second time I heard him say that. The other was when I was on my first war party beyond Mini Shoshay. He was only about thirty winters old, but he was like a father to us who followed him. So we scraped the snow away about the fires and slept with our bellies to the ground. I awoke right away, and it was early morning without wind. The sky was clear and the morning star looked big and sharp. It was very cold. The fires were still burning, and he was sitting as I saw him before I slept. He was *wakon*. Sometimes when I think about him now, I wonder and wonder. But then I did not think so much, for I was young.

"When the sun was high, another band of Gray Fox's horseback soldiers attacked us, and we shot at each other, but it was not much of a fight. The herd was strung out when the soldiers came, for the horses were very tired and it was hard to keep them going, so we lost some of them—maybe a hundred. Our band was not big enough to follow the soldiers and drive the herd too, so we kept on down the Powder valley with maybe four hundred. When we got back, the people were all ready to move and they were waiting for the horses. So we moved down the valley to Sitting Bull's village not far from the river's mouth. We were poor and they took us in with them. There we lived in patched tepees, waiting for the grass. And the anger of the people grew.

"The snow melted; warm winds came with rain; and when the new grass was high enough to make horses strong, our relatives began coming in to our village—sometimes a big band, sometimes a few *iglakas*; and more and more they came and the village grew and grew. Then we all moved over to the valley of the Rosebud, deeper into our own country. If Gray Fox wanted his soldiers killed, let him bring them to us there. We would not hunt the soldiers, and we would not go into the little islands the Wasichus made so that they could starve us and steal our country. There on the Rosebud more and more of our relatives came; also Cheyennes and Arapahoes. It was a long camp, and it grew and grew; seven hoops of people; Cheyennes, Oglalas, Miniconjous, Sans Arcs, Hunkpapas, some Santees, Yanktonais, Brûlés, Arapahoes; and horses, horses, many horses. Some of the people came from Red Cloud's agency; but Red Cloud did not come. We said maybe his skin was getting white and he was turning into a Wasichu. Spotted Tail also was eating Wasichu food. Some came from along the Mini Shoshay with guns they got from Wasichu traders. There were many, many guns in the camp. Many men with big names were there, Sitting Bull, Crazy Horse, Gall, Big Road, Black Moon, Crow King. The big names I always knew, but some of the men I never saw before. We knew there were soldiers on both sides of us, on the Yellowstone and on Goose Creek; but we waited there. If the soldiers wanted to be killed, let them come to us. That was our country.

"When the cherry seeds hardened, there was a big sun dance. I danced with the thong in my chest, and for a little I saw the other world; but after the thong tore out of the flesh, I could see only with my eyes. But I could feel a great power. Nobody noticed me that time, for many with big names were dancing.

"Sitting Bull was the principal dancer, and the people watched him most of all; for he was a great *wichasha wakon*, and he could see things far away and things that were going to happen. For a long time he danced and hung from the tree by the thong in his back. When it tore out, he fell to the ground and lay like dead for a while. Then he awoke; and when they carried him into the sacred lodge, he told a vision that came to him in the world of spirit, and it spread among the people so that everybody knew and talked about it.

"He was camped with all the people in a place that looked like the valley of the Greasy Grass [Little Big Horn]; but it was not the same, for it was glowing and made of spirit. He could see the happy people feasting, each band in its hoop, and the children playing; and on the glowing hills near by fat horses grazed and had their fill of grass that was greener than the youngest grass of this world. Then he saw that a whirling cloud of dust was coming fast from where the sun comes up; and as it came nearer it filled the heavens, so that a darkness fell upon the valley and the village. The cloud was full of shouting, as of men in battle, and screaming as of frightened horses, and thunder as of many guns shooting together. Then a strange rain began to fall out of the dust cloud, a dry rain full of shouting. For it was not water that fell, but soldiers, soldiers, soldiers; all dead and tumbling upside down and over and over as they came falling, until they were heaped and scattered in the twilight of the cloud.

"When the people heard about this vision, they said, 'There will be a great victory. Many soldiers will come, and they will die.' So there was a power among the people, and their hearts were strong.

"A little after this I was with a hunting party over on the Greasy Grass, and High Horse and I were together again, for he had come back with his people. Our breasts were very sore from the sun dance, but we both said the pain made us feel stronger. The hunting was not good, so we went back up the Greasy Grass to Ash Creek, and up the creek to where the people had moved while we were gone. Some Cheyennes came there and told about Gray Fox's soldiers coming down the Rosebud. So there was a council and it was decided that our warriors should go back there and attack the Gray Fox by surprise.

"The sun was going down behind us when we started, and I think there were more than a thousand of us, Sioux and Cheyenne. We rode in a long column with *akichita* in front and on both sides to watch for soldiers and hold the warriors back until we could all attack together. Sitting Bull and Crazy Horse were with us; but I heard that Sitting Bull was too sick and crippled from the sun dance to fight, and came along to encourage the warriors.

"When the morning star was just coming up in front of us, we stopped to rest the horses and let them eat; and while they grazed we ate what we had with us. Daybreak came, and when the hills began to stare at us, we started again, riding in a column four abreast with the *akichita* out ahead of us to watch for soldiers. We were coming close to the place on the Rosebud where we had the sun dance, and the river ran through a canyon there. If we could catch the soldiers in the canyon, maybe it would be like Sitting Bull's vision. High Horse and I talked about that as we rode. Maybe it was not the Greasy Grass he saw; maybe it was the Rosebud where there would be a rain of dead soldiers in the dust cloud.

"We were getting close, and the dawn was coming. The *akichita* rode up and down the column and made the warriors stop talking. Then we could see that the sun was up back of the ridge ahead of us and it was shining on the hilltops. The Rosebud was just the other side of the ridge, and the *akichita* out ahead were just coming to the top. High Horse and I were among the fronters because we had won honors.

"All at once there were horses' heads and men's heads on the ridge right in front of us! It was a small party of the Gray Fox's Crow scouts out looking around.

"When we saw the Crows, we all forgot about the surprise. Everybody was yelling. We whipped our horses and went over the ridge on the run. The *akichita* tried to stop us, but we rode right through them. *Hokahey! Hokahey!* Most of the Crows got away, but there were plenty of soldiers, walking and horseback, down there in the valley. When we swung to one side to attack the horsebacks, I could see all our warriors swarming over the ridge. Nobody was leading us. We did not circle the soldiers; we just rode in among them all mixed up, and killing the nearest ones with spears and knives and war clubs. Sometimes we would knock them off their horses, then jump down and beat them to death. I saw a Cheyenne cut off a soldier's arm and ride away with it. Once I saw Crazy Horse, and he was not trying to guide the warriors, he was just fighting like the rest of us. I did not see Sitting Bull, but they say he was in there shouting to the young warriors to give them courage.

"I do not know how long we were fighting there; but all at once the horseback soldiers were gone, and I saw our warriors charging up the valley where many Shoshonis and Crows were getting ready to charge us. We were fighting them, and I think we were going to rub them out; but all at once some horseback soldiers were coming from behind us. Then I could hear our people crying, 'Take courage! Let us die here! Think of the women and children!' So we charged back against the horseback soldiers and made them run; but while we were in among them, the Crows and Shoshonis felt braver because of the soldiers, and they charged us. Many of our people began to run away out of the fight crying, 'Yea-hey!' High Horse and I were with them. All at once we were on the hillside out of the fighting, and I could see the broad valley full of fighting in bunches—scattered and all mixed up. I do not think anybody was winning—just mixed up and fighting. When we had watched awhile we felt ashamed; so we charged down into the fighting, yelling to each other, 'This is a good place to die! Take courage! *Hokahey!*' Then there was dust, with shouting and guns shooting and men and horses in the dust. Nobody was leading us; we were just hitting the nearest soldier. High Horse and I were brother-friends and we kept together all the time, helping each other. Sometimes we would be out of the fighting, then we would be in again. It was that way all day. Then the sun was setting and our warriors were leaving the valley, riding back up the ridge towards the sunset. The soldiers did not follow us. I think they were as tired of fighting as we were. Most of us rode back to our village that night, but some stayed around there to see what the Gray Fox was going to do. In the morning he went back up the valley with all his soldiers. Some said we whipped him. Some said we did not. I do not know. But it was not the rain of dead soldiers that Sitting Bull saw in his vision.

Nothing touched me all day; I think it was the quirt that protected me. I did not think about my sore breast, but it was sorer that night. Nothing touched High Horse either. Maybe the quirt protected both of us that time because we stayed so close together.

"It Was a Great Victory"

"I was young then," Eagle Voice continued after we had sat silent for a while, hearing the high wind and the whipping of the canvas on the poles. "I was young and strong, and I could still believe that sometime we would drive all the Wasichus out of our country. But now, when I can look back and see how it was going to be, it makes me sad to remember the fight on the Greasy Grass. It was a few days after we fought the Gray Fox on the Rosebud, and it was a great victory. But you see us now.

"Our whole camp had moved over into the valley of the Greasy Grass near the mouth of Spring Creek. High Horse and I were with a small party scouting and hunting over towards where the Gray Fox went after the fight. We did not see any soldiers, and the hunting was not good. It was late in the morning when we got home to the village on the Greasy Grass. The hoops of the bands were strung out a long way on the flat beside the river; and across the water, towards where the sun comes up, there are high bluffs. It was an old camping place and we liked to be there. Plenty of good water, plenty of good grass for the horses, plenty of wood. It was a good place to swim and fish too, and we always had fun there. On the other side, away from the river towards where the sun goes down, was open prairie sloping, and with one look we could see all the horses grazing. There were many, many. There were thousands, I think.

"Our small scouting party came from up the river, and the hoop of Sitting Bull's people, the Hunkpapas, was the first one we came to. Not far from there were the Miniconjous, High Horse's band. The Oglalas were farther down stream.

"We were riding across the Hunkpapa hoop, and some of the people were asleep or just getting up, because they had been dancing the victory dance all night. There was an old, old woman who saw me. She was cooking some meat in a pot. I knew her because she was my grandmother's friend and they liked to help each other. As I rode by her, she looked up and said something. The wind had come up and it was getting stronger all the time, so I did not hear what she said at first. When I stopped my horse she spoke louder and said, 'Natan uskay! Natan uskay! [Attackers are coming fast].' And I said, 'Where are they coming, Grandmother?' And she answered in a high voice that sounded like scolding a dog that is stealing meat: 'Grandson, I said Natan uskay!' Then she went on stirring her pot.

"High Horse said to me, 'Do you think she knows?' And I said, 'I know that old woman, and there's something to it. I'm going home to get ready.' High Horse said he would do that too, and then we'd come back. So I galloped on towards our hoop farther down stream. I could see people were excited, and some men and boys were out catching horses. When I got home my stepfather was gone, but my mother and little brother and my grandfather and grandmother were there. They were tying some things up in bundles; and my mother said, 'Soldiers are coming, they say! You'd better get ready! There's meat in the pot.' But I did not stop to eat. I stripped myself and put some paint on my face. While I was doing this, my grandfather said, 'That's right, Grandson! It is good to be young and die for the people. Nothing lasts, and it is not good to grow old.' Then I took my fast-shooting gun that came from Wasichu traders on Mini Shoshay, and ran out to get a fresh horse.

"Just then there was shooting up river where the Hunkpapas were— like ripping a big blanket by jerks; and a big noise of yelling grew yonder.

"I ran into my cousin who was bringing in some horses, and one of them was mine; so I took it, and rode towards where the big noise came from. But it was spreading all along the valley now. Women and children and old people were running down the river towards me. Women were screaming, men were shouting and running for their horses. Some were riding or running on foot towards the attackers yonder. It was so crowded at first where I was that I could not ride fast. So I turned out to the right into the prairie, and the whole flat along the stream was covered with the big mixed, singing noise that floated above the people.

"Just then I ran into Red Feather, a young fellow like me, and he was bringing some horses. They were rearing and pulling at the lariats, and he was having a hard time with them, because they were excited too. One of them was my best horse, big and a good runner. Not Whirlwind; he was wolf-meat long before that. This one was a roan with a crooked white patch around his left eye and nearly over to his left ear. He had a white look in that eye when he was excited, and he never got tame. Sometimes he ran away with me, but he never got tired. So I got on this horse and gave the other to a man who was running on foot towards the attackers.

"I rode on the run towards where the big excitement was. There was an old Hunkpapa woman pointing a gun at a man on the ground. He was a Hunkpapa too and he was sitting holding himself up with his hands back of him. I stopped my horse to see what the old woman was doing to the Hunkpapa. His breast was all bloody. The woman pointed the gun at his head, and it snapped but did not go off. The man said, 'Don't kill me, Grandmother; I will be dead soon anyway.' The woman screamed at him and said, 'You sneaking dog! Why did you come with the soldiers to kill your relatives?' Then the gun went off and the man fell over.

"I could see that horseback soldiers were running away up stream. They were strung out along the river bank, and they were not fighting much, just running away, with many, many Lakotas swarming against them and pushing them towards the water that was running deeper than a horse's belly. I rode into the crowd and began knocking soldiers off their horses with the butt of my gun. It was easy to do. It was easier than shooting, for it was not like a fight. It was more like hunting cows. There was a Lakota on a white horse and he was killing soldiers with a sword he got in the Rosebud fight.

"The soldiers were jumping their horses into the river, and many Lakotas were jumping after them. It was bad in there—horses and men mixed up and fighting. Sometimes they would wrestle—like the game we used to call 'Throwing-them-off-their horses.' They would go under and come up fighting, and go under. I held back and shot fast at soldiers and horses climbing out on the other side. Maybe I killed some; I do not know. My horse was crazy and I shot while he was dancing and whirling; but the soldiers and horsebacks were all crowded together yonder, and maybe I hit some. It was like shooting into a stampeding buffalo herd crowding up a steep hill. I was staying out that way because I was looking for High Horse. He would be there because his camp was close to the excitement.

"There was a Ree scout trying to break through to the river bank, and I saw a Lakota leap from his horse onto the Ree. They went down together, and for a little I could not see them. Then the Lakota was up on his feet, trying to find his horse in the crowd of warriors. I saw his face, and it was High Horse. So I pushed in there and he got up behind me. He had a long knife and it was bloody. He was panting hard and he kept saying, 'I cut that one's neck off, the Ree dog!' He sounded crazy. I think we were all a little crazy by then.

"I pushed out through the crowd of warriors looking for another horse. There were some down and kicking, and some running this way and that way. Some Cheyennes were just getting into the fight from down river, and when they came swarming on the run towards us they chased a big Wasichu horse right into us. High Horse caught its bridle rein and leaped into the saddle.

"There was a big smoke down stream where our poeple were burning soldiers out of the brush and grass. Then all at once we saw that our warriors yonder were turning back down the valley, and those about us began yelling that more soldiers were coming that way. So High Horse and I started on the run towards where the others were going, and we kept close together. Where the fire was we saw some Lakota boys shooting with their bows and arrows at a soldier dodging around in the brush. I think he had lost his gun and was trying to get away from the fire.

"We were in a river of warriors, and I heard afterwards it was Crazy Horse who was leading yonder; but I did not see him. Yonder ahead of us on the hillside we saw horseback soldiers, and they were turning back up the hill. There is a fast shallow place in the river where we used to cross, and on the other side, towards where the sun comes up, there is a deep draw that runs back through the bluff. Our warriors and many Cheyennes were pouring up this draw like a flood running backwards, and we were in it. I heard afterwards that warriors farther down stream were coming up around the bluffs on the other side from us. I did not know anything then. High Horse and I were just charging up the deep draw with all the others, and men were yelling to each other, 'It's a good day to die! Take courage! Think of the women and children down there! *Hokahey! Hokahey!*' And we whipped each other's horses.

"When we got to the top, it was all a big noise and a big dust. The wind was very strong and the day was hot and the earth was dry. Horses, horses, horses, all mixed up and making a high dust in the big wind. Yelling and singing and shooting and horses' hoofs, thousands of horses' hoofs pounding. It was steady thunder with a long screaming on top of it. It was not like night, but it was not day either. Horses and men were shadows flying this way and that way.

"All at once there were soldiers around us, soldiers standing together. I did not see any swords. I did not try to shoot. I think I hit one with my gun butt. I did not see him fall. High Horse was still close beside me, and I saw him slashing with his knife. Then there was only dust and noise and no soldiers. So we swung around and charged back. There were soldiers again, all on foot and huddled together. Our horses knocked them over. I could feel them under my horse. Then there was dust with shadows flying. There were two soldiers coming on foot right towards us out of the dust. They were making motions like running, but they were only walking. When we were nearly on them, they shot their guns straight up. Both went down under our horses; and all at once there were three horseback soldiers. We all came together and the horses reared. I hit the nearest soldier on the head with my gun butt and he fell off. My gun flew out of my hands. Then I saw High Horse leap onto another one with his knife. I heard a gun go off. I think it was the third one shooting, but when I looked he was gone in the dust. High Horse and the soldier were on the ground. When I got off to help, my horse tried to break away. He was screaming and rearing. The rope was tied around his lower jaw, and I held him, but he dragged me. When I got him back to where High Horse and the soldier were on the ground, they were hugging each other. The knife was in the soldier's neck, and he was coughing spurts of blood. When I pulled High Horse away, the knife came too. Then he went limp. Blood was coming out of his back and chest. He did not hear me when I called to him. I think that was when my horse broke loose. Then I had High Horse on my back and I was running. There were shadows flying by. Then there was only dust. Then all at once there was a white sun shining, and I was on a hillside alone and the roaring was yonder.

"I sat beside High Horse and cried hard because I would never see him again in this world. While I was crying I felt his blood all over me, and a power came into me. I wanted to kill soldiers and die. So I called to High Horse, 'My brother, look back as you are going, for I will be coming too! Look back and wait, for I will be coming soon!'"

Eagle Voice fell silent, and for some time he sat gazing at the slatting canvas wall of the tepee, while the high wind carried on the story without words. At length he looked at me and, with a faint smile, said: "You can see that he has been waiting long. It is not good. I ran back towards the dust cloud and the roaring yonder, and I was crying hard. I wanted to die killing Wasichus. There was a gun on the ground and I picked it up for a club. There were soldiers' horses with their reins tied together and they were running around in a little circle, rearing and pulling against each other. I got on one and rode at a run into the dust, looking for soldiers to kill and one to kill me. Then I was out on the other side. Wasichu horses were breaking out of the dust and warriors were chasing them. I did not want any horses then. I wanted to kill and die. So I rode back into the dust and it was getting thinner. There were soldiers on the ground. There were no soldiers standing.

"The big noise died. The sun began to shine again. I rode back to High Horse and sat beside him awhile. I remembered and cried. The Wasichu horse did not try to run away. He stood with his head down. I think he was worn out. Afterwhile I lifted High Horse and put him behind the saddle. Then I started home with him. The power was gone out of me. There was no dust and no noise. Horseback warriors were standing scattered over the hill, just looking. The women and boys were swarming up from the valley looking for wounded soldiers to kill.

"I took him home to his father's tepee among the Miniconjous. Big fires burned that night and the people were dancing the victory dance until morning. I did not dance. I remembered and remembered, and the power was gone from me. I cried all night."

The Woman Who Died Twice

"It was a great victory," the old man said at last. He had been sitting like the embodiment of the brooding stillness outside. Yesterday's booming warm wind had died late in the night, and it had seemed that the still, soft dawn needed only a meadowlark to be April.

When he had filled and lighted his pipe, he drew a long draft and passed the pipe to me. "*Dho*," he said, "that was a great victory; but you see us now. I do not like to think of it. We all went away from there towards the mountains, and there was feasting and dancing, for we had killed many enemies. But my heart did not sing when I danced. High Horse was my brother-friend, and he was waiting for me yonder in the world of spirits." For a while the old man gazed in silence at the ground. Then he squinted at me with a pucker of suppressed amusement about his eyes, and said, "Maybe he will not know me when I come at last, bent low and walking on three legs." He chuckled and was still again.

"But what about Tashina, Grandfather?" I asked, and had to wait for an answer.

"I saw her at the sun dance on the Rosebud," he said. "She looked at me again the way she used to do, and I was glad she was not angry with me any more. But my head was full of war and great deeds to be done. I saw her once again after we had rubbed out Long Hair and his horseback soldiers on the hill. But then my heart was sick because of High Horse. It was the way I told you. There was a road I did not see until I had walked across the world.

"It was a victory, but now I can see that it was the end of the old days. The Wasichus were coming and coming, more and more Wasichus, and the bison would soon be gone. While we were camped near the mountains some of our people began to leave us, one *iglaka*, two, three *iglakas* at a time. They were going back to the agencies. We heard of many soldiers getting ready on Goose Creek south of us, many soldiers getting ready on the Yellowstone north of us. They would come together and surround us. So in the Moon of Black Cherries [August] the scattering of the people began. They always scattered in the fall after they had come together for the sun dance. But that time it was different. I did not know then that the hoop was breaking and would never come together again. When we broke camp, most of us started north together. Some were talking of Grandmother's Land [Canada]. They said if we went there, the soldiers could not chase us any more, and Grandmother England [Queen Victoria] was kind to our relatives who were living in her country. But many said they did not want to die in a strange land far from home.

"The prairie burned behind us, wide as the sky. This made it hard for the soldiers' horses to follow. We turned east towards Mini Shoshay [the Missouri River]. Then the rain came. Day and night it rained until the mud was deep and our horses could hardly pull the drags. There were still many, many of us, many, many horses; but some people were always leaving us—one *iglaka*, two, three *iglakas*, maybe a big party. Some would hunt awhile, but when they had made winter meat, they would go to the agencies.

"My grandfather and grandmother had some relatives in Grandmother's Land, and when Sitting Bull turned north again with about a hundred lodges, we went along with him and crossed the Yellowstone. Crazy Horse, with many of the people, went on towards where the sun comes up. I never saw him again. The Miniconjous went on with him, and when I saw Tashina again after many moons, everything was different. My step-father, Looks Twice, said if we went visiting in Grandmother's Land, afterwhile the soldiers might go away and we could come back home.

"Horseback soldiers came after us yonder, and there was a fight. It was not much. We got away in the night with Sitting Bull, and fled north. Then we camped and hunted and dried much meat. Soldiers did not come there. We had good tepees and plenty of *papa*.

"In the Moon of Dark Red Calves [February] we heard about Crazy Horse and his people. They had gone back through the burned-off land to Tongue River, and they were hungry there when the soldiers came, many soldiers. It was a bad fight in the snow and cold, and Crazy Horse had no powder; so he fled with his people in a snowstorm to Little Powder River, and there they were starving.

"The story was a moon old when it came to our village. Maybe many soldiers would attack us too. So we broke camp when a melting wind blew, as it did yesterday, and went into Grandmother's Land. There we had relatives to visit and the soldiers could not chase us.

"I thought maybe we would go back home when the new grass came; but when the valleys were green along the creeks, another story came to us. Crazy Horse had led his starving people into the Soldiers' Town on White River [Fort Robinson] so that they could eat. Then we thought it would be better to wait until it was time for the fall hunt. Maybe Crazy Horse and his people would be hunting, and we could join them, and be happy together again. But bad stories came to us that summer, and just before the winter we heard that the Wasichus had murdered Crazy Horse at the Soldiers' Town.

"We did not go home."

The old man ceased and sat with drooped head, his hands on his knees. When I held the pipestem towards him, he did not see it, and I felt alone in the tepee. "What then, Grandfather?" I said at length. He raised his head and seemed to come back slowly from a distant place. His gaze took on the crinkled, quizzical look, and what he said came with a shock of surprise: "I got married."

He took the pipe and smoked awhile. "*Dho,*" he continued, "we did not go home. Our relatives were kind to us. There were bison in plenty. There were no soldiers to chase us. There were valleys and streams like ours at home; but when I rode along a valley, something was not there; and when I looked at a hill, it was a stranger. There were no great deeds to be done and no great honors to win. When I was a boy, and the sun would come up, something wonderful might happen that day. It was not so any more. Stories came from the agencies, and they were about hunger and sickness and the forked tongues of the Wasichus. The soldiers even took away the people's horses. Pa Sapa was full of crazy Wasichus digging up the yellow metal.

"Grasses came forth and died, and the snow fell. Again the grass was new and died and there was snow. Maybe next grass everything would be better, and we would go home. We did not go home. The stories that came to us were not good. Afterwhile we got used to the strange land. Then I got married.

"She was a Hunkpapa girl and her right name was Plenty White Cows. People called her Woman Who Died, and they told about a strange power she had. She made charms for her two brothers, so that what they tried to do, they could do it; and with these charms they had won great honors in war. Also she could see things that were going to happen.

"She was older than I was, but she was a girl yet. I think maybe young men were a little afraid of her because of the stories people told, and she was not very strong—maybe because she had died once and gone to the world of spirits. I will tell you how it was, the way people told it; for it had been made into a story for anybody to tell.

"When Plenty White Cows was just a little girl, maybe five or six winters old, a strange sickness came upon her. The *wichasha wakon* could do nothing, and so she died. At that time her father and mother were camping with some other Hunkpapas at Slim Buttes, north of Pa Sapa. And when their girl was dead, they prepared her for the other world and put her on a scaffold, the way I have told you. Then the band broke camp and moved on towards Mini Shoshay, and the father and mother and brothers went wandering and mourning. This was when the Moon of Black Cherries [August] was young, and it was a time of no storms.

"There was a man whose name was Against the Clouds. He and his woman were Sans Arcs. They had been visiting with relatives in Grandmother's Land, and they were on their way back to Bear Butte near Pa Sapa, where the Sans Arcs would be camping. They were traveling alone with two horses to ride and one to pull the drag. It was not very far between sleeps, for they were getting to be old people and they would be tired when there was yet much day. Also, they were having a good time together, because the weather was so pleasant. They were not in a hurry to be at home, because their children were dead and they had no family.

"So Against the Clouds and his woman were riding along slowly where the trail left the creek and began to climb towards a pass in the sharp buttes. These buttes stand tall in a row that is bent like a great bow with the arrow aimed at the sunset; and that is the way the two were going. The man was ahead of the drag-horse and the woman came last. When they were not far from the pass, the woman said, 'Look! Look over there! Somebody has died here since we came through with the young grass.' So Against the Clouds stopped his horse and looked. 'It is so,' he said; for yonder high up on the side of the butte, not very far away, was a new scaffold. And the woman said, 'I wonder if it is somebody we know.' The man looked hard awhile, then he said, 'Do you see how the crows are doing? They fly around but do not come close. Something is scaring them.' And the woman said, 'There is something sitting on the scaffold. Maybe it is a buzzard.' And when the man had looked hard for a while longer, he said, 'That does not look like any buzzard I ever saw sitting. Let us go and see.'

"So they left the drag-horse grazing by the trail and rode over a

225

little way to see what was sitting yonder on the scaffold. All at once the woman cried out and stopped her horse. It surely was *not* a buzzard up there. 'Let us get away from here!' she said, and she could hardly make the words, she was so frightened. But Against the Clouds just sat still on his horse, looking and listening, with his woman behind him, looking and listening. It was the bundle that was sitting up there with its face turned the other way—a little bundle! And as they stared with their mouths open, hardly breathing, there came a thin sound like a sick child crying and whimpering. Then the man said, 'Nobody is dead here. I think they put somebody up there too soon. I will go and see.' So he did, while the woman waited, for she was still frightened. And when the man had looked, he called to his woman. 'Come here quick and do not be afraid! It is a sick child, and it may die if we do not hurry to help it.' Then the woman was not afraid any more, and she went in a hurry to help.

"So that is how the little girl who died came back to this world again. And when the two old people had unwrapped her, they made a camp by a spring that ran cool among pines just beyond the pass. And there they washed the little girl very carefully with warm water. Also they made some broth and put it in her mouth a few drops at a time, for she was still more in the spirit world than here.

"Against the Clouds and his woman did not sleep much all night. They sat beside the sick little girl and gave her drops of broth once in a while, for they were afraid she would die again and they wanted to keep her for their own. They had no children for their old age, and the woman was already too old to have any more. While the little girl was sleeping, they talked together and made a plan. If the girl lived, they would take her home with them and say they adopted her in Grandmother's Land. They were very good old people and always spoke straight words; but they wanted a daughter so much that they made this story to tell so that they could keep her. They prayed hard too; and when it was morning, they could see that the girl would live. And the woman said, 'Let us give our daughter a good name. I think it would be well to call her Plenty White Cows. It is a sacred name, and surely Wakon Tonka has sent her to us from the spirit land. Also, it is a pretty name. I always liked it.' And the man said, 'Let it be so. We will call her Plenty White Cows.' So they did.

"Against the Clouds and his woman stayed in camp there until the girl was well enough to talk, but she could not remember much. She would just look and look at the two old people, and sometimes she would cry a little. They asked what her father's name was, and she could not tell.

She did not know her own name either, so they told her the new name, and she would say it again and again.

"Afterwhile she could remember that she was sleeping and that a man came singing. He touched her and told her to 'waken, for some people were coming to take her back. So she awoke and tried to get up. It must have been hard to crawl out of the bundle, but somehow she did part way. And when she sat up, there was no man, but only a crow flying off. Then she was frightened and began crying, and right away the people that the singing crow-man told about were there. Then she did not remember any more until she was tasting broth.

"The old people were so good to her that in a little while she loved them very much and learned to call them father and mother. And when she was well enough to walk a little, they broke camp and started for Bear Butte with Plenty White Cows riding on the drag.

"When Against the Clouds and his woman came back home with their new daughter, their friends would come to see and bring gifts. But the little girl would hide behind her foster-mother and peek around at the faces. For a long while she seemed to be looking for somebody she knew, but when anyone spoke to her, she would hide behind her foster-mother and cry. Maybe she was looking for her own father and mother like people she had seen in a dream. Her foster-parents said she was very bashful; but people talked about it and said she was queer.

"So Against the Clouds and his woman had Plenty White Cows all for themselves, and they were so fond of her that people said they were foolish about her. Also, she loved them very much and was always helping her foster-mother. It was not long before the foster-parents noticed that she knew things she could not know unless a spirit told her. Sometimes she would talk to people they could not see and learn something that was true but that she could not know by herself. That is the way she found her foster-father's horse when it was lost and no one could find it.

"I think it was two snows after this, and the Sans Arcs were traveling. It was in the Moon of Black Cherries again. The people with their pony-drags were crossing a deep creek and Hunkpapas were camped on the other side. Some Hunkpapa men were at the crossing to help if any should have trouble with the drags in the mud. One of these Hunkpapas was the brother of the girl's father, and when Against the Clouds and his woman and Plenty White Cows came riding with their drag, this man looked very hard at the girl; and when they had crossed, he wondered and wondered. Then he went and told his brother, who was camping there, that he had seen a girl who looked just like the one who died, only maybe a little older. So when the Sans Arcs had camped not far from the Hunkpapas, the real father and his brother went over to see.

"When they had walked part way around the village circle, they saw Plenty White Cows helping her foster-mother at the fire in front of the tepee. And when the real father saw her, he just stood with his mouth open, looking, until the girl cried out and ran to hide behind her foster-mother. Just then Against the Clouds came from staking out his horses, and the real father said to him, 'Kola, you have a little daughter here who looks just like the little daughter I had, but she died two snows ago just about this time. It was at Slim Buttes. My woman still cries hard whenever we talk about our daughter.' But Against the Clouds and his woman looked down their noses and said nothing. Then the real father and his brother went away.

"In a little while, the real father came back with the girl's real mother. And when the mother saw the girl, she screamed and hid her face with her hands. Then she looked again, with tears running through her fingers, and she wailed, 'What do I see, O what do I see? My little girl is dead! My little girl is dead! What do I see?' This time the girl did not run and hide. She looked with big scared eyes at the woman who was crying so hard, and then she ran to the woman and the woman seized her and held her, crying very hard.

"By now Against the Clouds and his woman were just standing there with tears running down their faces, and the real father was crying too. And Against the Clouds said at last, 'Friends, it is true. This is your little girl. We saved her from the scaffold and made a story so that we might keep her.' And the foster-mother said, 'Yes, it is true, but we love her so much, and we are getting old and she is all we have.'

"Then the real father said to Against the Clouds, 'Kola, we are men, and we can smoke a pipe and talk this over.' So that is what they did, and this is how they agreed. The girl was born and had died. Then she was born again. So she had two mothers and two fathers, and the first parents would own her as much as the second parents, the second as much as the first. The girl would keep her second name because the first name died with her. She was born first in the Moon of Dark Red Calves [February], so in that moon she would go to live with her first parents. Then in the Moon of Black Cherries [August] she would go to live with her second parents, because it was then that she came back from the spirit land.

"And when this was agreed, the first father and mother and the second father and mother and their little girl were happy."

XXVI

The Moon of Black Cherries

"*Dho,*" said Eagle Voice, approving the conclusion of his silent meditation. "I got used to the strange land. By the stories that came to us, home was not yonder any more. The sacred hoop of the people was broken, and old men said it could never be mended. If Sitting Bull went back, maybe the soldiers would kill him. They had killed Crazy Horse already. My brother-friend was gone. The people yonder were hungry around the agencies. Where we were, there were bison in plenty, and no soldiers to chase us. I was young and I liked to live. So I got used to the strange land; and I got married too.

"We were on a fall hunt with some people from different bands of the Lakota, and a few Cheyennes and Arapahoes, maybe ten or twelve lodges altogether, and we were camping by a creek. Three of my horses strayed away and I was out looking for them. They had strayed far, dragging their lariats, and the sun was getting ready to go down when I got back to the creek. I was on my horse, holding the others while the four were drinking.

"There was going to be frost that night. The air smelled good and it was still. The smokes stood straight from the tepees yonder in the flat. Leaves were changing color and some plums were red in a clump of brush. A little sound was big. I was just sitting there leaning on my horse and holding the others. There was a whiff of meat cooking. Maybe I was thinking about something a long way off, but I do not remember what.

"All at once the brush cracked. The horses snorted. The two young ones reared and broke away, running and kicking and making sharp wind when they kicked. It was just like the other time I told you about; that time after my first sun dance when the people were getting ready to scatter and my horses broke away at the creek.

"She was standing there at the edge of the plum brush, and my heart jumped in me; for all at once it was that other time back home. Then I saw that it was Plenty White Cows standing there. She had red plums in a fold of her blanket, and she was looking at me and smiling. She was pretty.

"Our party was small, so I had seen her often since her family came to camp with us. Against the Clouds and his woman were dead, and she was living with her real parents. I had noticed her more than other girls because I knew the story about her and the strange power she had. That was not the only time she had smiled at me that way. The first time was when I was riding by her tepee and she was cooking out in front of it. She was bent over, stirring the pot, and she looked up at me surprised. Then she looked happy and smiled, and she was pretty, and she did not seem strange any more.

"Yes, it was like the time back home that I told you about. Maybe that is why I said it, or maybe I was bashful all at once. My mother and grandmother wanted me to get married, and they said I was too bashful because I did not notice girls much. Maybe I was bashful then. I said, 'Hold this horse for me while I catch the others.' So she took the lariat and I rode away on the run after my horses. While I was chasing them, I was wondering if the horse would be tied to the brush when I got back. The young horses felt good, and I had a long chase before I caught them in a bend of the creek against a high bank. It was dark before I got back with them, and I thought surely the other horse would be tied to the brush, just the way it was that other time.

"It was not so. She was standing in the same place, holding the horse. There was starlight."

The old man fell silent and began fumbling in his long tobacco pouch. When he had filled the pipe and tamped it with a leisurely thoroughness, he said, "That is how it was, Grandson; that is how it was." Then he lit the pipe, his lean cheeks hollowing.

When we had sat in silence for a while he began talking in a low voice, with little expression at first, as though remembering aloud with no thought of sharing.

"She was a good woman, and she made the strange land almost like home. She was always working and never angry. She would make low songs for herself when she was working. I think she could tan deerskin as soft as my grandmother could; and she made clothing of it, beautiful with beads and dyed porcupine quills. I always got plenty of tender meat for us, plenty for my grandfather and grandmother too. They would come to eat with us and bring other very old people with them. I could always get plenty, because she could tell me where to hunt. Sometimes she would be working and singing to herself; then she would stop singing and tell me where she saw some fat young deer drinking when the sun was going down. Maybe that would be in the morning, but she would see it. So I would be there waiting for the sun to set, and the fat young deer would come.

"She always looked after my moccasins, and when I had been hunting on foot and was tired, she would grease the bottoms of my feet by the fire. She was patient and wise, and sometimes she was more like my mother than my woman; maybe because she was older.

"She could see what others could not see, and what was going to happen, she could tell it. When someone was going to die, she would tell me, and it would be so. If somebody lost some horses, she could sit still with her eyes shut and dream, and in the dream she would go to where the horses were then; and when she opened her eyes, she would tell how she went there, and it would be so.

"She was a good woman, but not strong like other women, maybe because she had died once and come back for a while. No children came to us, and my mother said the women talked about this. I think they did not like her. Maybe they were afraid because of her *yuwipi* [spiritualistic] power. But sometimes when they wanted to know something hidden, they would come to her with little gifts.

"There were grasses and snows and the land was not strange any more. When Sitting Bull went back and surrendered to the Wasichus, we did not go back, for the stories that came to us from our people on White Clay Creek where their reservation [Pine Ridge] was were not happy stories, and we were used to the new land.

"There were more grasses and snows and more grasses. Then one day when the cherries were turning black Plenty White Cows did not get up in the morning. Her mother and mine came over to help and they made some soup for her, but she did not want to eat it. She did not talk to us, but sometimes she would talk to people we could not see. Afterwhile when she was sleeping hard and there was nothing to do, our mothers went home.

"When the sun was beginning to go down, she called to me, and I leaned close to hear. Her voice was far away. I thought she was dreaming and talking in her sleep. There were tears on her face, and she said, 'A little girl is crying. Do you not hear her crying far away?' And I said, 'No little girl is crying. You are dreaming.' Then she looked at me with a soft look from far away, and said, 'It is the little girl you think about when you are alone. I hear her crying far across snows and grasses.'

"She closed her eyes and when she looked at me again, it was a far

231

look that did not see me, and she was talking about a great water reaching to the sunrise, and a long road across it and strange peoples yonder in a strange land. 'It is a long road,' she said, 'but you will come back home. The little girl will grease your feet beside the fire, and she will not cry any more.'

"I thought she had gone to sleep and I sat there awhile listening to her breathing, and wondering. I went outside and while I stood there, the sun went under. Then I heard her call me again, and I went in and leaned close to hear what she would say. 'Cherries are getting black,' she said. 'They are getting black.' And I said, 'It is so; they are blackening.' At first I did not know what she meant. Then she looked at me from far away, and her voice was far away too, and she said, 'The young moon is low yonder. It is time to go. They are coming to take me home again.'

"Then there was a sudden wide look in her eyes, and I knew it was not for me. All at once I knew it was for her foster-parents, Against the Clouds and his woman. They had come for her in the Moon of Black Cherries, the way they used to do before they died; but I could not see them. I knew this all at once, and there was a big ache in my breast; but I said, 'Plums are beginning to ripen too. Soon they will be good to eat. We will go and pick some.' I was seeing red plums in a fold of her blanket. She closed her eyes and lay still, but I could hear her breathing deep.

"I was sitting there in the dark wondering and thinking many things with the ache in my breast. Her mother came back, but I did not tell her anything because I must not talk to her. I could see the old woman was leaning down over her daughter, and I think she was listening. Then she cried out and began mourning.

"My mother came and others too. They made a fire in front of our lodge, and there was mourning all night."

Eagle Voice was silent for a while, looking at the ground. At length he turned a squinting gaze on me and said, "There is a strange road ahead, Grandson, a road that leads far. Let us walk on it tomorrow. I want to sleep now."

XXVII

The Dark Hills of Water

The wind had sharpened, shifting eastward in the night, and now it filled the dull gray morning with the prickling smell of snow. When I arrived, Eagle Voice was up and eager to continue, beginning where he had ceased the day before, as though there had been no interruption.

"*Dho,*" he said when I had placed a cottonwood chunk in the stove, "it is a road that leads across the world.

"After Against the Clouds and his woman came and took her home to the world of spirit the land was strange again. Sometimes I rode all day, but there was nothing. Everywhere the valleys were empty, and if I stopped to listen, they would be listening too. The hills looked, and did not know me. Sometimes I thought I would go back home; but there was no home yonder. Sometimes I thought I would ride down to see the Rosebud and the Greasy Grass again, and maybe I would go over to the Little Piney country where my father's scaffold stood. Then I would think maybe there would be many Wasichus yonder, too many to kill. Or if there were no Wasichus, the valleys would be empty and I would be a stranger and the hills would stare. The bones of my father would be scattered and the blowing of the wind would be like mourning. So I did not go.

"The snow came and fell deep.

"Dreams came to me when I slept, and when I sat alone beside my fire and the wind whipped the smoke-flap, dreams came to me awake. Sometimes I would be sitting there looking at the fire, and she would be sitting yonder across the fire, maybe sewing quills and beads on a moccasin. Then I would look, and there would be nothing I could see; but when I looked away she would be there again sewing by the fire.

"I hunted much and got fresh meat for my grandparents and other old people. Often people invited me to come and eat with them, and there would be stories, so that I would be back in the good days awhile. But I liked to be alone too. I wondered much about the great water

233

reaching to the sunrise and the strange people in a far land and the little girl crying far away. Maybe the little girl was Tashina when I was a little boy. But I was a man, and how could she grease my feet?

"One night when the winter was old, Plenty White Cows came while I slept, and I saw her clear. She was standing by the plum brush, and she was smiling at me. Plums were red in the thicket and there were some in a fold of her blanket. She smiled at me and said, '*Shonka 'kan*, you made me proud.' Then I saw that it was not Plenty White Cows standing there. It was Tashina. And just as I knew her, horses snorted and broke sharp wind. Then there was only starlight and a voice that said, 'Hold fast, there is more.' And I was awake in the dark and the wind was whipping the smoke-flap."

The old man paused, fumbling in his long tobacco pouch. After a leisurely tamping of the pipe, he lit it, passed it to me and sat gazing at the ground. When it seemed that he had lost me in his meditation, I prompted him, 'And the long road, Grandfather?'

"Ah," he said, his gaze slowly focusing upon me; "the long road. I started south before the young grasses appeared, going to see my people, the Oglalas, again. Maybe there would be soldiers, so I rode nights, slept days. No soldiers. I saw the new iron road [Northern Pacific] that the Wasichus had made, and for a while I was afraid to cross it. My horse was afraid too; but we crossed it on the run. I was hiding when the great iron horse went by snorting smoke and pulling many big wagons. I rode down across the flat-lands, past the White Buttes and Bear Butte and Pa Sapa.

"When I came to Smoky Earth [White] River, my mind was forked. Maybe I would go over to the Miniconjous on the South Fork; maybe I would go to the Oglalas on White Earth Creek. I went to the Miniconjous, and I was a stranger. People were talking about the Wanekia [the Messiah] who was coming soon, they said. He was coming from where the sun goes down, and all the Wasichus would disappear like smoke when he came; and there would be a new heaven and a new earth for Lakotas. I did not believe it. I thought they were all *witko*."

"And Tashina Wanblee, Grandfather," I urged when he had been silent overlong. "Surely you went there to see her."

"She was not there," he said in a matter-of-fact manner, fixing his crinkled look upon me. "Too many snows and grasses. She had a Hunkpapa man. Living up on Grand River with Sitting Bull's people; five snows ago, they told me.

"I came to the Oglalas here on White Earth Creek, and I was a

234

stranger, at first, for I was not a young man any more, and they did not know me. It was not good. Red Cloud living in a square Wasichu tepee made of wood. *Akichita* wearing the blue coats of the Wasichu. All the people waiting for Wasichu food, like hungry dogs, and talking about the Wanekia. Some said he was coming right away, like a whirlwind across the prairie. No more Wasichus. The good days coming back and all the buffalo. I did not believe it. I thought they were all *witko*. There was a big ache in my breast and I wanted to go back to Grandmother's Land; but when I thought I would go, the ache got bigger. Then Pahuska came. You know Pahuska?"

"Everybody knew him, Grandfather," I said. "We called him Buffalo Bill. He was a great Wasichu chief, great hunter, great warrior. And you went with his big show to Paris."

"Ah," the old man agreed. "It is so. Pars, Pars; it is what they called that country. It is so. He wanted Lakota warriors to ride and play war and dance, so that the strange people across the great water could see. He would give us *maza ska* [white metal, money] to do this. When I heard about the great water and the strange peoples yonder at the sunrise, I knew I must go, for it was what she told me before she went home.

"The Wasichus had made another iron road along the Minitonka [Niobrara]. It was the way Wooden Cup said before my grandfather was born. A strange people would come from the sunrise, too many to be counted. They would kill all the bison and take the land and bind it with iron bands. I was going to see where all the Wasichus came from. We started for the sunrise on this iron road, and went faster than our horses could run. I was afraid, but I held on tight and looked at the land I knew since I was a boy. It was running away, and the hills looked scared. After a while it was dark, and I slept. Then I awoke and there was a big moon outside. The land was still running away. The wagon under me was jumping fast and crying, *'yea-hay, yea-hay, yea-hay,'* like warriors fleeing from too many enemies; and I could hear the iron horse running and snorting and puffing all out of breath. Sometimes he screamed like a war-pony shot in the guts. I held on tight, and the morning came.

"Then I saw the Mini Shoshay [Missouri River], and there was a big Wasichu village [Omaha], bigger than all the Lakotas camped in one hoop. Then there were more iron roads in a land I never saw before, and Wasichu villages—many, many. And the iron horse went on running as fast as before, snorting and puffing all out of breath and screaming.

"I wanted to go back, but I could not. Afterwhile I got used to it, but

235

my heart was not strong in me. When I was a boy we used to say that some time we would kill all the Wasichus; but now I knew there were more of them than grasshoppers. When Red Cloud went to see the Great Father, and we heard the big stories he told about the Wasichus and their villages yonder where the sun rises, we did not believe. We said he turned into a Wasichu when he put on their clothing, and his tongue was forked like theirs. But I could see his words were straight. And when we came to the biggest village of all where the great water begins [New York], I knew his stories were not big enough. Wasichus! Wasichus! They came crowding like a bison herd to look and look at us when we got on the big *peyta watah* [fire-boat] that was there.

"I cannot tell how big this *watah* was. They put all the horses and tepees and wagons in its belly; and the fire that made it go was in there too. When it started for the sunrise with us, it bellowed like bison bulls sending forth voices together when they paw the young grass and tear it with their horns. I saw the land begin to move. It did not run away fast. It floated away, and afterwhile it was all gone, and there was the great water to the sky. It was sleeping and breathing, up and down, up and down. I got sick, and I was afraid. Maybe I would die. I remembered what old men said, 'It is not good to grow old.' But I wore the quirt down my back, and you see I am alive yet.

"Twelve sleeps—water, water, water! Twelve sleeps! When the winds were asleep and the sun was showing, it was a flat blue prairie with no grass. Maybe it was like the prairie where the star nations live, and the sister in the story I told you fell through it! But no turnips on this prairie! The *peyta watah* shook itself and breathed hard, and smoke came out of its belly; but it did not move. The sun moved and the stars, and the sunrise was no nearer.

"The Thunder Beings came with lightning and a great wind that howled, and the flat blue prairie changed into dark hills that grew tall and fell, grew tall and fell. I was more afraid than I ever was before. All of us were afraid and the horses too. Sometimes I could hear them scream in the *watah's* belly. I was not afraid to die in a battle with enemies I could kill. But there was no enemy to fight. Maybe the quirt could not help me. If I died there in the great water, maybe I could not find the way to the spirit land, and I would be lost always in the dark hills. That is what made me afraid. If I died in the hills of water, maybe I could never find my relatives again. But I had my pipe with me, and I remembered what my father said with the voice of the eagle in my vision, 'Hold fast to your pipe, for there is more.' So I held fast to my pipe. Also, Pahuska was like a father to us. He laughed and told us to be brave. He had a strong heart.

"We came to where the hills were smaller and the winds were asleep. Then we saw the sun again and the blue prairie; and the strange land came floating to us out of the sunrise."

In the Village Called Pars

"There was another iron road," the old man continued after a period of silence, "and we came to the village they called Pars. This village was so big that we could never see how big it was, and the tepees were made of stone. The Wasichus there could not be counted. They piled tepees on top of tepees and climbed up there so that they could have places to live. These places were full of people, all looking out like prairie dogs from their holes. There were big roads and little roads going everywhere in this village, and the people and the horses and wagons were always going everywhere with much noise and many cries. I do not know what they were doing.

"Pahuska wanted the people to see us, so he led us all on a big road made of stone where there were tall trees and green grass; and there the people came crowding like a bison herd to look at us. Pahuska went first, and he was riding a big white horse. He did not look like other Wasichus. His hair was long like a Lakota's, but it was not braided and it was yellow. Also his clothing was made of buckskin. We followed him on our ponies, riding two together, and we were painted and dressed as for victory and our ponies were painted too. And after us were *iglakas* with their pony-drags. And after them there were Wasichu horsebacks with lariats on their saddles, riding two together. Then there were Wasichu wagons with tepee tops on them, and other wagons with four horses pulling them and people riding on top and inside. And there were horseback soldiers, and they were riding two and two.

"I think the people liked the Lakotas best of all. When we knew they were not enemies and were glad to see us, we were glad too, and we began singing a riding song all together. It was the way young warriors would do when they were going somewhere and there were no enemies around. When we stopped singing, the herd of people roared and crowded in to us, shouting and reaching up to touch us. A young woman took hold of my arm, but some horsebacks came and pushed the people back. These horsebacks looked like soldiers, but I think they were *akichitas*.

"When we started riding through this green place with the tall trees, I could see where water was coming up out of the ground, many streams of water rising and falling. I do not know what it was. I have heard there is shooting water like that over in Shoshoni country, but I never saw it.

"Afterwhile we came to a great high stone with a big hole in it, and we all rode through this hole. From that place I could see roads that led to the four quarters of the world. The stone was standing where the Sacred Tree should grow and bloom, the way Blue Spotted Horse told me when I was a boy. I wondered much about this. Maybe these Wasichus had the sacred hoop too; and maybe the Wasichus back home across the great water had forgotten about the hoop and so were not good any more. Maybe that was why Grandmother England's soldiers did not chase us when we fled to Grandmother's Land. Maybe they had the hoop too. That is what I thought then, but now I do not believe it.

"There was a place where all these people came in a herd to see us twice nearly every day. It was a little round flat valley with a steep hill all around it, and on this hill the people sat to see, and roared when they saw.

"Pahuska would ride into the middle of the round flat valley and make his tall white horse stand on its hind legs. Then he would take his big hat off and wave it at the people on the hill all around him; and the hill would roar. Sometimes he would throw shining balls into the air, and he would shoot at them, and always they would break. The people liked him, but I think they liked us more. We did many things the way we used to do at home. Sometimes we would dance and sing. Sometimes we would attack Wasichu wagons, going up Shell River [Platte], maybe, or maybe up the road to Pa Sapa. Or we would chase the other kind of wagon with people sitting on top and inside and four running horses pulling it [stage coach]. There would be shouting and war-cries and a great dust of hoofs, and many guns going off; but there were no bullets in the guns. Some of us would get killed and roll in the dust, and our brothers would ride by and lean to pick us up and take us out of the fight. We did many things, and always a roaring wind blew across the hill of people when they saw. It was fun; and sometimes when we were alone together and the dead ones were alive again, we would laugh about it.

"We stayed there while moons came and went, and always the hill of people was there to see us and roar.

"*Washtay!* It was good! Pahuska had a strong heart and he was like a father. He gave us plenty of fat *papa*, all we could eat; and there was plenty of *paezhuta sapa* [black medicine, coffee] with plenty of *chun humpi* [tree juice, sugar] to put in it."

The old man ceased and fell to brooding. "*Dho!*" he said at long last, slowly fixing his crinkled look upon me. "It was the same young Wasichu woman. When Pahuska led us through the place of grass and trees to show us to the people, it was the same young woman who came crowding with the other Wasichus and took hold of my arm. She looked up at me then and I saw her face, but the horseback *akichitas* came and pushed the people back. I wondered about this, and sometimes I would think about her face and the way she looked up at me. Then I wanted to see her again. I am wearing the white war bonnet now, and it is thin. My teeth are uprooted and I am bent so that I am not even as tall as you, my grandson. But then I was straight and tall and strong, and maybe I was good-looking. Also I was a good dancer.

"It was the time when leaves would be falling in my country; and when I thought about this I would feel sad, because it was far across the dark hills of water. It was in the night when she came back. Some of us Lakotas were standing outside, for it was not our time to play war in there. Sometimes we heard the hill of people roar. There was a light that flickered in a cage where we were, and Wasichus came close to look at us. They would look and look, and we were making jokes about them, but they did not know it because we made our faces stone. Sometimes we would growl and the people near us would push back, and we would look angry, but we were laughing inside. They were funny, the way they looked and looked and peeked around each other to see us.

"She came out of the shadow. One of her hands was on my naked arm and one upon my naked breast—thin white hands—and she was looking up at me."

The old man ceased again and gazed awhile upon the ground with half-closed eyes. "Leaves were falling at home," he said in a low voice, still looking at the ground. Then, raising his eyes and fixing upon me a squinting gaze that had a question in it, he continued. "She had much hair. Sometimes I think about it yet, and I see a bright cloud when the sky is white in the morning and the sun is just beginning to come. Her look was soft and kind. There was a power that went through me from her hands. Sometimes when I think about this, I remember when I was a boy and Blue Spotted Horse gave me the sacred pipe to touch, and the power went through me."

Again the old man paused, and the focus of his gaze fell beyond me.

"If it was good or bad," he continued, "I do not know. It is far away and I am old; but sometimes when I think about it, I am a boy in the night and the moon makes him want to sing, but something is afraid in the shadows. She pulled me with her look and with her white hands. I went into the dark with her. There was laughing and there were voices back there, but they were far away, far as across the hills of water.

"Out in the dark was a little wagon with two wheels, and one horse pulled it. These were always going up and down the many roads in that village, and a man sat high on top to make the horse go. We got in there and the whip popped and we went fast. Her mouth was on my face; her hair was on my eyes; her hands were about my neck. I did not know what she was saying again and again, but it was like singing; and I could smell young grass when rain has fallen and the sun comes out.

"There was a place where two dark roads crossed, but some little fires burned in cages on poles and made shadows. That is where we got out of the wagon, and the man on top laughed and popped his whip and went away. We climbed twice to where she lived and we were alone in that high place."

The old man ceased and began fumbling in his long tobacco sack. When he had prepared the pipe with more than necessary attention to detail, he lit it and blew a cloud.

"Three suns, three sleeps my heart sang there," he continued, handing me the pipe. "My heart sang and I thought she would go back with me and be my woman always. We would go to Grandmother's Land where I could kill plenty of good meat for her, and she would learn to tan buckskin very soft, and make clothing and moccasins beautiful with beads and porcupine quills. Also, there would be children and grandchildren. This is what I thought when my heart was singing, but I could not tell her, for my tongue was strange to her and hers was strange to me.

"It was in the fourth sleep that she came back to me, all the way across the dark hills of water."

"Who came?" I asked.

"Plenty White Cows came back while I slept," he said, "the same way she came before I left Grandmother's Land. Plums were red in the brush behind her and plums were red in a fold of her blanket. She was looking at me and her eyes were sad. Then a wind came moaning through the brush and she drew her blanket over her face, and there was a shadow that hid her. But when the shadow passed, the blanket was open about her face, and it was Tashina, and she was crying. I could see tears on her face and hear her crying like a little girl far away, but she did not look at me.

"Then all at once it was dark and I was awake in that strange place. I was afraid of something and my heart was sick. I do not know what I was afraid of. I could hear the woman sleeping, and the dark was still. I listened and listened, and there was nothing. In battle my heart sang, and I was not afraid. But in that still dark place I feared more and more and I could not stay.

"So I got up without making a noise, and walked softly. I felt for the little handle that turned. It clicked loud when I turned it, but nothing heard. I went out where a thin little fire was burning on a stick, and I went down and down, walking softly. There was another little handle that turned to let me out. When I was in the road outside, where the lights flickered in their cages, I ran. Some people came out of the shadows and yelled at me, but I did not stop.

"Then four *akichitas* came running out of the shadows and took hold of my arms. These men were not big and they were not angry. They patted me on the back and made soft sounds and kept saying, 'Bufflo Beel, Bufflo Beel.' And I said 'Ah, *kola*, it is so,' for I knew they meant Pahuska.

"I was glad to go with these Wasichu friends, for I was lost in that village of many roads. They took me to a place and two of them stayed with me. They made soft sounds and wagged their heads up and down and said, 'Bufflo Beel, Bufflo Beel,' and I knew they were friends. We stayed in that place until it was morning, and then they took me to Pahuska.

"He was not angry. He slapped me on the back and laughed like a big wind. I do not know why he did this, for my heart was sick. My heart was sick for home.

"I did not want to play war any more. I did not want to eat. The dream would not go away. I thought and thought about it and about my country many sleeps across the dark hills of water. I wanted to die, but there was no enemy to kill me; and I thought if I got weaker and weaker and died, maybe I could not find the way back to my relatives. I wondered how she found the way to me. Maybe it was her *yuwipi* power that helped her, and maybe I would be lost always out there.

"Then Pahuska said he would send me home, for he was like a father. Two others were going back, and one of these knew the Wasichu tongue, so we went together.

"Then, after many sleeps, I was here again."

XXIX

The Girl's Road

When I returned from the woodpile, the old man sat with closed eyes, listening to the random plaintive sounds he was making with his eagle-bone whistle. I fed the stove against the snow-chill that had begun to creep into the tepee. The wind had ceased and the listening world outside was filled with whispering flakes that clad the hills in gauze.

"You walked across the world," I said, "and then you found the road at last?"

Emerging slowly from his meditation and ignoring my question, he began.

"Looks Twice and my mother had come from Grandmother's Land. My grandfather and grandmother wanted to come home to their people, for they were very old and they did not want to die up there. So my step-father brought them back. They were all living in a little gray house of logs yonder on White Horse Creek, and I went to live with them. Winter was coming, and people were talking about the Wanekia [Messiah]. Some believed, and some said it was all foolishness. Looks Twice and my mother did not believe yet and I did not believe either; but my grandfather and grandmother said maybe it was true.

"I heard that Kicking Bear had gone with Good Thunder and some others to see the Wanekia far away where the sun sets and a people they called the Paiutes lived. They would come back with the young grass, and then, some said, we would know that it was all true. But others said it was a long way yonder, and stories that traveled far always got bigger. I did not care much about the Wanekia; but I wanted to see Kicking Bear again and talk about the things we used to do together before the hoop was broken. We could remember the time we got all those Crow horses, and we could talk about High Horse and Charging Cat; and maybe we would laugh about the way the fat old woman bounced on her pony-drag.

"It was a hard winter with much snow, and there was not much to eat. There was nothing to hunt, and the Great White Father did not

243

send all the cattle he promised. Sometimes I could kill a jack rabbit. The people grew angry and many were sick. I thought about the dream that came to me across the great water. Maybe this was why Plenty White Cows did not look at me in the dream and Tashina was crying. I remembered what Plenty White Cows told me before she went to her parents in the spirit world. I would go across a great water, and when I came back I would find the little girl she heard crying far away. I was back from across the great water, and there was only hunger and sickness.

"Afterwhile the snow melted and the young grasses appeared. Then Kicking Bear and the others came back. There was a big meeting at No Water's camp on White Clay Creek, and we went there to hear. Before the talking began I saw Kicking Bear, and it made my heart sing to see him again. He was older, but I knew him. So I went to him, and I think he did not know me. He looked hard at me and his eyes looked angry. I said, 'Cousin, I am Eagle Voice. Do you remember High Horse and Charging Cat and all those Crow horses we got that time? And do you remember the fat old woman, how she bounced when her pony ran away?' I made a laugh, for I thought he would remember and laugh too. He just looked hard at me like a stranger. His eyes were cold, his face was sharp. Then he cried out, 'Believe! Believe! For those who do not believe shall be lost!' And he went away.

"My heart was sick, for nothing was the same any more. I heard all they said at the meeting, and many, many were there to hear. The Wanekia would come like a whirlwind. Then all the Wasichus would disappear like a smoke. The earth would be made new and green forever and all the spirits would come from the other world and be alive here again. And with these the bison would return and the people would be happy together under a blue, blue sky; and there would be no crying any more, no hunger or sickness, no growing old or dying. A long while ago this same Wanekia came to the Wasichus, and they killed him. This time he would come to us, and we would know him. This is what we heard.

"The man they saw yonder where the sun sets was a Paiute and his name was Wovoka. He had died and gone to the other world a little while. There he had seen the Wanekia and talked to him; and when this Wovoka came back to our world here, he had to tell all the people everywhere, so that they would be ready. The Wanekia had given a sacred dance and sacred songs for the people to learn, and these would bring the new heaven and the new earth. This would happen after one more winter when the young grasses came again.

"I think most of those who heard, believed. Red Cloud was there, and he believed too. My step-father and my mother and my grandparents believed, but I was not sure. Maybe I was thinking how Kicking Bear looked at me. Also, I had gone across the world and back. It was so big and there were so many, many Wasichus. I wondered how one Wanekia could rub them all out and make the world new.

"After the big meeting, the people began dancing the sacred dance and singing the sacred songs. They held hands and made a hoop as they danced and sang, and at the center of the hoop there stood the *chun wakon* [sacred tree]. It was like the sacred hoop that Blue Spotted Horse told me about when I was a boy going on vision quest, and the tree at the center should fill with leaves and blooms and singing birds. But the tree was dead and the few leaves on top were dry.

"People danced and danced, singing to the Father who would come. And afterwhile some of them would fall down and lie dead a long while. And when these came alive again, they would tell of the spirit world where they had been and of the dear ones they saw yonder. My grandmother saw my father and he was young and happy and they talked together. And when she told us, her face was all bright and she was so glad that she cried and cried.

"Many saw people I used to know, and what they told seemed true. Afterwhile I began to think maybe this was the way the sacred hoop would be mended; and my grandmother told me I ought to help the people. So I danced, and sang the sacred songs to the Father who should come. But while I danced I would think about the sun dance in the good days before the hoop was broken, and how the people feasted together then and were happy and there was no crying. Now there was little to eat and much crying, and only the spirit world was happy. I did not see anything, and my heart was sick.

"The Agent told the people to stop dancing, but they would not; and in the Moon of Falling Leaves [November] we heard that the soldiers were coming to stop us. So the people fled north to the Top of the Badlands [Cuny Table], and I went with them. It would be hard for the soldiers to come to us there, and we did not want to fight them. The people said we could dance there until the Wanekia came, and then there would be no soldiers any more. The young men found some Wasichu cattle and these they took so that the people could eat.

"Kicking Bear was there and he was the big man in the teaching of the people; but he was a stranger. Sometimes I thought only his body was in this world, and sometimes I wondered if he was *witko*. Afterwhile he left us and went to Sitting Bull's camp on Grand River to start the dancing there.

"I danced hard because I was sorry for my people, and maybe I could help; I did not know. Once while I was dancing I was thinking about the sun dance the way it used to be in the good days. And all at once I was there again, and I could feel the power go through me; but it did not stay. And when I could not dance any more and lay down to sleep, there was no vision.

"In the Moon of Popping Trees [December] we heard that Sitting Bull was dead. The metal breasts [Indian police] killed him in his camp on Grand River, and they were his own people. It was cold, and we were beginning to starve, so we came back here and camped around the Agency [Pine Ridge], and they gave us some cattle to butcher. Soldiers were camped there too, but they did not bother us because we did not dance. Some of the people did not believe any more, and many were not sure that the Wanekia would come with the young grass; but many still believed."

The old man ceased, and it was some time before he shared with me the pictured past that flowed behind his closed eyelids.

"*Dho*, Grandson," he said, regarding me with a gentle look, "I found the road.

"The Moon of Popping Trees was old and dying when we heard about Sitanka [Big Foot] and his band. They were fleeing towards us from Grand River where Sitting Bull was killed. They were starving and many of them were sick, and it was cold. There were about two hundred of them and some were Hunkpapas. We heard that they had crossed White River and were coming up the Porcupine. Then we heard that the horseback soldiers surrounded them over yonder by Porcupine Butte and took them down to Wounded Knee Creek. That is where they camped that night with the soldiers all around them.

"Next morning the wind was still and it was warmer. There were thousands of us camped around the Agency, and all at once we heard shooting over there across the hills. Much shooting—wagon-guns shooting very fast! *Boom-boom-boom-boom-boom!* Very fast! And many other guns too, like tearing a blanket! They did not stop. They kept on shooting fast. Somebody shouted, '*Aah-hey! Aah-hey!* They are butchering over there!'

"The people were cooking and eating when they heard the guns and they went crazy. Everybody was crying, 'They are butchering them! *Aah-hey!* The soldiers are butchering them yonder!' Young men were running for their horses. Many started riding fast towards the shooting over across the hills, and I rode with them. The soldiers did not try to stop us, for our men back there were getting ready to attack. There

246

was a fight, but I did not see it. We rode fast, and when I looked back from the top of the hill, I could see others riding fast after us, and the people running.

"The shooting ahead yonder was louder when I was over the first hills. I was riding my step-father's horse that he brought from Grandmother's Land, and it was a strong horse; so I was up with the fronters. My heart sang again. Maybe I would die on the prairie after all, and High Horse would be waiting and he would see me far off and come running to meet me.

"Then all at once the wagon-guns stopped shooting. It was still over there.

"When we came to the top of the last hill, we saw the butchering. There is a long crooked ravine and it runs down to a flat valley beside the Wounded Knee. Along the ravine horseback soldiers were galloping this way and that way, all mixed up. They were hunting down the women and children who were still alive. The men were dead down yonder in the valley where the butchering began.

"There were not many of us on the hilltop yet, but we could see others coming behind us, and we charged down along the ravine. *Hokayhey! Hoka-hey!* But our horses were worn out and could hardly gallop. I think the soldiers did not know that we were few; and when they saw others coming over the hill, they did not wait to fight us there. They ran away towards the valley where there were more soldiers, and they were getting off their horses to dig and fight lying down.

"When we charged down beside the ravine, there were dead women and children scattered in it where the wagon-guns-that-shoot-twice [Hotchkiss guns] caught them running away. Up on the hillside above the ravine, there were some women and children huddled together in a gully, and they screamed to us as we passed.

"It was not much of a fight. There were too many soldiers and we were few, and the wagon-guns shot at those coming over the hill behind us.

"We circled back up along the hillside to where a few women and children were still living."

The old man paused and sat for a while with closed eyes. When he looked at me again his face was aglow with a pervasive smile. "That is where I found the road, Grandson," he said. His voice was low and gentle, with a quaver of age in it. "That is where I found the road.

"I did not know her at first. The last time I saw her she was a girl yet; but that was when I went to Grandmother's Land after the Rubbing Out of Long Hair. She was older and heavier, and she was holding a child under her blanket. I did not know her until she looked up at me, crying hard, and said, 'O *Shonka 'kan! Shonka 'kan!* They have killed him! They have killed him!' Then I knew Tashina's eyes with the tears in them."

The light went out of the old man's face, and again he sat silent.

"It was not very far from there across the hills to the little gray log house on White Horse Creek," he continued at length. "I put her on my horse and led him, walking, and all the while she held the child close under her blanket, crying hard. It was a little boy and he was dead.

"That night the snow came and a great wind blew, and we were alone in the little gray house. When the storm died, and it was very cold, some people came and we heard that her man was dead in the valley where the butchering began.

"Looks Twice and my mother came back with my grandfather and grandmother. We lived together there until the young grass came. And then one day when she did not cry any more, and we were talking about the good days, I said, 'I want to be your horse again. Do I have to go and eat grass?'"

The old man chuckled over the memory for a while, and then he said, the warm glow spreading from his smile: "That is when we made this little gray house here where my daughter lives, and now she is getting old too.

"It was a good road that we walked together, Grandson. Sometimes we were hungry, but it was a good road. Our children came to us, and when we were old, we saw our grandchildren too. It was a good road."

At this point it seemed that I had suddenly dropped out of the old man's world, and a great distance lay between us. He sat with closed eyes, making low, plaintive sounds on his eagle-bone whistle. When he had sat thus over long, I said, "Grandfather, you still have your eagle-bone whistle; but what became of the sacred quirt?"

Slowly he returned to awareness of my presence, the smile and glow warm upon his time-carved face.

"When she died—" he said in a low, gentle voice that quavered a bit—"when she died, I just put it down beneath her dress, between her breasts. I would not need it any more."

The End